T0062595

Building Solutions with Microsoft Teams

Understanding the Teams App Developer Platform

Jenkins NS

Apress®

Building Solutions with Microsoft Teams: Understanding the Teams App Developer Platform

Jenkins NS
Chennai, India

ISBN-13 (pbk): 978-1-4842-6475-1
https://doi.org/10.1007/978-1-4842-6476-8

ISBN-13 (electronic): 978-1-4842-6476-8

Managing Director, Apress Media LLC: Welmoed Spahr
Acquisitions Editor: Smriti Srivastava
Development Editor: Matthew Moodie
Coordinating Editor: Shrikant Vishwakarma

Cover designed by eStudioCalamar

Cover image designed by Pexels

Distributed to the book trade worldwide by Springer Science+Business Media LLC, 1 New York Plaza, Suite 4600, New York, NY 10004. Phone 1-800-SPRINGER, fax (201) 348-4505, e-mail orders-ny@springer-sbm. com, or visit www.springeronline.com. Apress Media, LLC is a California LLC and the sole member (owner) is Springer Science + Business Media Finance Inc (SSBM Finance Inc). SSBM Finance Inc is a **Delaware** corporation.

For information on translations, please e-mail booktranslations@springernature.com; for reprint, paperback, or audio rights, please e-mail bookpermissions@springernature.com.

Apress titles may be purchased in bulk for academic, corporate, or promotional use. eBook versions and licenses are also available for most titles. For more information, reference our Print and eBook Bulk Sales web page at http://www.apress.com/bulk-sales.

Any source code or other supplementary material referenced by the author in this book is available to readers on GitHub via the book's product page, located at www.apress.com/978-1-4842-6475-1. For more detailed information, please visit http://www.apress.com/source-code.

Printed on acid-free paper

Dedicated to
My parents,
Mr. N. Sundararaj and Mrs. T. Renjitham.

My Wife,
Dr. PJ. Jeyashree.

My lovely sons,
Master J. Johann Chris and Master J. Jordan Chris.

Table of Contents

About the Author

 **Jenkins NS** is the Founder and Director of JPOWER4, an MVP in Office Development and a Microsoft Certified Trainer (MCT) who has been working on SharePoint for more than 16 years, focusing on building custom solutions for Microsoft Teams, SharePoint Framework, Power Platform, Office 365, and SharePoint.

He is passionate about SharePoint; actively blogs; organizes events; and speaks at events and international conferences, most recently on the topics of Microsoft Teams, SharePoint Framework (SPFx), and Power Platform. Jenkins blogs at http://jenkinsblogs.com and he is very active on social media.

About the Technical Reviewer

 **Vijai Anand Ramalingam** is a Microsoft MVP in Office Apps and Services, an experienced Modern Workplace Architect with deep knowledge in SharePoint and Office 365. He is a blogger, author, speaker, and has published 1300 blogs/articles on C# Corner. He works as a Technology Architect in Cognizant Technology Solutions in the United Kingdom. Vijai has worked on Microsoft SharePoint on-premises/online, Office 365, and Azure.

Acknowledgments

I thank my Lord and savior Jesus Christ for making my dream come true.

I would like to thank everyone at Apress for giving me this opportunity to publish my first book. Thank you to Matthew Moodie, my editor, for supporting my writing endeavors and helping me to achieve this dream.

I would also like to thank the technical reviewer, Mr. Vijai Anand, for his valuable suggestions and comments.

Introduction

Microsoft Teams is the new modern way to communicate, collaborate, and enable teamwork as everyone is now looking for flexible approaches to the work environment. There are many collaborations, communications, and teamwork tools available. However, when it comes to a one-stop solution to work in a way that is simple, flexible, and effective, Microsoft Teams is the only solution that tops it all. Now that everyone is working remotely, Microsoft Teams provides the best way for employees to collaborate extensively from remote locations; from any devices like mobiles, laptops, and browsers; and without the risk of governance and security compliance.

Today Microsoft Teams provides a platform to automate business processes, and the customer wants to customize their workplace, especially as they are working with a group of people working jointly on many of the same projects. If you are reading this book and you are looking for a solution to extend your team's platform with your line of business, then you are in the right place.

Microsoft Teams is an extensible platform with many capabilities like tab, bot, task modules, messaging extension, webhooks, connectors, and solution accelerators like SPFx, Power Platform. You can create custom apps for an individual, team, group of people, and your organization.

This book helps you to build, test, and deploy apps for your lines of business. The book has 11 chapters and it provides detailed descriptions about the apps and contains many examples with step-by-step descriptions of how to build, test, and deploy locally; and be the host for a production environment. This book helps you to learn basic to advanced apps development with your existing client-side development model using JavaScript. Moreover, this book provides an invaluable resource for those who are planning to extend their Microsoft Teams platform with their line of business apps.

CHAPTER 1

Overview: Microsoft Teams Developer Platform

This chapter covers the way in which organizations work has evolved and how employees interact with your application and your application interacts with employees. We will talk about the Teams extensible platform and capabilities with different types of business solution opportunities for your line of business.

We will also discover the high-level architecture and how Teams clients and key services work together to deliver Teams capabilities. This includes a high-level understanding of how messaging works, where data is stored in Teams, how data flows in and out of Teams, and where the compliance boundary is.

Finally, the chapter covers why you have to build apps for Teams and invest in building custom solutions for Teams.

Objectives

This book helps to understand what developer platforms are available in Teams and the types of applications that can be created. As Teams integrates with many Microsoft 365 services, we need to understand how the Teams architecture supports extensibility and how our application can use existing system components. Next, we will take a deep dive into solution development for Teams. The book explains bots, message actions, message extensions, task modules, personal apps, and more.

Next is to make development lightweight by using accelerators. PowerApps and Flow and other no-to-low code tools help build solutions for Teams quickly. You can also leverage your existing skills from SharePoint development.

At the end, we will refine our learning by understanding the best practices, app packaging and publishing and making it available via the store, and understand what developers can do in Teams.

© Jenkins NS 2021
J. NS, *Building Solutions with Microsoft Teams*, https://doi.org/10.1007/978-1-4842-6476-8_1

Microsoft Teams Overview

Today's workforce is more mobile, social, and global than ever. People have different backgrounds in technology and different expectations about communication and collaboration tools. But whatever calling and meeting tools people prefer, one thing is clear: most of their time is now spent collaborating. We want to make that easier.

What happens when you don't provide tools to support these new workstyles? To do the immediate task at hand, end users download consumer-grade tools, which create friction for end users as they have to manage multiple logins and move between different experiences, and it creates risk for the organization as shadow IT develops.

One of the things all leaders are concerned about is making sure that all their IP and information are secure. People are looking for a collaborative solution that works for a diverse workforce that includes aspects of social use, based on something that is modern and secure, and that is what Teams and Microsoft 365 deliver.

Microsoft 365 helps to communicate more effectively when you communicate within a team with the people that you are working on with the project. It enables people to work from any device, whether it's a mobile device or your computer. One of the most important goals for businesses is to automate business processes, and as a platform, Teams provides a way to achieve this.

Additionally, people really want to customize their workplace and especially as they are working with a group of people, they want to customize that space based on what they are working on. And while doing all of that, they are thinking about securing access to the business so that they are protecting their information and defending against cyber threats.

Teams Architecture

When we discuss architecture and security and compliance, it is important to keep in mind these three principles:

- Designed for the cloud
- Agility at scale
- Amplify the value of Office 365

If it is designed, it is built for the cloud. (Can it be run on-premises? No.) Teams want to be able to take advantage of all the latest and greatest Microsoft 365 services and features as they become available.

Another advantage of Teams architecture is that it can be agile at scale. Fast delivery and being able to roll out new features quickly are some of the main goals. If you have been using Teams for a while, you will have experienced this rapid development. Teams currently has about one build per week. But it is not only new features; if there is also something that is needed to be fixed, a Teams engineering team can fix it quickly and get the change out to the clients.

If you are familiar with Teams, you know that it is a chat-centered workspace, a hub for teamwork that brings together a lot of the capabilities that are in Office 365: groups, Planner, Power BI, SharePoint, Office, Excel, Word, Visual Studio Teams System, and services from partners that you can bring in via tabs, connectors, and bots. All these different pieces are to be integrated in a way that makes them better together and allows your team to collaborate using all of them.

Teams Joins Microsoft 365 with Intelligent Communications

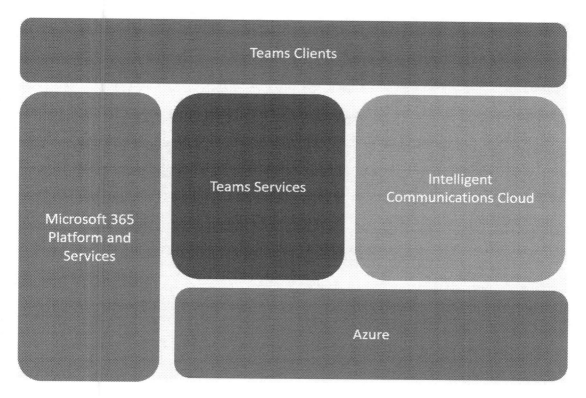

Figure 1-1. *Microsoft Teams Architecture*

From an architecture perspective, Teams brings together Office 365 and Skype, so Teams sits between Office 365 and Skype and on top of Azure. The services inside Teams are really an orchestration layer that brings the other pieces together and then enables you to attach a modern group to a set of chats or to make sure a SharePoint site is provisioned when you create a Team and scalable Azure infrastructure that can be used by anyone. Things like attach a modern group to a set of chats or to make sure a SharePoint site is provisioned when you create a Team and scalable Azure infrastructure that any of you can use. See Figure 1-1.

Teams Services

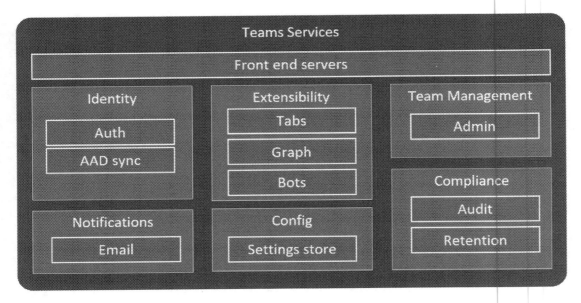

Figure 1-2. *Teams Services*

Let's take a closer look at what we call the "middle tier." These are the services that the Teams engineering team built to create Teams vs. the other services that take dependencies. It is a collection of microservices that all have a specific function. It has been built to allow it to deploy each piece separately. See Figure 1-2.

Most of these have more of an orchestration component to them. But what is being done in Teams is that all O365 (Office 365) capabilities are taken, and all of the modern Skype infrastructure is brought together in this modern chat-centric workspace, the hub for teamwork. It is a set of front-end servers that allows it to send out that HTML/JavaScript/TypeScript payload and enables us to handle configurations so that you're getting the right version of the product with the right set of features turned on.

Identity: Microsoft Teams owns and manages an active directory sync to make sure that your teams and modern groups stay in sync. They also have authentication. This is the magic where they figure out if you have a license and if teams are turned on or if you have the right to use it. Then for compliance, they own two services. One is called an audit and the other is called a retention hook.

The audit service is a place where all the events from Teams, including events like creating a team, creating a channel, and deleting a channel are captured. It is all those things that your IT admin wants to know about. Teams pumps these into the standard O365 infrastructure, so you can see them in the audit log in the security and compliance center. Teams keeps a persistent chat that keeps the data indefinitely. But some organizations see the data as a liability and want to get rid of it as soon as they deem it no longer useful.

Teams also handles notifications. There is a fire hose from the chat service that gives us every message, and if you haven't been online for the last 60/ 90 minutes but you have a new message, Teams can then send you an email or a push notification.

Team management is where all the administration is done like creating a team, creating a SharePoint Team site, and creating an Office 365 group. For extensibility, Teams has a set of services to support, graph APIs, tabs, and bot creation/management. And then for config, Teams stores metadata in a lot of different places, some in the chat service in Skype, some in groups, but there is also some specific Office 365 configuration stored in user settings, profiles, and tenant mappings.

Intelligent Communications Cloud

Teams took a big dependency on what Skype was good at – Chat, Meeting, Calling, and all the services that power it. The set of microservices you see in the next image are the next generation converged core services between Skype and Skype for Business (Figure 1-3).

Because Teams is chat centric, it takes a big bet on a lot of our Skype messaging services. Teams has a very powerful search functionality, and there is a set of microservices on the modern Skype side - chat, media - where images are stored.

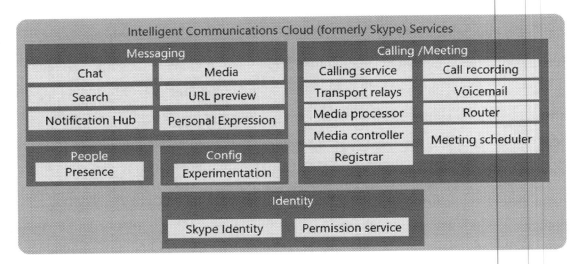

Figure 1-3. *Intelligent Communication Cloud*

Teams also has the URL preview service, like any other modern app. When you put in the URL, Teams gives you back the little preview, so you can easily share a URL, and everybody knows what it is that they are clicking on. The notification hub lets you know when new messages arrive to your client.

The services calling/meeting are all important and power the meeting/calling experience in Teams. The goal of Teams here is to converge the best of Skype and Skype for Business, and the Teams engineering team has the same developers working and owning these.

For example, the cloud recording service aggregates content across from users/clients in a call or meeting that is being recorded, messages them into the right data structure, and sends them off to Microsoft streams where all cloud recordings are stored for later.

Then Teams has the identity and permission service, which is how Teams maps AAD users into the Skype world, which relies on a Skype token. Permission service is a place where, for example, some changes to enable guest users are to be made.

Logical Architecture

Figure 1-4 is the logical architecture of Microsoft Teams. The diagram shows how everything is connected. Every team has a Microsoft 365 Group and SharePoint Team Site as its underlying membership construct. All files are stored in a SharePoint Team site document library folder for public channels, and private channels store all files in a separate SharePoint site and OneDrive for chats.

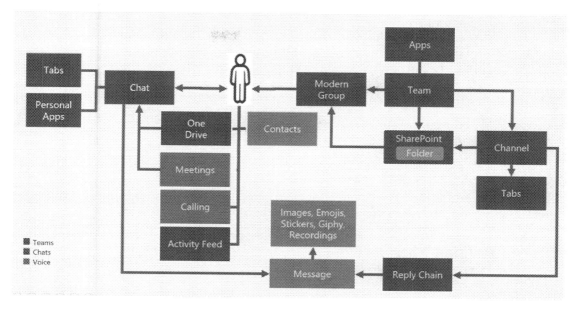

Figure 1-4. *Logical Architecture*

Where Are Conversations Stored?

Chat Service

- In memory processing for speed

- Leverages Azure storage (blob, tables, queues)

There is a chat service behind Teams, and it has its own physical storage. But you can imagine that when you send a chat from sender to receiver, you expect it to get there instantly. So, most processing happens in memory, and that is backed by Azure storage.

Substrate / Exchange

- Chat and channel messages are also stored in Exchange for information protection.

Teams stores the chat information in Exchange to enable information protection. If you chat in Teams, that goes down to the chat service. Teams has service internally that is referred to as a substrate, which looks at the chat and decides what to do with it.

There are two options:

- If it's a digital chat, then it gets published into a hidden folder in the mailbox of each participant of the chat.

- If you are in a team conversation, that team conversation gets published into a hidden folder in the group mailbox associated with that team.

Conversation Images and media

Inline Images/Stickers are stored in a media store, but Giphys are not stored.

Where Are Files Stored?

1: N Chats

Files are uploaded to OneDrive for Business, and permissions are set for the members of the chat.

Team Conversations

Files are uploaded to SharePoint. A folder is associated with each channel in the team.

Cloud Storage

Dropbox, Box, Citrix ShareFile, Google Drive.

How Teams Enables O365 Information Protection

When you chat in Teams, that goes down to the chat service (Figure 1-5). And then Teams has a service internally that it refers to as s substrate. That looks at the chat and decides what to do with it. If you have a 1:1 chat with someone, then that chat is posted to a hidden folder in the user mailbox of all participants of that conversation. If you have a team conversation, that chat is posted to the group mailbox. Then files, either SharePoint or OneDrive for Business and OneNote/Wiki, are physically stored in SharePoint as well.

In doing that, all the information protection tools that you might be using with Exchange and SharePoint today become available for you. Today the information protection features only work when the mailbox is online (it will not work when the mailbox is on-premise).

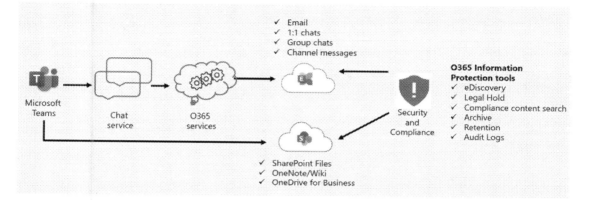

Figure 1-5. O365 Information Protection

Teams Extensible Platform Capabilities

Teams is the single hub for an office, to reduce the information overload you get every day and focus on the content that is most relevant to you to get your job done, better. It brings together all the apps and tools your organization is already using, into one user interface; for IT that means better and easier management, reduced security threats, and more time you can spend on valuable, forward-looking projects.

This delivers superpowers to people through proactive intelligence and is the core to the extensibility of the Teams platform. Teams delivers intelligent experiences using our APIs and/or our partner community that do the following: First, make the most difficult and time-wasting tasks at work easy. Thereafter, drive intelligence to your people that allows them to understand how they add more value to the organization, and then deliver it more efficiently and quickly. See Figure 1-6.

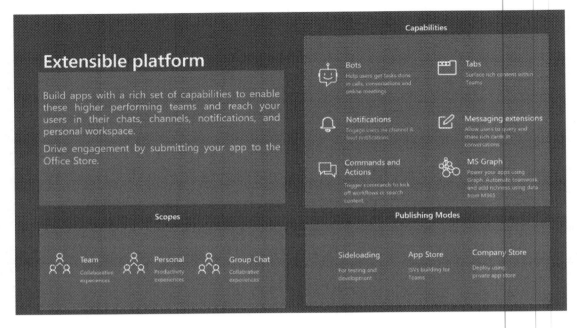

Figure 1-6. *Extensible Platform*

Teams is a very extensible platform with many capabilities. Think of this as the way for your employees to interact with your application or for your application to interact with employees, whether that is through chats, channels, notifications, or in their personal workspace or on their Teams workspace.

Some of these are **bots**. Most people are familiar with bots. A popular one would be where you are asking questions and getting answers by just pulling up a bot. Bots help users get tasks done in conversations in Teams. Bots can do things like kick off workflows and provide status on them, give and receive kudos from team members, create lightweight surveys to gauge employee satisfaction, and answer natural language questions about sales and customer usage data.

Tabs give you a rich surface, where you can really post your application in any of the information from your app in a tab so it's right there for users or you can post an application in a tab.

Tabs allow you to surface rich content within Teams, so you can bring the tools and services your team cares about right into a channel or private chat. You can then add rich dashboards and data visualization, collaborate on documents and note taking, manage tasks across the group, and share designs.

🔔 **Notification** engages users via feed notifications, whether it is in a feed or whether it is in a channel so you can notify people, for example, if something is changed in your application that you are extending into Teams, you can provide that notification to users.

📝 **Message extensions** allow users to query and share rich cards in conversations. Messaging extensions provide a way for people to actually pull something up and query and share rich cards in conversations; and by the way, users can take actions on those cards, give you input back, and based on that input you provide additional information. You have commands and actions that could kick off a workflow source search content. With Actionable messages, you can add rich content to your connector cards.

🗔 **Task modules** let you open a dialog from bot cards or tabs. When you need to do a little form entry, a lookup, or keep a 1:1 interaction out of a channel, pop open a dialog.

📝 **Connectors** help bring useful information and rich content from external services into channels in Microsoft Teams. You can get social media notifications, updates about pull and push requests, and news updates.

🔗 **Microsoft Graph** is a unified REST API and comprehensive developer experience for integrating the data and intelligence exposed by Microsoft services.

📹 **Voice and video** - Add rich calling and meeting automation and media.

🖥 **Adaptive cards** are a new cross-product specification for cards in Microsoft products including Bots, Cortana, Outlook, and Windows. They are the recommended card type for new Teams development. You can use adaptive cards, existing Hero Cards, Office 365 cards, and Thumbnail cards.

One of the things that's important to think about is that you have the ability to put something in a team environment where it's something that, for example, is putting in a channel with multiple people, or you're putting into someone's personal channel where it's really something geared just for the individual and in terms of how you can publish things. Teams allows you to sideload things for testing and development. If it's a fully customized packaged solution, that's something you could build and publish in the Teams app store or if it's a custom application, which has really been customized for just one individual customer, that's something you can deploy using the app store. Think of each customer as having a private app store for their company where you can load it.

Evolve How Your People Work, with the Tools They Need

One of the beauties of Microsoft Teams is that Teams really is the hub for where people get work done and so they want to make sure that all the tools they need are a part of Teams. This is so they don't have to change contacts and we think of this as two different types of applications.

The first part of customizing and extending Teams is bringing together all the Microsoft Office applications you know, allowing you to reduce context switching and create conversations around content.

The second part of this infusion of tools is where all the other apps and services you need every day are brought together to get your job done. Microsoft Teams store currently has over 250+ partner applications and integrations available today and is growing (Figure 1-7).

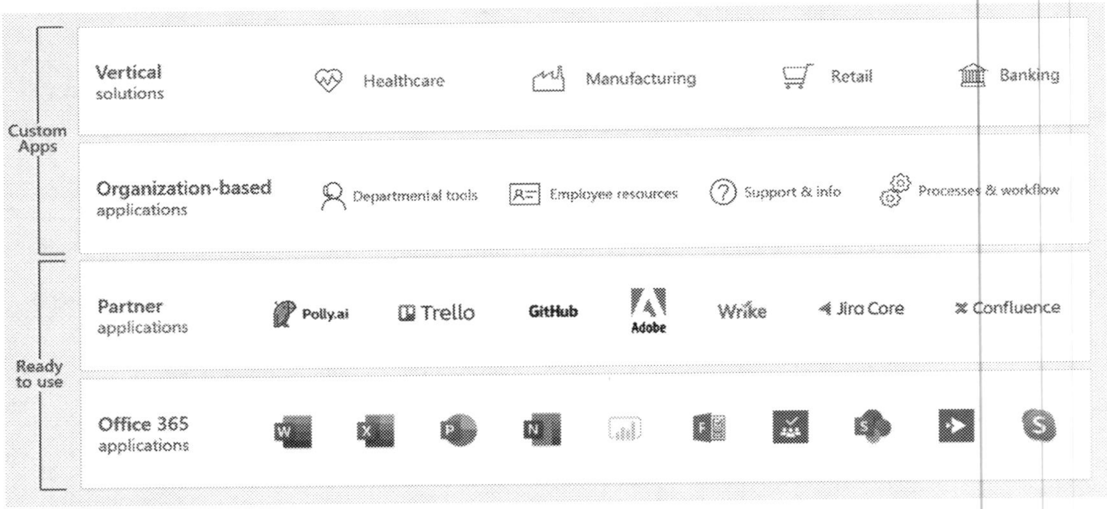

Figure 1-7. *Types of Teams Apps*

These first two layers here are ready-to-use applications available for you, as soon as you download Teams, should your IT admins make them available to you.

Microsoft Teams also gives you the ability to extend your experience to leverage the apps and services that your organization has built for you; these are the tools you need to leverage every day as an employee to get work done and as part of your role. It is called line of business (LOB) applications (Custom Apps).

App Scenarios Across Different Industries and Horizontals

The purpose of this section - App scenarios across different industries and horizontals is to give you some ideas and to start thinking about what your customers need (Figure 1-8).

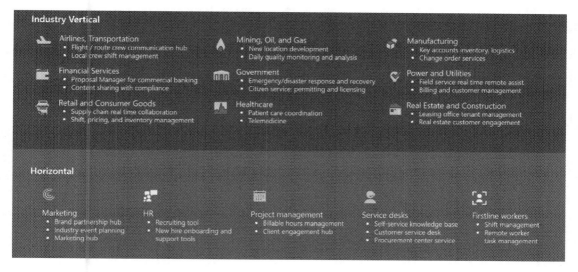

Figure 1-8. Teams App Scenarios

These types of business solution opportunities around teamwork are pretty much endless: from airline, retail, health care, legal firm, real estate, different industries, and different functions. You can envision with your customers, understand their business process and teamwork needs, and connect Teams to the tools and services they use every day to help them fully realize Teams' value.

Why Do You Have to Build Apps for Teams?

The Microsoft Teams Platform is a powerful, flexible platform for creating apps for Microsoft Teams. However, that doesn't mean it will fit all scenarios. In this section, some key scenarios where Teams apps excel are discussed.

Enhancing Communication and Collaboration

Teams apps shine when they are focused on enhancing collaboration and communication. Most successful Teams apps involve either some form of pulling information in from another system, having a conversation about it, and allowing users to take action about that information from directly within the Teams client, or pushing information to a targeted audience based on an event or action in an external system.

Encouraging Social Interactions

Apps that focus on encouraging social interactions between team members work. These are apps that send polls, let people send feedback to each other, connect them together, or are just for fun (don't underestimate the power of a few "just for fun" apps can have on team morale). Teams is a social platform; custom social-focused apps encourage your team to extend your company culture into your collaboration space.

Initiating and Facilitating Common Business Processes

Teams can be an effective platform for launching, and facilitating the completion of, common business processes. Things like creating and sharing a sales call report, tracking your time against a project, reserving common resources, submitting help desk requests, and more can make for effective Teams apps. Quite often there is already some other system responsible for completing these actions. In those cases, using Teams as a bridge to initiate the process and for communicating during the process can create an effective hybrid app.

Surfacing Some (or All) of Your Existing Apps

If you've got an existing web app, SharePoint site (or SPFx extension), PowerApps, or other web-based application, it may make sense to enable some or all of it in Teams. Just be sure to consider the context and scope carefully. If you enable your navigation and form a heavy website as a channel tab, it probably won't work very well.

Personal Apps with Tabs and Bots

One-to-one conversational bots are one of the most open-ended extensibility points within Microsoft Teams. The conversation is just between the bot and your user, you have the flexibility of including task modules to simplify the collection of complex sets of information, and you can combine them with personally scoped tabs. With this canvas you can create a complete traditional app experience within the Teams client.

Why Do You Have to Invest in Building Custom Solutions for Teams?

The first reason is to differentiate your offer. There are a lot of partners out there who are doing deployment around Office 365 or Microsoft Teams, but the partners who are building custom solutions and showcasing custom solutions are really achieving two things:

- They are getting their customers excited, because it shows the customer the true vision of what Microsoft Teams can do for them.

- It helps them stand out and differentiate themselves from all the other deployment partners.

It enables you to increase your profitability. Microsoft did a study with Forrester and found that building custom solutions for Microsoft Teams increases your profitability by 17%, and it enables you to charge for your higher-margin developer resources.

It helps you with outreach to a broader audience. This gives you that ability to go in and talk to the business decision makers and to the end users who really value this, and it helps you to really add value to the business groups. It also helps increase your relevancy to specific industries.

Conclusion

In this chapter, we have learned the ways in which organizations' work has evolved and understand that we are building a platform, and Teams is a very extensible platform with many capabilities and different types of business solution opportunities for your line of business.

We have also learned about high-level architecture how the Teams clients and key services work together to deliver Teams capabilities. We have also gained a high-level understanding of how messaging works and how/where data is stored in Teams, data flows in and out of Teams, and compliance boundaries.

Finally, in this chapter we have discussed why you have to build apps for Teams and why you have to invest in building custom solutions for Teams.

Now that we have learned the basics of the Microsoft Teams Development Platform, we will start with the development of the Microsoft Teams apps in our upcoming chapters.

CHAPTER 2

Building Apps and Solutions with Microsoft Teams

This chapter covers the setup environment and explains how to create apps for Microsoft Teams using Yeoman Generator, .NET with c#, and Nodejs. It also describes various contexts and scenarios about Teams' apps lines of business.

Microsoft Teams Developer Platform Overview

The Microsoft Teams developer platform makes it easy for you to extend Teams and integrate your own applications and services seamlessly into the Teams workspace. These apps can then be distributed to your enterprise or to teams around the world.

To start developing for Teams, it is important to decide many points. First, when you are building any application, you need to ask yourself, does it really solve a real-world problem for a team? You don't want to build something that is not solving any business problem, because there will be no users of your app. Next, an important decision point will be how often the user will use this application. If your app value proposition is not well balanced with the effort and costs associated with it, then one might need to explore other options.

Teams is all about users' experiences and their interactions with the tool. If you want an app to win a people's choice award, then think about user personas and how your app can improve their lives.

© Jenkins NS 2021
J. NS, *Building Solutions with Microsoft Teams*, https://doi.org/10.1007/978-1-4842-6476-8_2

Here are the integration points for Teams apps.

- Messaging extensions with search commands

    - Search external systems and share the results as an interactive card.

- Messaging extensions with action commands

    - Collect information to insert into a data store or perform advanced searches.

- Tabs

    - Create embedded web experiences to view, work with, and share data.

- Connectors and webhooks

    - A simple way to push data into and send data out of the Teams client.

- Task modules

    - Interactive modal forms from wherever you need them to collect or display information.

Set Up the Development Environment for Microsoft Teams

To extend Microsoft Teams, you need to create a Microsoft Teams app. A Microsoft Teams app is a web application that you host. This app can then be integrated into the user's workspace in Teams.

As a Teams developer you can use different approaches and knowledge to extend the Teams platform. You can leverage your earlier knowledge of .Net with C# / NodeJS / SPFx to develop Teams Apps.

You can extend the Teams developer platform capabilities by creating custom apps by leveraging your existing knowledge. The Microsoft Teams Development platform currently supports three languages: .Net, JavaScript, and Python. Refer to Figure 2-1.

Figure 2-1. *Microsoft Teams Apps Supported Language*

Also, the Microsoft Teams Development platform supports six different IDEs to develop Microsoft Teams apps (Figure 2-2).

Figure 2-2. *Microsoft Teams Apps different IDEs*

1. Microsoft Teams platform with C#/.NET and App Studio

2. Microsoft Teams platform with Node.js and App Studio

3. Microsoft Teams platform with Yeoman generator

4. Microsoft Teams platform with SharePoint Framework

5. Microsoft Teams Toolkit for Visual Studio Code

6. Microsoft Teams platform with Phyton and App Studio

Prepare Your Office 365 Tenant

Let's prepare the development environment. Make sure custom app uploading is enabled for the Microsoft 365 organization you want to build your app in. Sign up for the Office 365 developer program if you need a dedicated development tenant. Make sure you have an environment where you can upload and test your Teams app.

1. Sign up for a Microsoft 365 developer Subscription.

   Follow this post : `http://jenkinsblogs.com/2020/03/06/set-up-a-microsoft-365-developer-subscription-for-learning/`

2. Enable custom Teams apps and turn on custom app uploading.

   a. There are three settings relevant to enabling custom apps and custom app uploading:

   - Org-wide custom app setting ➤ Allow interaction with custom apps ➤ On

   - This setting enables or disables custom apps for your organization. It needs to be on.

   - **Team custom app setting ➤ Allow members to upload custom apps ➤ On/Off**

   - This setting applies to each individual team inside Microsoft Teams. If you want to install your app for a specific team, this will need to be on for that team.

   - User custom app policy ➤ User can upload custom apps ➤ On/Off

     This setting controls the permissions for an individual user. You'll need to enable this for individuals that can upload custom apps.

Next, prepare your development environment based on your knowledge and customer-preferred method. We have four different options to develop Microsoft Teams apps.

- Prepare your development environment for .Net

- Prepare your development environment for NodeJS

- Prepare your development environment for Yeoman generator

- Prepare your development environment using Microsoft Teams Toolkit for Visual Studio Code

Based on your knowledge, select one and prepare your development environment.

Prepare Your Development Environment for .Net

Here are the steps:

- **Install Visual Studio**

    - https://www.visualstudio.com/downloads/

    - You can install the free community edition.

- **Install Microsoft Teams App**

    - https://marketplace.visualstudio.com/
      items?itemName=TeamsDevApp.vsteamstemplate

    - Create, debug, and deploy Teams apps directly from Visual
      Studio.

- **Install Git**

    - https://git-scm.com/downloads

If you see an option to add git to the PATH during installation, choose to do so. It will be handy. Verify your git installation by running the following in a terminal window:

```
$ git --version
git version 2.17.1.windows.2
```

Make sure to launch the latest version of Visual Studio and install any updates if shown.

MICROSOFT TEAMS TOOLKIT FOR VISUAL STUDIO

The Microsoft Teams Toolkit extension enables you to create, debug, and deploy Teams apps directly from Visual Studio Code.

Features

- Project generator

- App configuration manager

- Package validator

- Publishing to your tenant app catalog from Visual Studio

Prepare Your Development Environment for NodeJS

Here are the steps:

- Install Git

    - `https://git-scm.com/downloads`

- Node.js and NPM

    - `https://nodejs.org/dist/latest-v8.x/`

    - You need to have NodeJS installed on your machine. You should use the latest LTS version.

- Install a code editor

    - `https://code.visualstudio.com/`

    - Get any text editor or IDE. You can install and use Visual Studio Code for free.

If you see options to add git, node, npm, and code to the PATH during installation, choose to do so. It will be handy. Verify that the tools are available by running the following in a terminal window:

```
$ git --version
git version 2.19.0.windows.1

$ node -v
v8.9.3

$ npm -v
5.5.1

$ gulp -v
CLI version 4.0.2
```

You may have a different version of these applications. This should not be a problem, except for gulp. For gulp you will need to use version 4.0.0 or later. If you don't have gulp installed (or have the wrong version installed), do so now by running **npm install gulp** in your terminal window.

Prepare Your Development Environment for Yeoman Generator

For completeness, here is how to prepare for Yeoman generator:

- Install NodeJS

- Install a code editor (I'm using Visual Studio Code for this too).

- Install Yeoman and Gulp CLI

    To be able to scaffold projects using the Teams generator you need to install the Yeoman tool as well as the Gulp CLI task manager.

    Open a command prompt and type the following:

    ```
    npm install yo gulp-cli typescript -global
    ```

- Install the Microsoft Teams Apps generator

- The Yeoman generator for Microsoft Teams apps is installed with the following command:

    ```
    npm install generator-teams -global
    ```

Prepare Your Development Environment Using Microsoft Teams Toolkit for Visual Studio Code

The Microsoft Teams Toolkit extension enables you to create, debug, and deploy Teams apps directly from Visual Studio Code.

Prerequisites

- Visual Studio Code v1.44 or newer

    - `https://code.visualstudio.com/download`

- NodeJS 6 or newer

    - `https://nodejs.org/en/`

- Install Microsoft Teams Toolkit

  - `https://marketplace.visualstudio.com/`
    `items?itemName=TeamsDevApp.ms-teams-vscode-extension`

  - Create, debug, and deploy Teams apps directly from Visual Studio
    Code

Host an App

Apps in Microsoft Teams are web applications exposing one or more capabilities. For the
Teams platform to load your app, your app must be reachable from the internet. To make
your app reachable from the internet, you need to host your app. You can either host it
in Microsoft Azure for free or create a tunnel to the local process on your development
machine using ngrok (`https://ngrok.com/`). When you finish hosting your app, make a
note of its root URL. It will look something like the following:

- `https://yourteamsapp.ngrok.io`

- `https://yourteamsapp.azurewebsites.net`

Tunnel Using ngrok

For quick testing you can run the app on your local machine and create a tunnel to it
through a web endpoint. Ngrok is a free tool that lets you do just that. With ngrok you can
get a web address such as `https://d0ac14a5.ngrok.io` (this URL is just an example).
You can download and install ngrok for your environment. Make sure you add it to a
location in your PATH.

Once you install it, you can open a new terminal window and run the following
command to create a tunnel. The sample uses port 3333, so be sure to specify it here.

`ngrok http 3333 -host-header=localhost:3333`

Ngrok will listen to requests from the internet and will route them to your app
running on port 3333. You can verify this by opening your browser and going to `https://`
`d0ac14a5.ngrok.io/hello` to load your app's hello page. Please be sure to use the
forwarding address displayed by ngrok in your console session instead of this URL.

The app will only be available during the current session on your development machine. If the machine is shut down or goes to sleep, the service will no longer be available. Remember this when sharing the app for testing by other users. If you must restart the service, it will return a new address and you will have to update every place that uses that address. The paid version of ngrok does not have this limitation.

A Microsoft Teams App

Whenever we want to create an app, first we start a process of registering a new Bot Channel Registration for any app for Teams other than Tabs. See Figure 2-3.

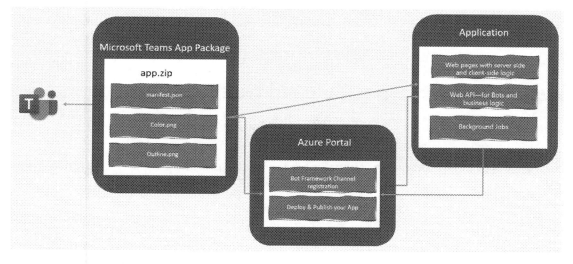

Figure 2-3. *A Microsoft Teams App*

Next develop the application using any one of the development environments based on your preference. Then create an App Package using App Studio.

Exercise 1: Create a First Microsoft Teams App Using Yeoman Generator

Creating and distributing an app built on the Microsoft Teams Platform involves Bot Channel registration, Teams apps in various contexts, Define App using App Studio, deciding what to build, building your web services, creating an app package, and distributing that package to your target end users (Figure 2-4).

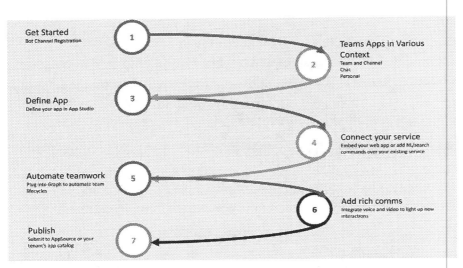

Figure 2-4. *Building a Teams App flow*

Register the Bot with Microsoft Azure's Bot Framework

The first step is to create a new Microsoft Teams bot for your Microsoft Teams App.

Open a browser and navigate to the Azure portal (`https://portal.azure.com/`. Sign in using your **username@tenantname.onmicrosoft.com** that was used from the Azure subscription.

Select **Create a resource** in the left-hand navigation. See Figure 2-5.

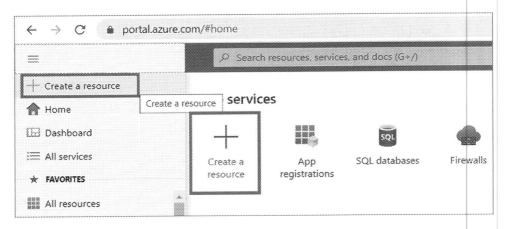

Figure 2-5. *Create a resource*

Enter resource group in the Search the marketplace input box, and select Resource group. See Figure 2-6.

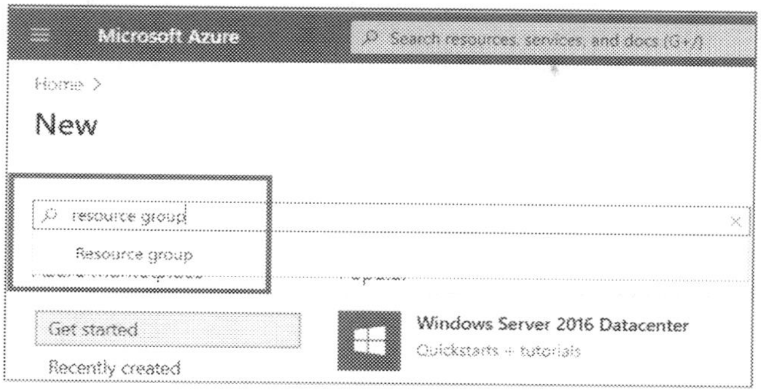

Figure 2-6. *Resource Group*

On the **Resource Group** page, select the **Create** button to create a new resource group. See Figure 2-7.

Figure 2-7. *Create resource group*

Select a valid subscription, enter a name for the resource group **Ex: Teams**, and select the wanted region. None of these choices will impact the bot registration and are up to you. See Figure 2-8.

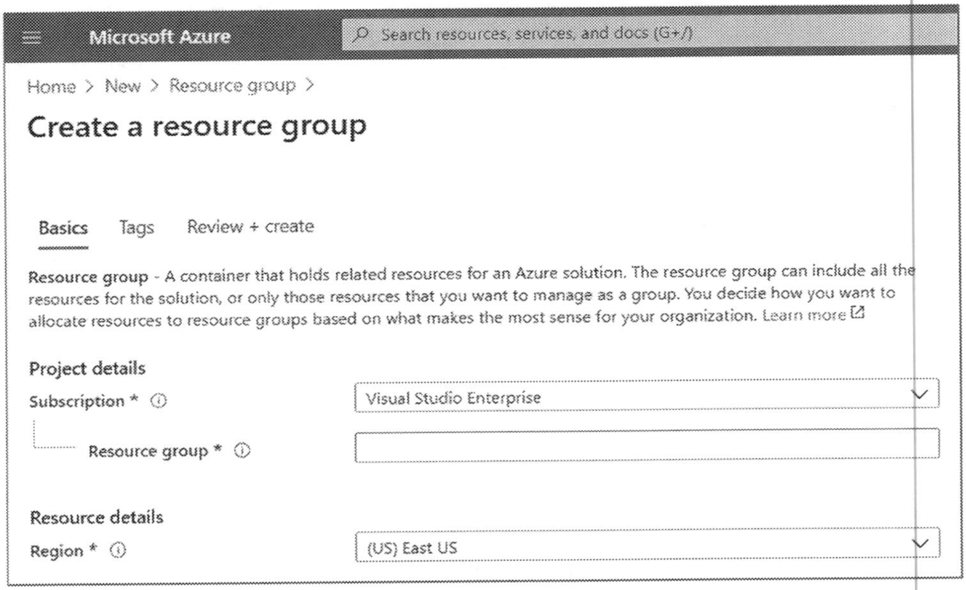

Figure 2-8. *Create resource group form*

Complete the wizard to create the resource group. See Figure 2-9.

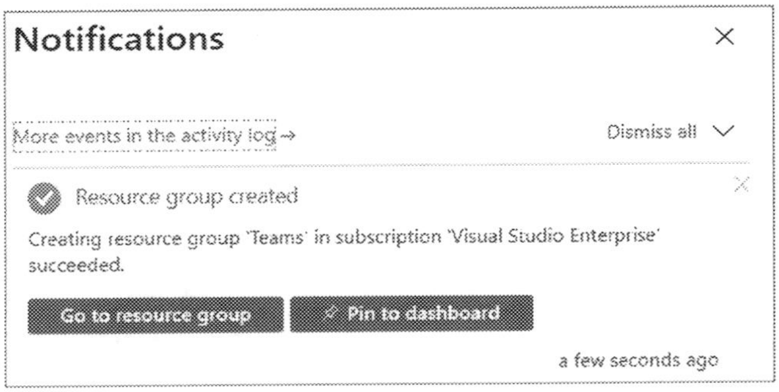

Figure 2-9. *Resource Group Created Notification*

Once Azure has completed the resource group creation process, navigate to the resource group.

From the resource group, select the **Add** or **Create resources** button as shown in Figure 2-10.

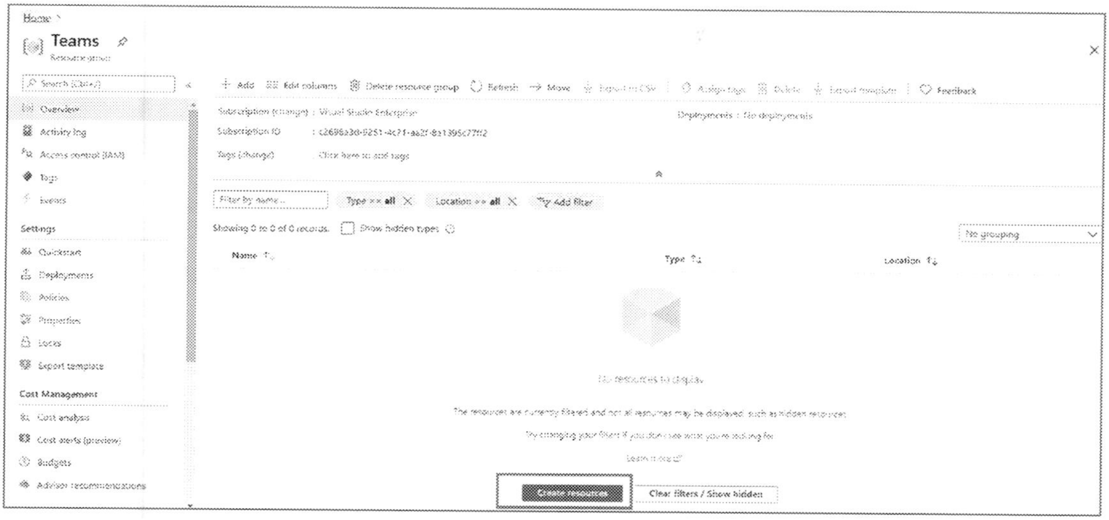

Figure 2-10. *Create Resources*

Bot Channel Registration

Enter **bot** in the **Search the marketplace** input box and select **Bot Channels Registration** from the list of resources returned. Then select **Create** on the next page to start the process of registering a new bot resource. See Figure 2-11.

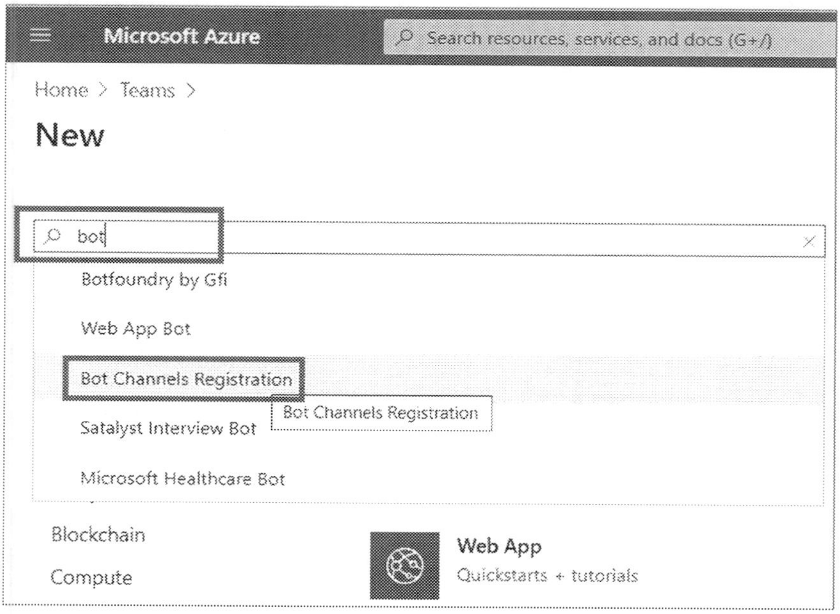

Figure 2-11. *Search Bot Channel Registration*

In the **Bot Channels Registration** Page, click to initiate create Bot Channels Registration. See Figure 2-12.

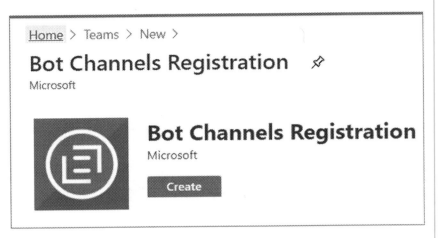

Figure 2-12. *Bot Channel Registration*

In the **Bot Channels Registration blade**, enter the following values and then select **Create** as shown in Figure 2-13.

- **Bot handle**: Enter a globally unique name for the bot.

- **Subscription**: Select the subscription you selected previously when creating the resource group.

- **Resource group**: Select the resource group you created previously.

- **Location**: Select your preferred Azure region.

- **Pricing tier**: Select a preferred pricing tier; the F0 tier is free.

- **Messaging endpoint**: `https://REPLACE_THIS.ngrok.io/api/messages`

  The bot registration needs to know the endpoint of the web service where the bot is implemented. This will change each time you start the ngrok utility used in previous exercises.

- **Application Insights**: Off

- **Microsoft App ID and password**: Auto create App ID and password

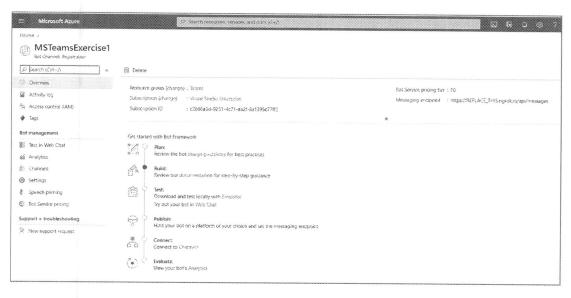

Figure 2-13. *Create Bot Channel Registration*

Azure will start to provision the new resource. This will take a moment or two. Once it's finished, navigate to the bot resource in the resource group. See Figure 2-14.

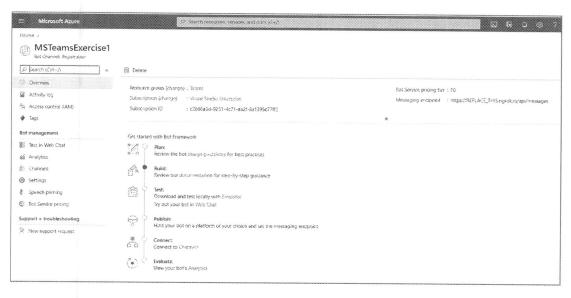

Figure 2-14. *Bot Channel Registration*

Enable the Microsoft Teams Channel for the Bot

For the bot to interact with Microsoft Teams, you must enable the Teams channel as shown in Figure 2-15.

- From the bot resource in Azure, select **Channels** in the left-hand navigation.

- On the **Connect to channels** pane, select the **Microsoft Teams channel**, then select **Save** to confirm the action.

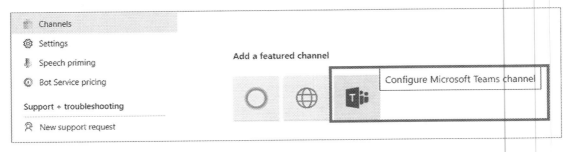

Figure 2-15. *Select Teams Channel*

- Agree to the Terms of Service (Figure 2-16).

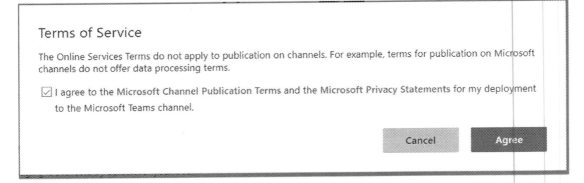

Figure 2-16. *Teams Channel Terms of Service*

Once this process is complete, you should see both the Web Chat and Microsoft Teams listed in your enabled channels (Figure 2-17).

Connect to channels			
Name	Health	Published	
Microsoft Teams	Running	--	Edit
Web Chat	Running	--	Edit
			Get bot embed codes

Figure 2-17. *Connect to channels*

Retrieve the Bot App Id and Password

When Azure created the bot, it also registered a new Azure AD app for the bot. You need to generate this new bot app as a secret and copy the app's credentials.

Select **Settings** from the left-hand navigation. Scroll down to the Microsoft App ID section.

Copy the ID of the bot as you'll need it later. See Figure 2-18.

Figure 2-18. *App ID*

Create a Client Secret for the App

Click **Manage** link to navigate to the **Azure AD app**.

For the daemon app to run without user involvement, it will sign into Azure AD with an application ID and either a certificate or secret. In this exercise, you'll use a secret.

Select **Certificates & secrets** from the left-hand navigation panel.

Select the **New client secret** button under the Client secrets section (Figure 2-19).

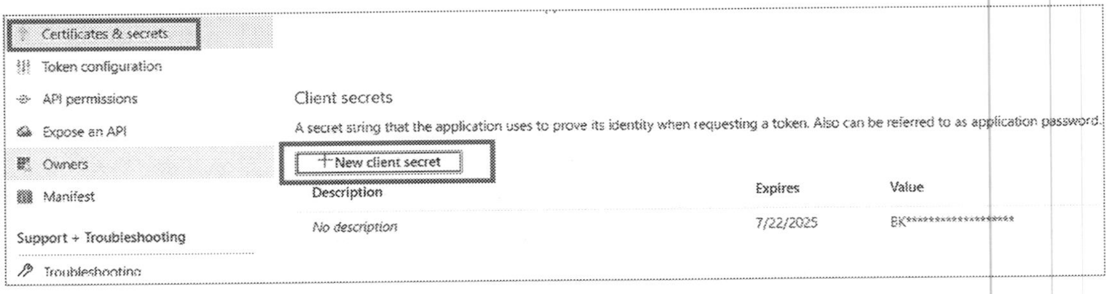

Figure 2-19. *New client secret*

When prompted, give the secret a description and select one of the expiration duration options provided, for example: Never and select **Add**.

Note   Copy the new client secret value. You won't be able to retrieve it after you perform another operation or leave this blade.

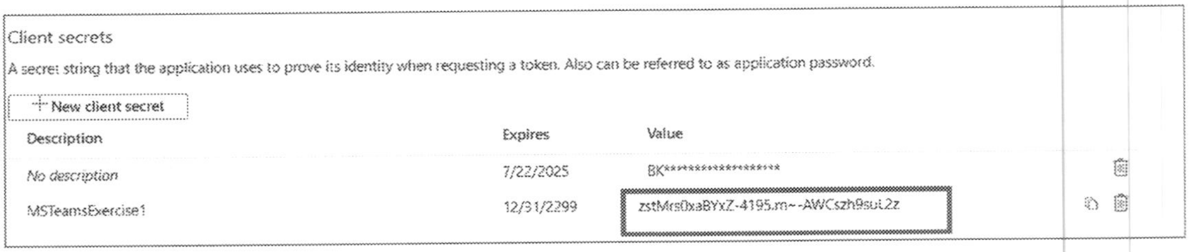

Figure 2-20. *New client secret value*

The Certificate & Secrets page will display the new secret. It's important you copy this value as it's only shown this one time; if you leave the page and come back, it will only show as a masked value (Figure 2-20).

Copy and store the value of the secret value as you will need it later.

Teams Apps in Various Contexts

We have three types of contexts available for Teams App.

- Team and channel

- Chat

- Personal

Team and channel

Enable public collaboration and workflows with all team members.

Example: share, discuss, and get notified about new service incidents

Chat

Lightweight collaboration in 1:1 or group setting without complex permissions

Example: 1:1 topic between manager and direct report

Personal

User-centric view, showing aggregate content along with private bot chat

Example: list of all tasks assigned to me

Scopes

Your app might require contextual information to display relevant content based on scope. The list of supported scopes to get context from tabs, bots, and connectors are given below.

Configurable Tabs

Currently, configurable tabs support only the team and group chat scopes. That is, configurable tabs are supported only in the Teams' scope (not personal), and currently only one tab per app is supported.

```
"scopes": ["team","groupchat"]
```

Static Tabs

Currently, static tabs support only the personal scope, which means it can be provisioned only as part of the personal experience, that is, static tabs declared in personal scope are always pinned to the app's personal experience. Static tabs declared in the team scope are currently not supported.

```
"scopes": ["personal"]
```

Bots

This specifies whether the bot offers an experience in the context of a channel in a team, in a group chat (groupchat), or an experience scoped to an individual user alone (personal). These options are nonexclusive.

```
"scopes": ["team","personal","groupchat"],
```

Bots – Command Lists

You must define a separate command list for each scope that your bot supports. This specifies the scope for which the command list is valid. Options are team, personal, and group chat.

```
"scopes": ["team","groupchat"]
"scopes": ["personal", "groupchat"]
```

Connectors

This specifies whether the Connector offers an experience in the context of a channel in a team, or an experience scoped to an individual user alone (personal). Currently, only the team scope is supported.

```
"scopes": ["team"]
```

Create an App Using Yeoman Generator

In this section, you will create a new Teams app using Yeoman generator (yo teams):

- To create a new web part project

- Create a new project directory in your favorite location

- Open command prompt

- Navigate to a newly created directory, create a new folder "yoTeamsMessagingExtension"

- Run the Yeoman generator for Microsoft Teams by running the following command: **yo teams**. See Figure 2-21.

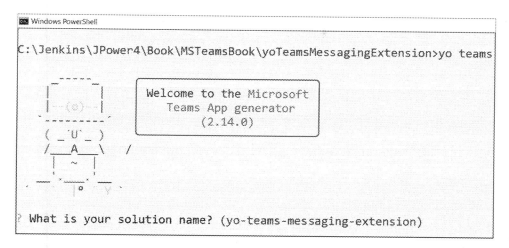

Figure 2-21. *Create Teams app using yo teams*

Yeoman will launch and ask you a series of questions. Answer the questions with the following values (Figure 2-22):

- What is your solution name?: yo-Teams-messaging-extension

- Where do you want to place the files?: Use the current folder

- Title of your Microsoft Teams App project? yoTeamsMessagingExtension

- Your (company) name? (max 32 characters): JPOWER4

- Which manifest version would you like to use? 1.6

- Enter your Microsoft Partner Id, if you have one? (Leave blank to skip)

- What features do you want to add to your project? A Message Extension Command

- The URL where you will host this solution? https:// yoteamsmessagingextension.azurewebsites.net

- Would you like to include Test framework and initial tests? No

- Would you like to use Azure Applications Insights for telemetry? No

- Where is your message extension hosted? In a new bot

- What is the Microsoft App ID for the bot used by the Message Extension? 00000000-0000-0000-0000-000000000000

- What type of messaging extension command? Search based messaging extension

- Would you like a Settings option for the messaging extension? Yes

- What is the name of your Message Extension command? searchCmd

- Describe your Message Extension command? Search books from google books api

```
? What is your solution name? yo-teams-messaging-extension
? Where do you want to place the files? Use the current folder
? Title of your Microsoft Teams App project? yoTeamsMessagingExtension
? Your (company) name? (max 32 characters) JPOWER4
? Which manifest version would you like to use? v1.6
? Enter your Microsoft Partner ID, if you have one? (Leave blank to skip)
? What features do you want to add to your project? A Message Extension Command
? The URL where you will host this solution? https://yoteamsmessagingextension.azurewebsites.net
? Would you like show a loading indicator when your app/tab loads? No
? Would you like to include Test framework and initial tests? No
? Would you like to use Azure Applications Insights for telemetry? No
? Where is your message extension hosted? In a new bot
? What is the Microsoft App ID for the bot used by the Message Extension?  00000000-0000-0000-0000-000000000000
? What type of messaging extension command? Search based messaging extension
? Would you like a Settings option for the messaging extension? Yes
? What is the name of your Message Extension command? searchCmd
? Describe your Message Extension command? Search books from google books api
```

Figure 2-22. *Answer yeoman questionaire*

Note   Most of the answers to these questions can be changed after creating the project. For example, the URL where the project will be hosted isn't important at the time of creating or testing the project.

Open Visual Studio Code using **code .** in the command prompt. See Figure 2-23.

Figure 2-23. *Visual studio code OOB*

- Go to env file ➤ Open and update

  MICROSOFT_APP_ID=1ad3a766-9629-44e5-b76c-c1256a8080ec
  MICROSOFT_APP_PASSWORD=zstMrsOxaBYxZ-4195.m~-AWCszh9suL2z

- Then open SearchCmdMessageExtension.ts file and find const card = CardFactory.adaptiveCard(

- Replace the body section to the code below

```
body: [
                    {
                        type: "TextBlock",
                        size: "Large",
                        text: "Title of the Item"
                    },
                    {
                        type: "TextBlock",
                        text: "Desc: Command Search Messaging
                        Extension"
                    },
                    {
                        type: "Image",
                        url: `https://${process.env.HOSTNAME}/
                        assets/icon.png`
                    }
                ]
```

- Find const preview = {

- Replace the content section title and text to the code below

```
title: "Title of the Item",
    text: "Desc: Command Search Messaging Extension",
```

Test the Messaging Extension App

Open the command Prompt, navigate to the project folder, and execute the following command:

gulp ngrok-serve

This gulp task will run many other tasks all displayed within the command-line console. The ngrok-serve task builds your project and starts a local web server (http://localhost:3007). It then starts ngrok with a random subdomain that creates a secure URL to your local webserver.

40

In development, testing can be done using the tool ngrok that creates a secure rotatable URL to your local HTTP webserver. Ngrok is included as a dependency within the project so there is nothing to set up or configure.

```
[11:54:22] Starting 'nodemon'...
[11:54:22] Finished 'nodemon' after 14 ms
[11:54:22] Starting 'watch'...
[11:54:22] HOSTNAME: 1d42b1a1cfc8.ngrok.io
[tslint-plugin] Linting complete.
  msteams Initializing Microsoft Teams Express hosted App... +0ms
  msteams Creating a new bot instance at /api/messages +0ms
  msteams Found 1 MessagingExtension(s) on the Bot object +6ms
  msteams Adding Messaging extension: searchCmdMessageExtension +0ms
  msteams Server running on 3007 +591ms
```

Figure 2-24. *ngrok-serve execution*

Ngrok has created the temporary URL 1d42b1a1cfc8.ngrok.io that will map to our locally running web server (Figure 2-24).

Then go to the Azure portal and open the Bot Channel registration App. Update the Messaging endpoint using the temporary URL 36236469245b.ngrok.io (Figure 2-25).

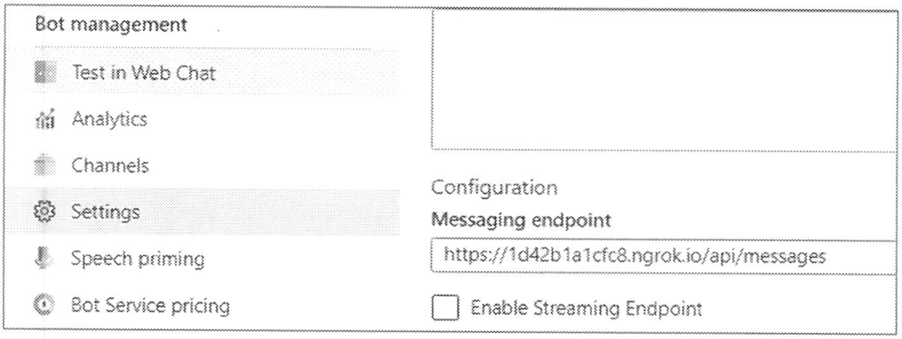

Figure 2-25. *Update Messaging Endpoint*

Note   The free version of ngrok will create a new URL each time you restart the web server. Make sure you update the Messaging endpoint of your URL each time you restart the web server when you are testing the app.

Install the Custom App in Microsoft Teams

Now let's install the app in Microsoft Teams. In the browser, navigate to `https://teams.microsoft.com` and sign in with the credentials of a Work and School account.

Microsoft Teams is available for use as a web client, desktop client, and mobile client.

Using the app bar navigation menu, select the More added apps button. Then select More apps followed by Upload a custom app and then Upload for me or my teams (Figure 2-26).

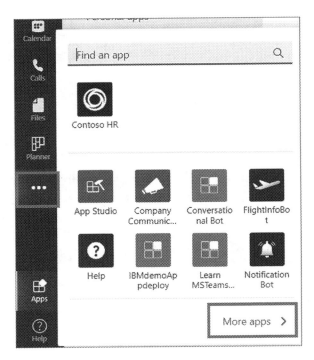

Figure 2-26. *Add apps to MS Teams*

In the file dialog that appears, select the Microsoft Teams package in your project. This app package is a ZIP file that can be found in the projects **./package** folder (Figure 2-27).

Figure 2-27. *Upload apps*

After installation, you will be able to see the app in the apps list (Figure 2-28).

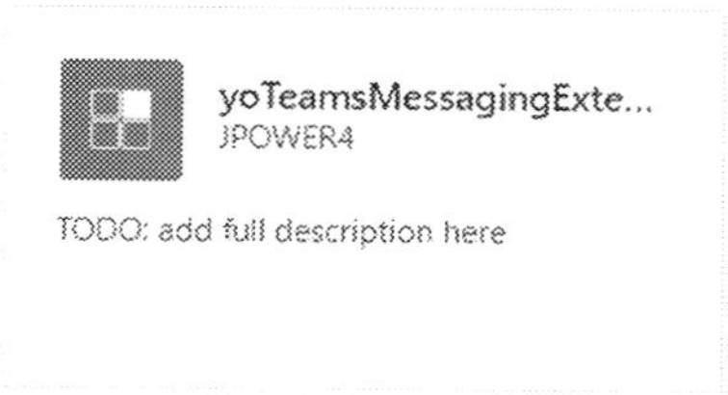

Figure 2-28. Installed app

Once the package is uploaded, Microsoft Teams will display a summary of the app.

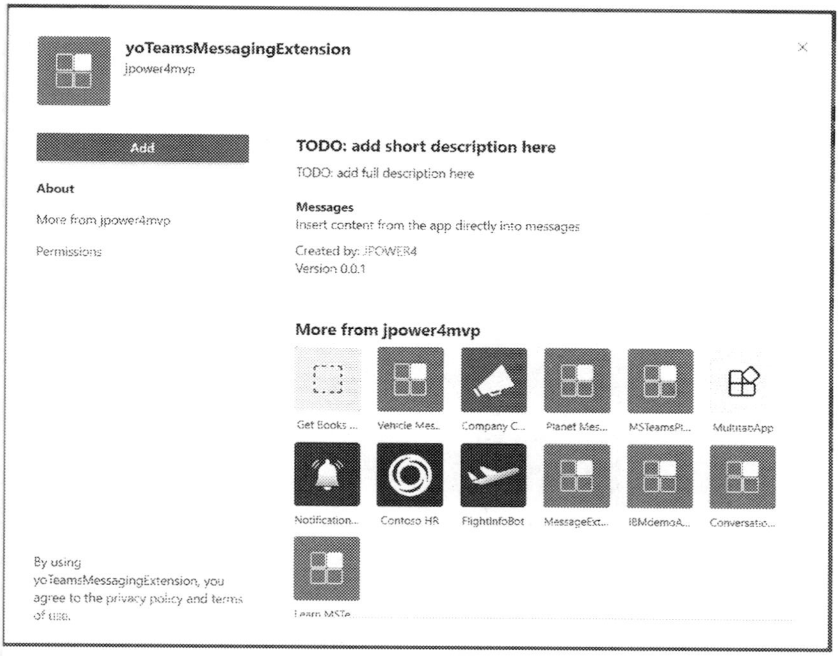

Figure 2-29. Add the app to teams & channels

Select the **Add** button to install the app (Figure 2-29).

After installing the app, Microsoft Teams will take you to the 1:1 chat with the Microsoft Teams app.

Go to your Teams conversation section (Figure 2-30).

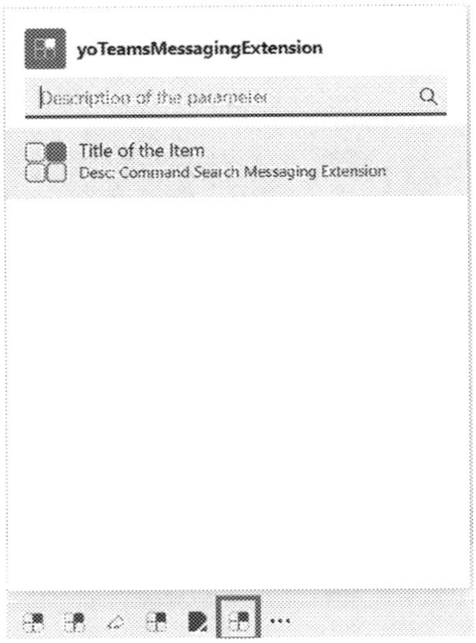

Figure 2-30. *Access the messaging extension from channel*

Select the Item and click it; it will send the detail content to your team members via a channel (Figure 2-31).

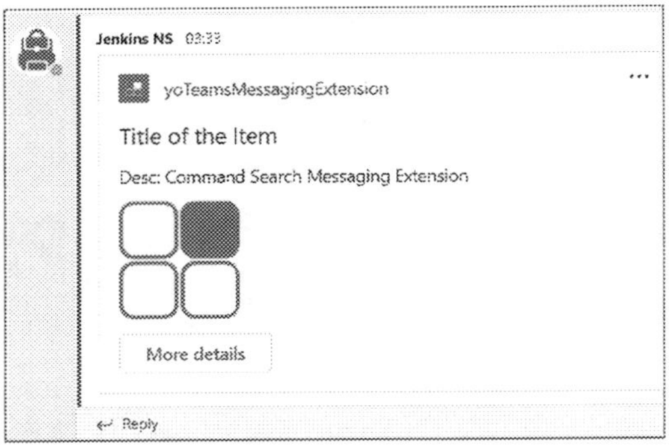

Figure 2-31. *Send the message to your team members*

In this exercise, you have created a simple out-of-box action command messaging extension using Yeoman generator for the Microsoft Teams app. We will see this in detail and more messaging examples in Chapter 4.

Exercise 2: Create a Message Extension App Using Nodejs

The Microsoft Teams developer platform makes it easy for you to extend Teams and integrate your own applications and services seamlessly into the Teams workspace. These apps can then be distributed to your enterprise or for teams around the world.

To extend Microsoft Teams, you need to create a Microsoft Teams app. A Microsoft Teams app is a web application that you host. This app can then be integrated into the user's workspace in Teams.

Messaging extensions allow users to query or post information to and from your service and post that information, in the form of cards, right into a message.

Verify that the tools are available by running the following in a terminal window:

```
$ node -v
v8.9.3
$ npm -v
5.5.1
$ gulp -v
CLI version 4.0.2
```

In this exercise, I am going to create a Message extension app using NodeJS and public google books REST API and show you how to use App Studio and deploy the app into Microsoft Teams.

Step 1: Create New Nodejs Project

First, open a command prompt and create a new directory for your favorite location, then navigate into it (Figure 2-32).

```
md nodeJSMessagingExtensions
cd nodeJSMessagingExtensions
```

```
C:\Jenkins\JPower4\Book\MSTeamsBook\nodeJSMessagingExtensions>
```

Figure 2-32. *Creating new folder for nodejs app*

Create a new NodeJS project by creating your package.json file with the following command (Figure 2-33).

npm init

```
package name: (nodejsmessagingextensions)
version: (1.0.0)
description: Message Extension with nodejs
entry point: (index.js) getBooks.js
test command:
git repository:
keywords:
author: JPOWER4
license: (ISC)
```

Figure 2-33. *Creating new app using npm init*

Enter your project details and then install ngrok

npm install ngrok

then open the project using Visual studio code, type the command below

code (Figure 2-34).

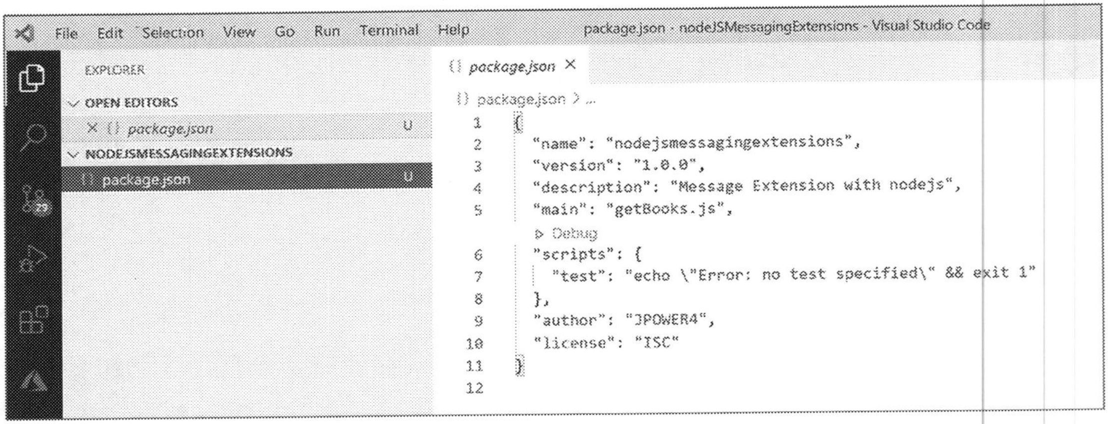

Figure 2-34. *package.json*

Create a file called getBooks.js and paste the following code:

```
const ngrok = require('ngrok');

var request = require('request');
var util = require("util");
var restify = require('restify');
var builder = require('botbuilder');
var teams = require('botbuilder-teams');

var connector = new teams.TeamsChatConnector({
    appId: "<update the bot ID>",
    appPassword: "<update the bot ID password>"
});

const port = 8080;

var server = restify.createServer();

server.listen(port, function() {
    console.log(`Node.js server listening on ${port}`);
    ngrok.connect(port, function(err, url) {
        console.log(`Node.js local server is publicly-accessible at ${url}`);
    });
    console.log('%s listening to %s', server.name, util.inspect(server.
    address()));
});

// this will reset and allow to receive from any tenants
connector.resetAllowedTenants();

var bot = new builder.UniversalBot(connector);

server.post('/api/composeExtension', connector.listen());
server.post('/api/messages', connector.listen());
server.post('/', connector.listen());

var composeExtensionHandler = function(event, query, callback) {
    var attachments = [];
```

```
var url = "https://www.googleapis.com/books/v1/volumes?q=" + query.
parameters[0].value + "&limit=100&offset=0";
if (query.parameters[0].value == undefined | query.parameters[0].value
== '') {
    url = "https://www.googleapis.com/books/v1/volumes?q=ISBN:978078974
    8591&limit=10";
}
request(url, {
    json: true
}, (err, res, body) => {
    if (err) {
        return console.log(err);
    }
    var data = body;
    for (var o of data.items) {
        try {

            console.log(o.volumeInfo.title);

            var logo = {
                alt: o.volumeInfo.title,
                url: o.volumeInfo.imageLinks.thumbnail
            };

            var card = new builder.HeroCard()
                .title("Title: " + o.volumeInfo.title)
                .text("" + o.volumeInfo.description)
                .subtitle("Publisher: " + o.volumeInfo.publisher)
                .images([logo])
                .buttons([{
                    type: "openUrl",
                    title: "View Image",
                    value: o.volumeInfo.imageLinks.thumbnail
                }]);

            attachments.push(card.toAttachment());
```

```
        } catch (err) {
            console.log(err);
        }
    };

    var response = teams.ComposeExtensionResponse
        .result('list')
        .attachments(attachments)
        .toResponse();

    // Send the response to teams
    callback(null, response, 200);

    //}
    });
};

connector.onQuery('searchCmd', composeExtensionHandler);

var composeInvoke = function(event) {
    console.log(event);
};

connector.onInvoke('composeInvoke');
```

The code above is fairly straightforward; first declare required modules and create a TeamChatConnector to map the **appId** and **appPassword**. Then create a server and listen using ngrok to execute locally.

Next, searching books using google books REST API and building as a Hero Card and sending to the chat window by an attachment object, the user can search by ISBN number.

Install restify is a framework utilizing connect style middleware for building REST APIs:

npm install restify

Microsoft Teams App only supports Microsoft Bot Builder framework, and for that I am compiling the bot framework our NodeJS project.

Install the headers below to refer to the BOT Framework:

```
npm install botbuilder@3.13.1
npm install botbuilder-teams
```

Now that we have completed the get books messaging extension coding, next we can create an app package to install in Microsoft Teams.

Step 2: Use App Studio to Create Your Apps for Microsoft Teams

Let's use App Studio to create and integrate our Teams apps:

- Go to `https://teams.microsoft.com`

- Log in with your Office 365 credentials

- Go to Apps to find the App Studio, and if App Studio is not available, then install it.

  - Get **App Studio** from Store

  - In Teams, click Apps button, search for "App Studio," install (Figure 2-35).

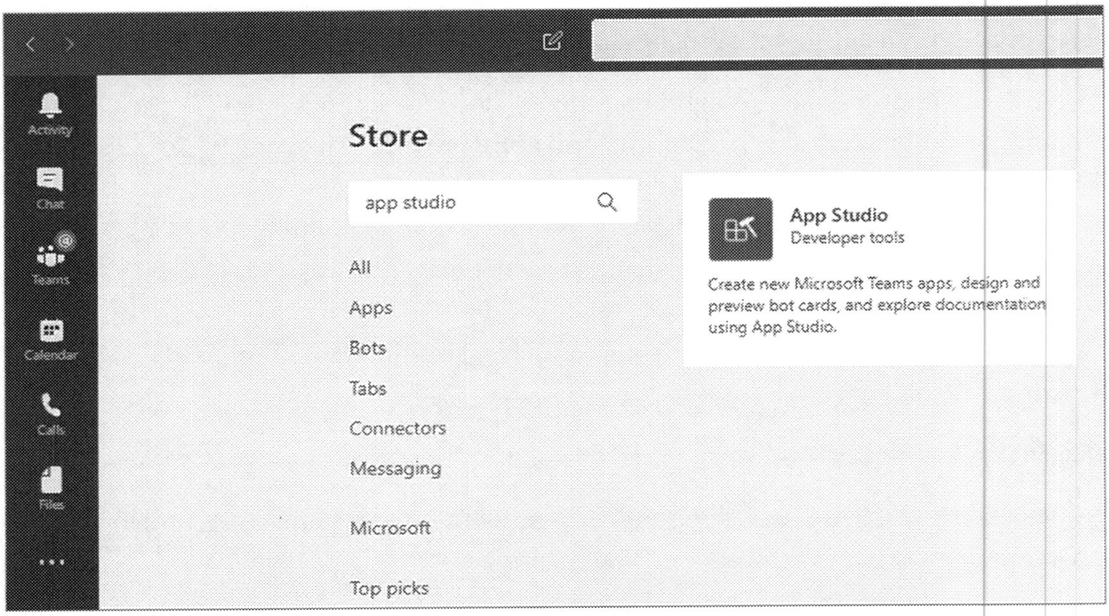

Figure 2-35. *Install App Studio*

- Go to apps and find App Studio to create an App package configuration (Figure 2-36).

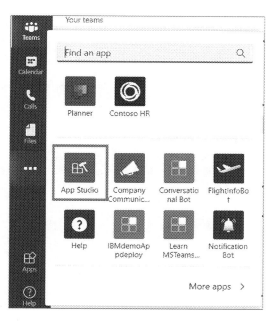

Figure 2-36. *Create App Package*

- Click App Studio and open it.
- Move to Manifest editor, and create a new app (Figure 2-37).

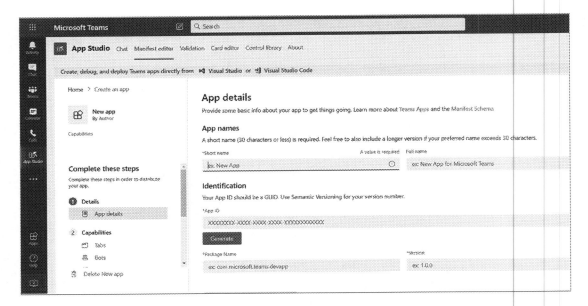

Figure 2-37. *Manifest editor*

- **Short Name**: Get Books App

- **Full Name:** To get books using ISBN number

- Click **Generate** button to create App Id

- **Package Name**: jpower4.msteams.messagingextension

- **Version**: 1.0.0

- **Short Description**: Messaging extension Teams App development

- **Long Description**: Messaging extension Teams solution development

- **Developer**: JPOWER4

- **Website**: https://github.com/jenkinsns

- **Privacy Statement** : https://github.com/jenkinsns

- **Terms of use :** https://github.com/jenkinsns

- **Branding:** upload Full color 192 x 192 image, Transparent outline 32 x 32 image, and select the theme color

Select **Messaging extension** under Capabilities

- Click Setup and give a Bot Name (Figure 2-38).

Messaging Extension   ✕

Please create a new bot, or select an existing one for your messaging extension.

Create new bot   Use existing bot

To create a messaging extension you'll need a bot. Give it a name and click the "Create" button below. This will register your bot with Microsoft and generate a new App ID for your bot.

*Bot name

MyExtensionBot

☑ Can update configuration?

Create

Figure 2-38. *Create new bot for Messaging extension*

- Click **Create** to create the bot
- Then get the bot ID and app password (generate new password) from the messaging extension section (Figure 2-39).

New password generated   ⊗

This is the only time when it will be displayed. Please store it securely.

LTx_O2N3xE3qLLC9KJ_IQG-7~GaNii3OOF

OK

Figure 2-39. *New Password generated*

- App Id and App Passwords are generated (Figure 2-40).

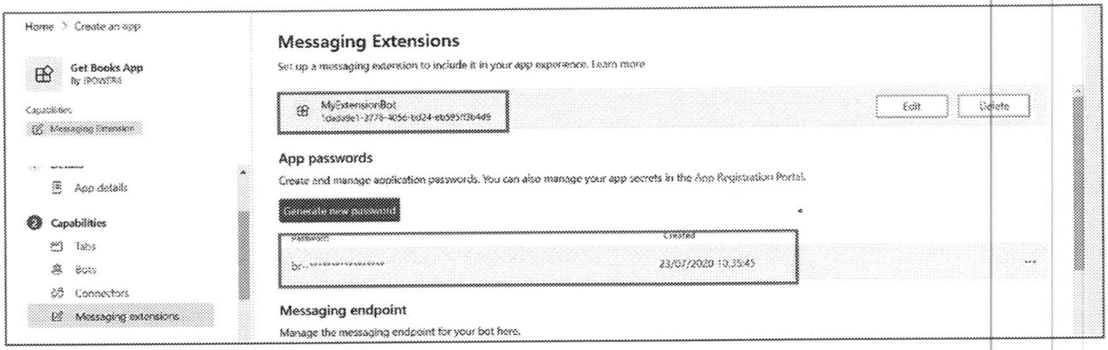

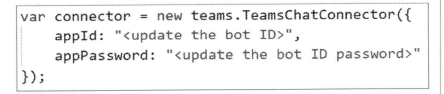

Figure 2-40. *Messaging Extensions AppID*

- Go to the getBooks.js file to update **appID** and **appPassword;** refer to the section below (Figure 2-41).

```
var connector = new teams.TeamsChatConnector({
    appId: "<update the bot ID>",
    appPassword: "<update the bot ID password>"
});
```

Figure 2-41. *Create TeamsChatConnector*

After it is updated, the code looks like this:

```
var connector = new teams.TeamsChatConnector({
    appId: "1dada9e1-3776-4056-bd24-eb595ff3b4d9",
    appPassword: "br~RN7iX6W.ckM93M8EU5Q-_v29IKtzF2~"
})
```

Then add a Messaging endpoint URL to get a public URL with https because we need ngrok to execute locally.

Step 3: Use ngrok to Start Listening on Port 8080

Go to the Command prompt and type the below command to start the application (Figure 2-42):

node getBooks.js

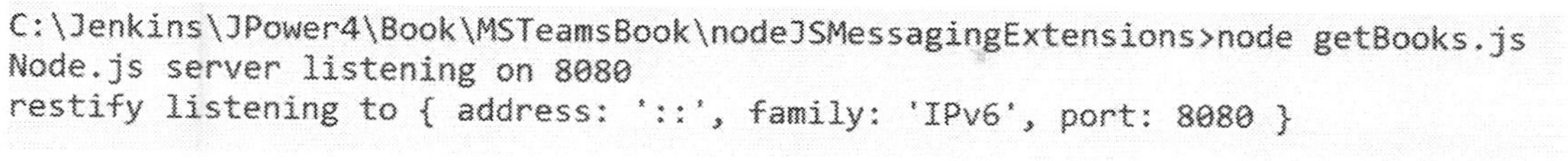

```
C:\Jenkins\JPower4\Book\MSTeamsBook\nodeJSMessagingExtensions>node getBooks.js
Node.js server listening on 8080
restify listening to { address: '::', family: 'IPv6', port: 8080 }
```

Figure 2-42. *node execution*

Then open a new browser and access
`http://localhost:4040/inspect/http`

Then you are be able to see the public URL: `https://a0a0e7883beb.ngrok.io`
(Figure 2-43).

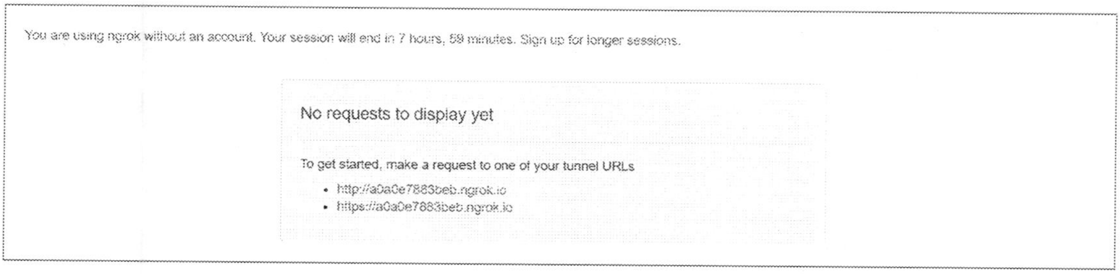

Figure 2-43. *ngrok request url*

Then go to App Studio and update the Bot endpoint address (Figure 2-44).
`https://a0a0e7883beb.ngrok.io/api/messages`

Messaging Extensions

Set up a messaging extension to include it in your app experience. Learn more

Messaging endpoint

Manage the messaging endpoint for your bot here.

Bot endpoint address

`https://a0a0e7883beb.ngrok.io/api/messages`   ⊘

Figure 2-44. *Messaging endpoint address*

Then Click Add button under the command section, and select "Allow users to query your service for information and insert that into a message" (Figure 2-45).

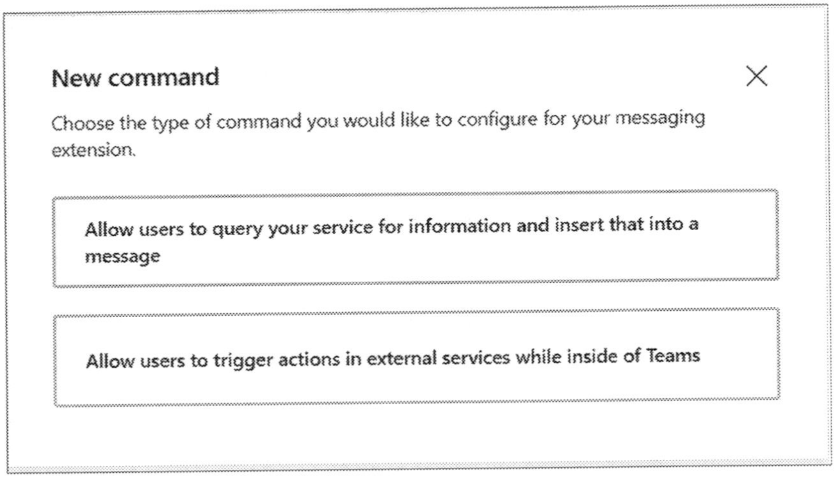

New command   ✕

Choose the type of command you would like to configure for your messaging extension.

Allow users to query your service for information and insert that into a message

Allow users to trigger actions in external services while inside of Teams

Figure 2-45. *Messaging extension action command*

Then fill in the New command form:

- Command Id: searchCmd

- Title: Search

- Description: Search for your book

- Then Add Parameters

- Name: searchKeyword

- Title: ISBN Number

- Description: Enter your ISBN Number (Figure 2-46).

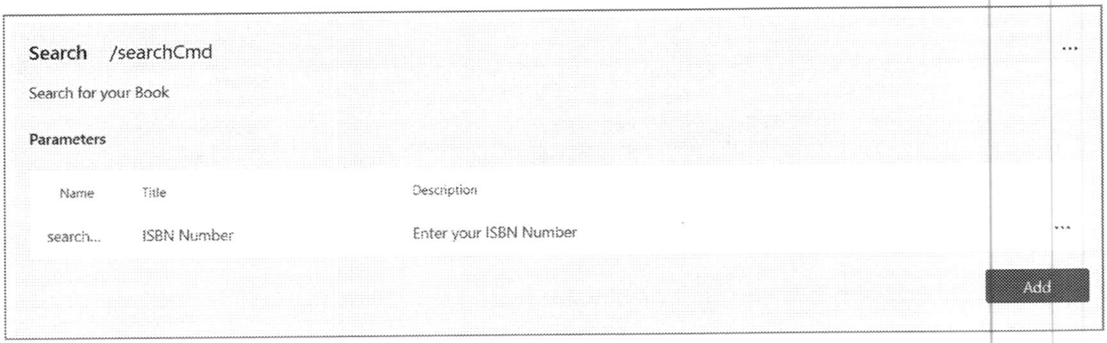

Search   /searchCmd   ...

Search for your Book

Parameters

Name	Title	Description
search...	ISBN Number	Enter your ISBN Number

Add

Figure 2-46. *Messaging extension parameters*

Click **Test and distribute** under the **Finish** section to test the app (Figure 2-47).

Test and Distribute

Choose what you'd like to do with your app. Learn more

Install

Install your app in Teams for testing.

> Install

Download

Download and save your app package for distribution and submission.

> Download

Submit

Submit your app to the Teams app store for approval.

> Submit

Figure 2-47. *Test and Distribute*

Then download the app package to test from your channel.

Step 4: Install the App to Your Team

Go to your team ➤ navigate to Manage Team ➤ Apps ➤ moreapps (Figure 2-48).

Figure 2-48. *Upload the app in to Teams*

Upload a custom app (select the downloaded zip file to upload).
Then click the **Add** button to install it (Figure 2-49).

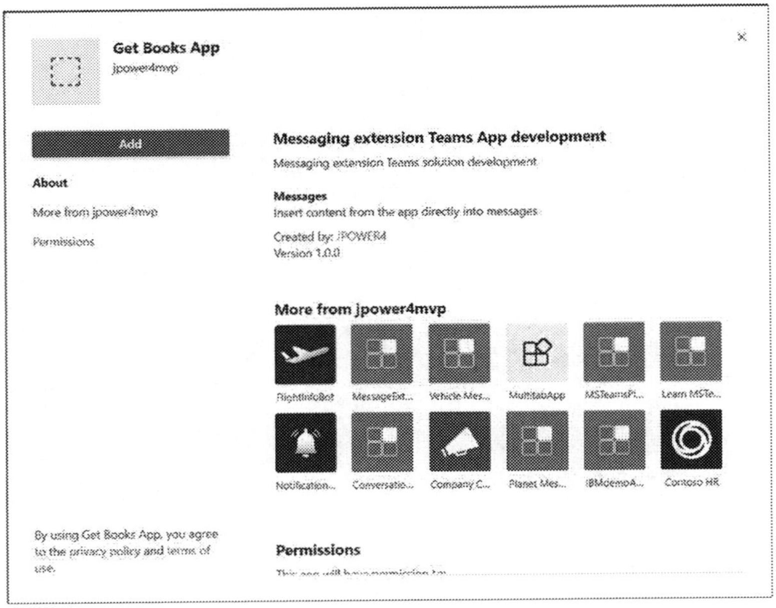

Figure 2-49. *Add the app to Teams*

Now google books search app is available in your Team, so go to your channel and access the app.

Click **...** in the conversation section and search the messaging extension app as it is highlighted below (Figure 2-50).

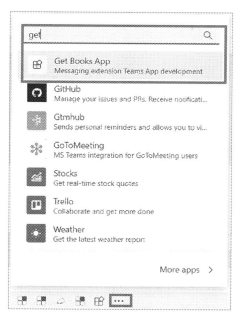

Figure 2-50. *Search the messaging extension app*

Then select the app; it loads a list of books and you will be able to select and send to your team members (Figure 2-51).

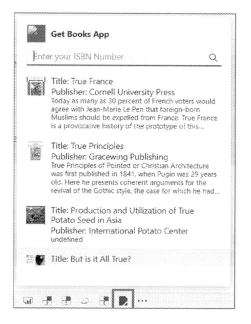

Figure 2-51. *Messaging extension loaded books list*

Then you can search books by the ISBN number and get the relevant books (Figure 2-52).

Figure 2-52. *Search books by ISBN number*

Select the Book and it will build a Hero Card with the title, publisher, image, and description to your teams' members. Then send to your team members as conversation (Figure 2-53).

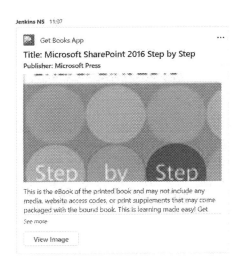

Figure 2-53. *Send the messaging extension card to team members*

Conclusion

In this chapter, you have learned the different IDE options and setup environments for various generators. It also explained how to create simple custom apps for Microsoft Teams using Yeoman Generator (yo teams), and Nodejs. You have also learned about various contexts and scenarios about Teams apps line of business and about Bot Channel registration, App Studio, and deploying the apps into Teams.

Now you have learned how to create simple custom apps using Yeoman generator and using NodeJS for Microsoft Teams. Along with this you will start learning different options and features of Microsoft Teams apps in our upcoming chapters.

CHAPTER 3

Interactive Conversational Bots

Everyone is talking about bots and every business wants to figure out how to use them. We want to believe that we live in a world full of intelligent automation. Organizations are always on the lookout for new ways and better approaches to bolster business by easily associating with buyers and providing customer support that adjusts and develops with changing communication propensities. Conversational bots allow users to interact with your web service through text, interactive cards, and task modules.

In this chapter, you will learn about various features of conversational bots and how to create and add bots to Microsoft Teams.

Overview of Conversational Bots

Bots help users get tasks done in conversation in Teams. Bots can do things like kick off workflows and provide statuses on them, give and receive kudos from team members, create lightweight surveys to gauge employee satisfaction, and answer natural language questions about sales and customer usage data.

A conversation bot allows users to interact within multiple forms like text, adaptive cards, forms, etc., from the Microsoft Teams client.

Microsoft Bot Framework

The Microsoft Bot Framework handles all the complexities of state management, message routing, etc. You need to build the web API using a Bot Framework and host it in Azure and add intelligence to your bot using Azure cognitive services such as the LUIS (Language Understanding Intelligent service), which helps to parse your message into intents and entities.

© Jenkins NS 2021
J. NS, *Building Solutions with Microsoft Teams*, https://doi.org/10.1007/978-1-4842-6476-8_3

If you already have a bot that is based on the Bot Framework, you can easily adapt it to work in Microsoft Teams. The available packages extend the basic Bot Builder SDK classes and methods as follows:

- Use specialized card types like the Office 365 Connector card.

- Consume and set Teams-specific channel data on activities.

- Process messaging extension requests.

Teams Activity Handlers

Like other bots, when a bot is designed for Microsoft Teams, it receives an activity, and it passes it on to its activity handlers. Under the covers, there is one base handler called the turn handler, which all activities are routed through. The turn handler calls the required activity handler to handle whatever type of activity was received. Where a bot designed for Microsoft Teams differs is that it is derived from a Teams activity handler class that is derived from the Bot Framework's activity handler class.

Bots in Microsoft Teams Channels and Group Chats

The basic architecture of bots starts from Microsoft cognitive services, which help to create AI-based apps and provide various APIs like Vision, Speech and Language, and Video. Microsoft cognitive services provide the LUIS, which helps to convert messages to the meaningful data. See Figure 3-1.

Microsoft Bot framework is a framework to build and deploy your bots for Microsoft Teams channels. Bot framework handles all the complexities of state management, message routing, etc. You only need to build the web API using Bot Framework, for bot, you need to build using bot framework and host it in Azure and add intelligence to your bot using Azure cognitive services – LUIS (Language understanding Intelligent service) which helps to parse your message into intents and entities.

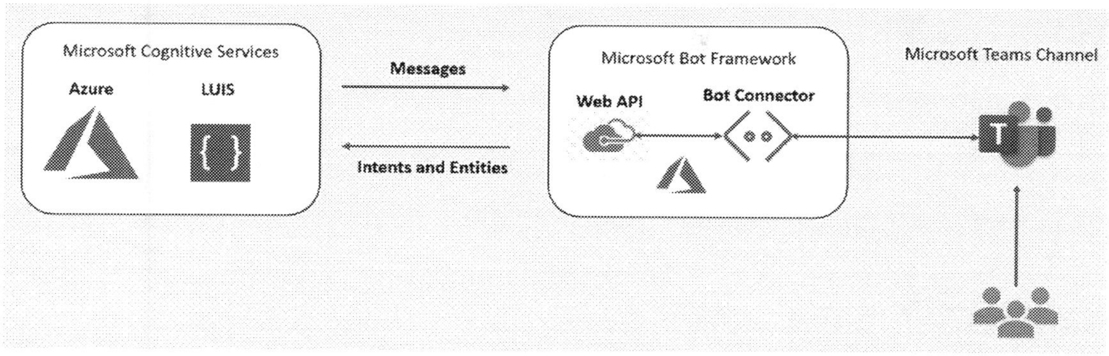

Figure 3-1. *Teams BOT Architecture*

There are three types of conversation bots within the Microsoft Team Client:

- Bots in personal chats - Personal Conversation or Personal Chat

- Bots in group chats - Group Conversation or Group Chat

- Bots in channels - Teams Channel

A bot behaves slightly differently depending on what kind of conversation it is involved in:

- Bots in channel and group chat conversations require the user to **@mention** the bot to invoke it in a channel.

- Bots in a one-to-one conversation don't require an **@mention**. All messages sent by the user will be routed to your bot.

Proactive Messages from Bots

Proactive messages are sent by a bot to start a conversation. Welcome messages and poll responses or external event notifications are common scenarios to use proactive messages.

Proactive messages generally fall into one of two categories:

- Welcome messages

- Notifications

Welcome Messages

When you use proactive messages to send a welcome message to users, you must keep in mind that for most people receiving the message, they'll have no context for why they're receiving it. Welcome messages are also the first time they'll have interacted with your app; it's your opportunity to create a good first impression.

Notification Messages

When you use proactive messages to send notifications, you need to make sure your users have a clear path to perform common actions based on your notification, and a clear understanding of why the notification occurred.

Exercise 1 - Creating a Conversational Bot for Microsoft Teams

Before starting the exercise, verify your environment. In this exercise, I am using the tools mentioned below, installed in my environment:

- Node.js - v10.16.0
- NPM - 6.9.0
- Gulp
  - CLI version: 2.3.0
  - Local version: 4.0.2
- Yeomen Generator of MS Teams - 2.14.0
- Visual Studio Code

and

- Microsoft Azure Subscription
- Office 365 Subscription

In the exercise, you will learn how to create and add a new bot to a Microsoft Teams app and interact with it from the Microsoft Teams client.

You need:

- To host a publicly accessible web service.

- To register your bot with the Bot Framework.

- To create a Teams app package with an app manifest.

The following steps are to be followed to create a new Microsoft Teams bot app for your Microsoft Team client:

1. Register the bot with Microsoft Azure's Bot Framework.

2. Bot Channel Registration.

3. Enable the Microsoft Teams channel for the bot.

4. Retrieve the bot app ID and password.

5. Create Microsoft Teams app using Yeoman generator.

6. Test the conversation bot.

Register the Bot with Microsoft Azure's Bot Framework

Open a browser and navigate to the Azure portal (`https://portal.azure.com/`. Sign in using your **username@tenantname.onmicrosoft.com** that was used from the Azure subscription.

Select **Create a resource** in the left-hand navigation (Figure 3-2).

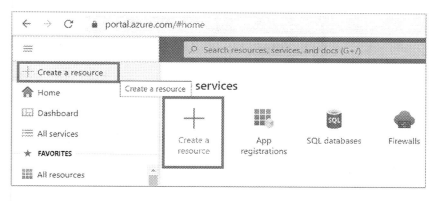

Figure 3-2. *Create a resource*

Enter a resource group in the Search the marketplace input box and select Resource group (Figure 3-3).

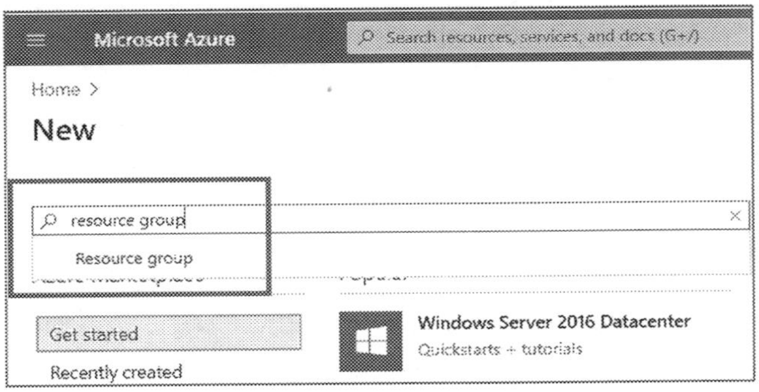

Figure 3-3. *Resource group*

On the **Resource Group** page, select the **Create** button to create a new resource group (Figure 3-4).

Figure 3-4. *Create resource group*

Select a valid subscription, enter a name for the resource group, **Ex: Teams**, and select the wanted region. None of these choices will impact the bot registration and are up to you (Figure 3-5).

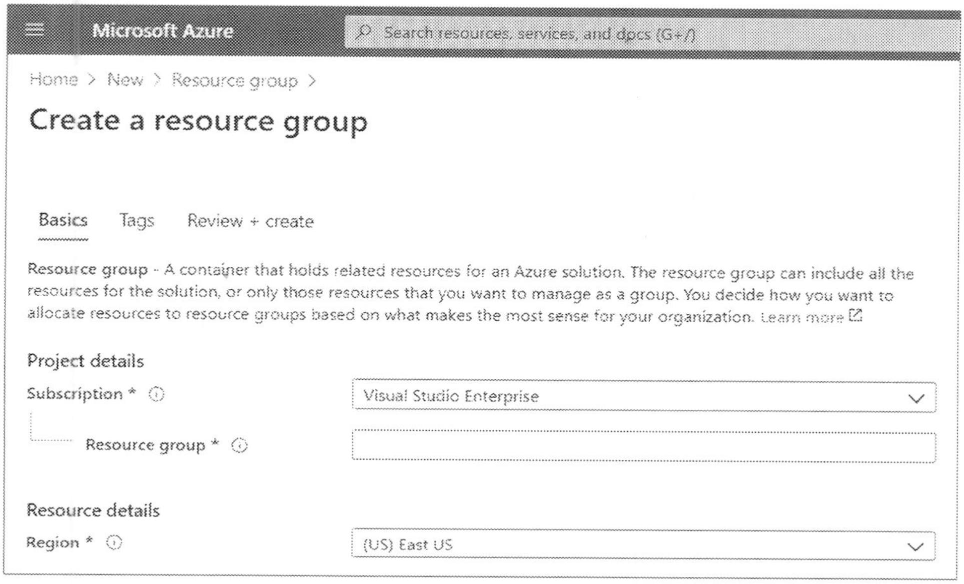

Figure 3-5. *Create resource group form*

Complete the wizard to create the resource group.

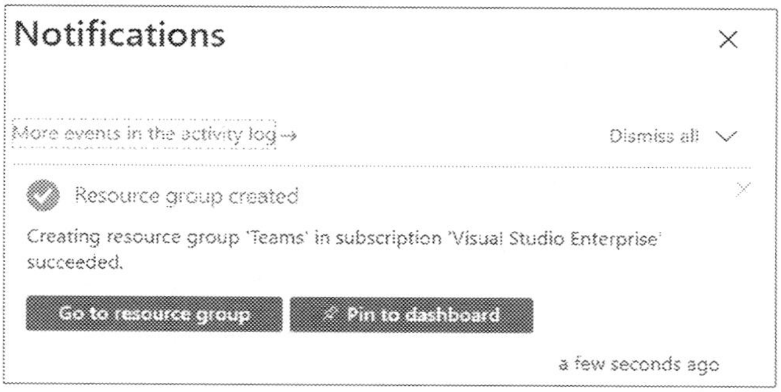

Figure 3-6. *Resource Group Created Notification*

Once Azure has completed the resource group creation process, navigate to the resource group (Figure 3-6).

From the resource group, select the **Add** or **Create resources** button (Figure 3-7).

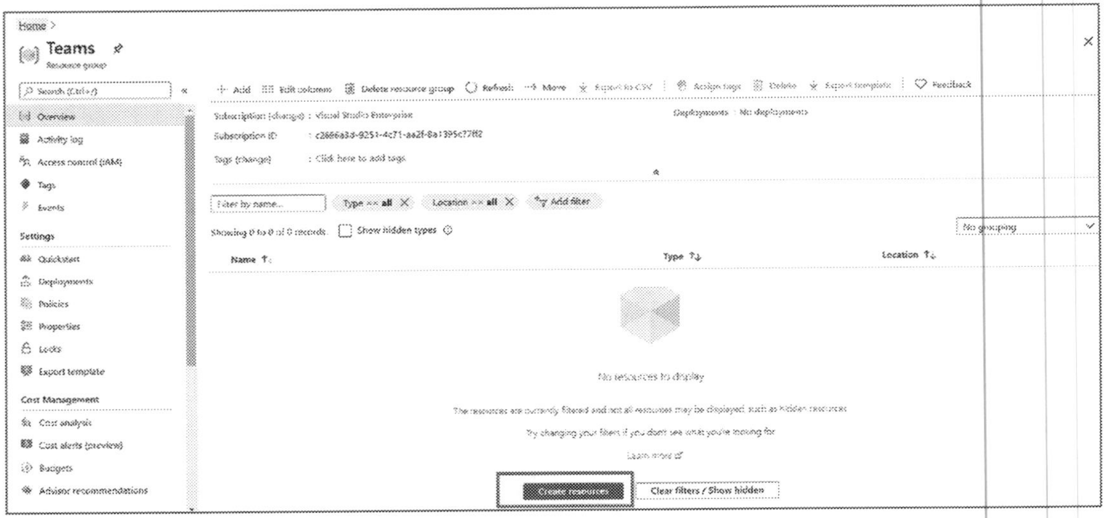

Figure 3-7. *Create Resources*

Bot Channel Registration

Enter **bot** in the **Search the marketplace** input box and select **Bot Channels Registration** from the list of resources returned. Then select **Create** on the next page to start the process of registering a new bot resource (Figure 3-8).

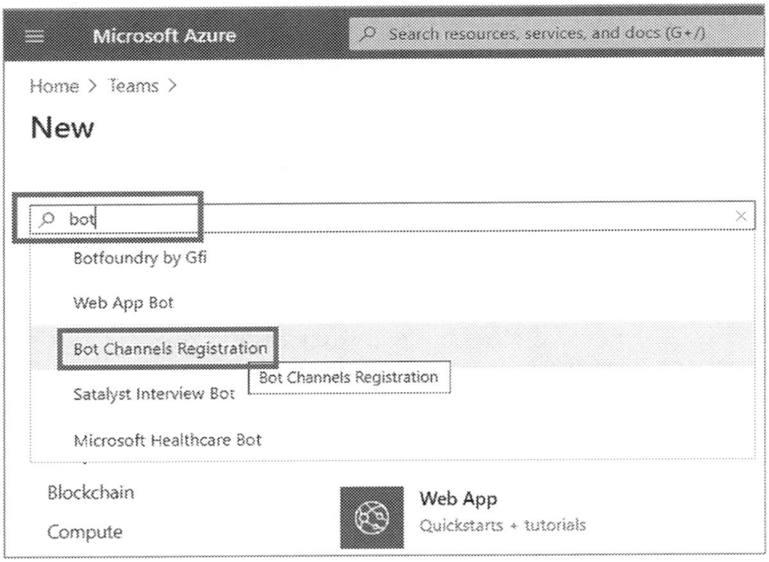

Figure 3-8. *Search Bot Channel Registration*

In the **Bot Channels Registration** Page, click to initiate create Bot Channels Registration. See Figure 3-9.

Figure 3-9. *Bot Channel Registration*

In the **Bot Channels Registration blade**, enter the following values and then select **Create**:

- **Bot handle**: Enter a globally unique name for the bot
    - **Ex:** MSTeamsExercise2
- **Subscription**: Select the subscription you selected previously when creating the resource group
- **Resource group**: Select the resource group you created previously - **Ex:** Teams
- **Location**: Select your preferred Azure region
- **Pricing tier**: Select a preferred pricing tier; the F0 tier is free
- **Messaging endpoint**: `https://REPLACE_THIS.ngrok.io/api/ messages`

The bot registration needs to know the endpoint of the web service where the bot is implemented. This will change each time you start the ngrok utility used in previous exercises (Figure 3-10).

- Application Insights: Off
- Microsoft App ID and password: Auto create App ID and password

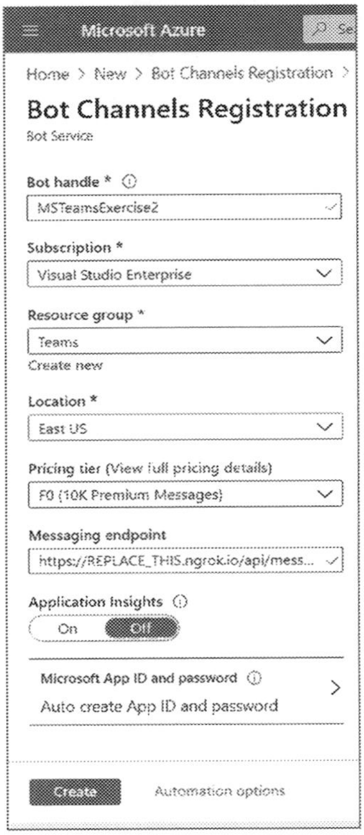

Figure 3-10. *Create Bot Channel Registration*

Azure will start to provision the new resource. This will take a moment or two. Once it is finished, navigate to the bot resource in the resource group as shown in Figure 3-11.

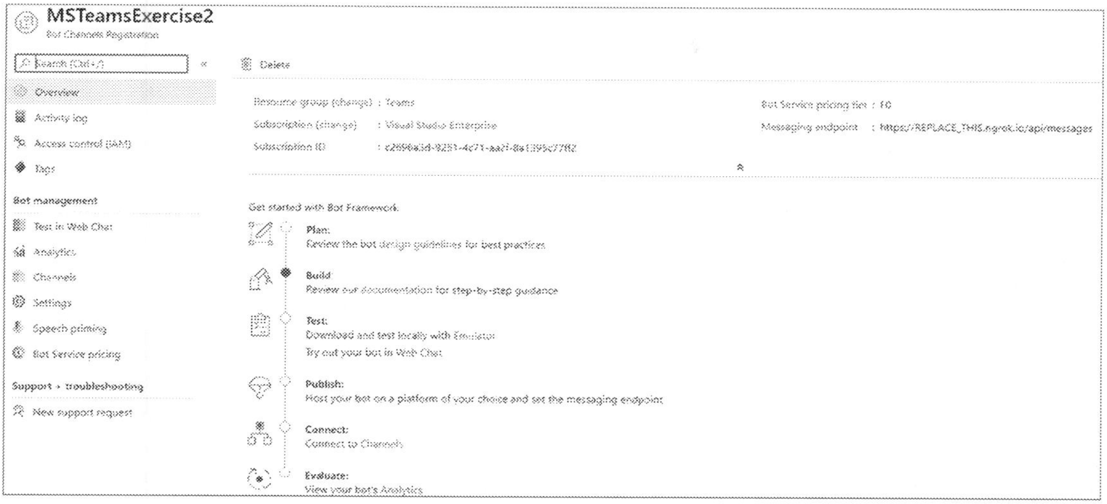

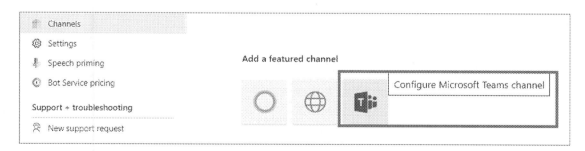

Figure 3-11. *Bot Channel Registration*

Enable the Microsoft Teams Channel for the Bot

For the bot to interact with Microsoft Teams, you must enable the Teams channel.

- From the bot resource in Azure, select **Channels** in the left-hand navigation.

- On the **Connect to channels** pane, select the **Microsoft Teams channel**, then select **Save** to confirm the action (Figure 3-12).

Figure 3-12. *Select Teams Channel*

- Agree to the Terms of Service

Once this process is complete, you should see both the Web Chat and Microsoft Teams listed in your enabled channels (Figure 3-13).

Figure 3-13. *Connect to channels*

Retrieve the Bot App Id and Password

When Azure created the bot, it also registered a new Azure AD app for the bot. You need to generate this new bot app as a secret and copy the app's credentials.

Select **Settings** from the left-hand navigation. Scroll down to the Microsoft App ID section.

Copy the ID of the bot as you'll need it later. See Figure 3-14.

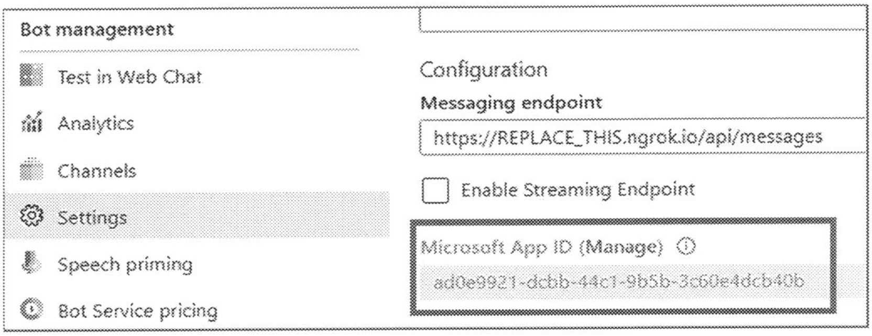

Figure 3-14. *App ID*

Create a Client Secret for the App

Click the **Manage** link to navigate to the **Azure AD app.**

For the daemon app to run without user involvement, it will sign into Azure AD with an application ID and either a certificate or secret. In this exercise, you'll use a secret.

Select **Certificates & secrets** from the left-hand navigation panel.

Select the **New client secret** button under Client secrets section

When prompted, give the secret a description and select one of the expiration duration options provided: for example: Never and select **Add**.

Note: Copy the new client secret value. You won't be able to retrieve it after you perform another operation or leave this blade. See Figure 3-15.

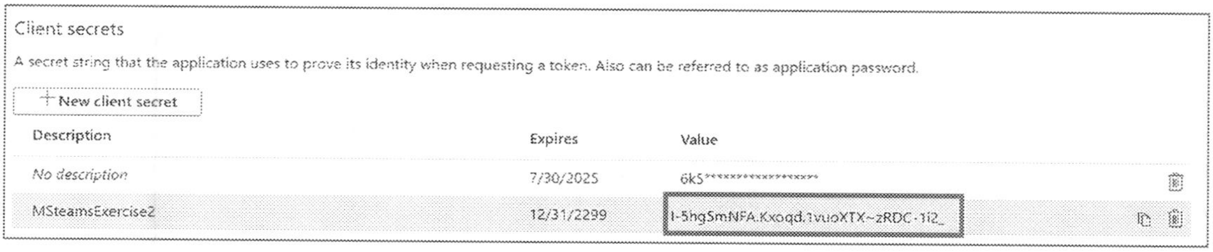

Figure 3-15. *App Client Secret*

The Certificate & Secrets page will display the new secret. It's important you copy this value as it's only shown this one time; if you leave the page and come back, it will only show as a masked value.

Copy and store the value of the secret value as you will need it later.

Create Microsoft Teams App Using Yeoman Generator

In this section, you will create a new Teams app using Yeoman generator (yo teams):

- To create a new web part project
- Create a new project directory in your favorite location
- Open command prompt
- Create a new folder "**conversationalBot**"
- Navigate to a newly created directory
- Run the Yeoman generator for Microsoft Teams by running the following command: **yo teams** (Figure 3-16).

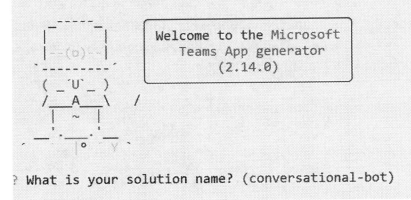

```
C:\Jenkins\JPower4\Book\MSTeamsBook\conversationalBot>yo teams
```

Welcome to the Microsoft
Teams App generator
(2.14.0)

```
? What is your solution name? (conversational-bot)
```

Figure 3-16. *yo teams*

Yeoman will launch and ask you a series of questions. Answer the questions with the following values (as shown in Figure 3-17):

- What is your solution name? conversational-bot

- Where do you want to place the files? Use the current folder

- Title of your Microsoft Teams App project? Conversational Bot

- Your (company) name? (max 32 characters) JPOWER4

- Which manifest version would you like to use? v1.6

- Enter your Microsoft Partner ID, if you have one? (Leave blank to skip)

- What features do you want to add to your project? A bot

- The URL where you will host this solution? https://conversationalbot.azurewebsites.net

- Would you like show a loading indicator when your app/tab loads? No

- Would you like to include a Test framework and initial tests? No

- Would you like to use Azure Applications Insights for telemetry? No

- What type of bot would you like to use? A new Bot Framework bot

- What is the name of your bot? conversationalbot

- What is the Microsoft App ID for the bot? It's found in the Bot Framework portal (`https://dev.botframework.com`). ad0e9921-dcbb-44c1-

- 9b5b-3c60e4dcb40b

- Do you want to add a static tab to your bot? No

- Do you want to support file upload to the bot? No

```
? What is your solution name? conversational-bot
? Where do you want to place the files? Use the current folder
? Title of your Microsoft Teams App project? Conversational Bot
? Your (company) name? (max 32 characters) JPOWER4
? Which manifest version would you like to use? v1.6
? Enter your Microsoft Partner ID, if you have one? (Leave blank to skip)
? What features do you want to add to your project? A bot
? The URL where you will host this solution? https://conversationalbot.azurewebsites.net
? Would you like show a loading indicator when your app/tab loads? No
? Would you like to include Test framework and initial tests? No
? Would you like to use Azure Applications Insights for telemetry? No
? What type of bot would you like to use? A new bot Framework bot
? What is the name of your bot? conversationalbot
? What is the Microsoft App ID for the bot? It's found in the Bot Framework portal (https://dev.botframework.com). ad0e9921-dcbb-44c1-
9b5b-3c60e4dcb40b
? Do you want to add a static tab to your bot? No
? Do you want to support file upload to the bot? No
```

Figure 3-17. *Answer Yeoman questionnaire*

Note   Most of the answers to these questions can be changed after creating the project. For example, the URL where the project will be hosted isn't important at the time of creating or testing the project.

Open Visual Studio Code using **code.** in the command prompt (Figure 3-18).

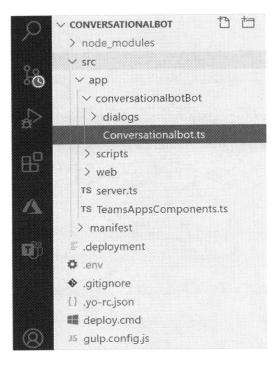

Figure 3-18. *Visual studio code OOB*

- Open .env file ➤ and add the MICROSOFT_APP_PASSWORD copied from the new client secret value

*MICROSOFT_APP_PASSWORD= I-5hg5mNFA.Kxoqd.1vuoXTX~zRDC-1i2_*

This bot will respond to the message MentionMe in a 1:1 chat conversation and @MentionMe in Channel Conversation.

Figure 3-19. *Personal Conversation response*

Update the Bot Code for 1:1 Chat Conversation

Go to the ./src/app/conversationalbotBot/Conversationalbot.ts file and add the
following code.

- At first, add the headers given below:

```
import * as Util from "util";
const TextEncoder = Util.TextEncoder;
```

- Then Include Message Factory object reference to the existing
  botbuilder package:

```
TeamsActivityHandler,MessageFactory } from "botbuilder";
```

It looks like what is below:

```
import { StatePropertyAccessor, CardFactory, TurnContext, MemoryStorage,
    ConversationState, ActivityTypes, TeamsActivityHandler,
    MessageFactory, ChannelInfo, TeamsChannelData, ConversationParameters,
    teamsGetChannelId,Activity, BotFrameworkAdapter, ConversationReference,
    ConversationResourceResponse
} from "botbuilder";
```

- Go to **Conversationalbot** class and find handler **this.onMessage()**
  within the public constructor(conversationState: ConversationState).

- In the **this.onMessage()** handler, proceed with the following code to
  handle one-to-one conversation and channel conversation.

- Find the code given below:

```
let text = TurnContext.removeRecipientMention(context.activity);
                text = text.toLowerCase();
if (text.startsWith("hello")) {
```

- Replace the code given below:

```
const text: string = context.activity.text.trim().
toLowerCase();
    if (text === "mentionme") {
        await this.handleMessageMentionMeOneOnOne(context);
        return;
```

```
        } else if (text.endsWith("mentionme")) {
            await this.handleMessageMentionMeChannelConversation
            (context);
            return;
        } else if (text.startsWith("hello")) {
```

- The above code is handling the personal chat and channel conversation request from the conversational bot.

- Then add the code given below in the Conversationalbot class.

```
private async handleMessageMentionMeOneOnOne(context:
TurnContext): Promise<void> {
    const mention = {
      mentioned: context.activity.from,
      text: `<at>${new TextEncoder().encode(context.activity.from.
      name)}</at>`,
      type: "mention"
    };

const replyActivity = MessageFactory.text(`Hi ${mention.text} from
a 1:1 chat.`);
    replyActivity.entities = [mention];
    await context.sendActivity(replyActivity);
  }

  private async handleMessageMentionMeChannelConversation(conte
  xt: TurnContext): Promise<void> {
    const mention = {
      mentioned: context.activity.from,
      text: `<at>${new TextEncoder().encode(context.activity.from.
      name)}</at>`,
      type: "mention"
    };

    const replyActivity = MessageFactory.text(`Hi ${mention.text}!`);
    replyActivity.entities = [mention];
    const followupActivity = MessageFactory.text(`*We are in a
    channel conversation group chat in the !*`);
```

```
await context.sendActivities([replyActivity,
followupActivity]);
}
```

- ***handleMessageMentionMeOneOnOne*** method is used to handle chat conversation.

- ***handleMessageMentionMeChannelConversation*** method is used to handle channel conversation.

Modify Manifest File to Handle the Commands

Here's the process:

1. Go to the ./src/manifest/manifest.json file.

2. In the ./src/manifest/manifest.json file, verify icons' property values, and update if necessary file names to match what's in the project.

3. Locate the property bots. Add a new bot to the collection of bots registered with this Microsoft Teams app by adding the following JSON to the array. This code will add our bot to the **personal and team** scopes of the user when it is installed. It includes a single help message that will show the command it supports, MentionMe.

4. Find the "commands" section under bots ➤ commandLists and replace it with

```
"commands": [
    {
      "title": "Help",
      "description": "Shows help information"
    },
    {
      "title": "MentionMe",
      "description": "Sends message with @mention of the sender"
    }
```

5. ***File ➤ Save All*** to save the changes.

At this point, your bot is ready to test!

Test the Conversation Bot

Open command Prompt, navigate to the project folder. and execute the following command:

```
gulp ngrok-serve
```

This gulp task will run many other tasks that are displayed within the command-line console. The ngrok-serve task builds your project and starts a local web server (http://localhost:3007). It then starts ngrok with a random subdomain that creates a secure URL to your local web server.

In development, testing can be done using the tool ngrok that creates a secure rotatable URL to your local HTTP webserver. Ngrok is included as a dependency within the project so there is nothing to set up or configure (Figure 3-20).

```
Starting 'nodemon'...
[00:31:49] Finished 'nodemon' after 29 ms
[00:31:49] Starting 'watch'...
[00:31:49] HOSTNAME: 832b174576e7.ngrok.io
[tslint-plugin] Starting linter in separate process...
[tslint-plugin] Linting complete.
  msteams Initializing Microsoft Teams Express hosted App... +0ms
  msteams Creating a new bot instance at /api/messages +0ms
  msteams Server running on 3007 +405ms
```

Figure 3-20. ngrok-serve execution

Ngrok has created the temporary URL 832b174576e7.ngrok.io that will map to our locally running web server.

Then go to the Azure portal and open the Bot Channel registration App. Update the Messaging endpoint using the temporary URL 832b174576e7.ngrok.io (Figure 3-21).

Figure 3-21. Update Messaging Endpoint

Note   The free version of Ngrok will create a new URL each time you restart the web server. Make sure you update the Messaging endpoint of your URL each time you restart the web server when you are testing the app.

Install the Conversation Bot in Microsoft Teams

Now let's install the app in Microsoft Teams. In the browser, navigate to `https://teams.microsoft.com` and sign in with the credentials of a Work and School account.

Microsoft Teams is available for use as a web client, desktop client, and mobile client.

Using the app bar navigation menu, select the More added apps button. Then select More apps followed by Upload a custom app and then Upload for me or my teams (Figure 3-22).

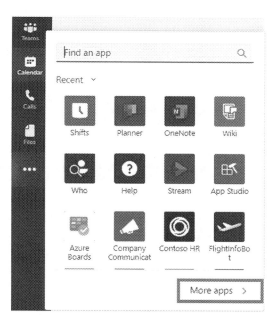

Figure 3-22. *Add apps to MS Teams*

In the file dialog that appears, select the Microsoft Teams package in your project. This app package is a ZIP file that can be found in the projects **./package** folder. See Figure 3-23.

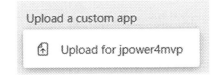

Figure 3-23. *Upload apps*

After installation, you will be able to see the app in the apps list (Figure 3-24).

Figure 3-24. *Installed app*

Once the package is uploaded, Microsoft Teams will display a summary of the app (Figure 3-25).

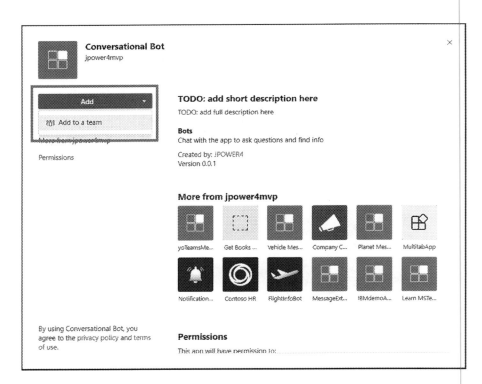

Figure 3-25. *Add the app to teams and channels*

Testing as Personal Bot

Click the Add button to navigate to chat with the bot as shown in Figure 3-26.

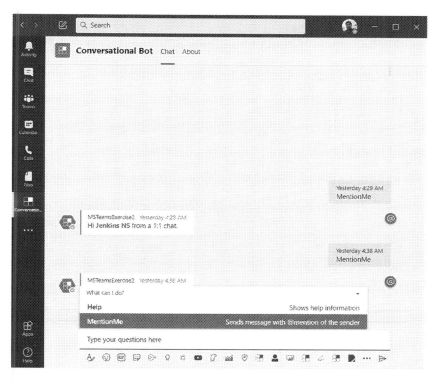

Figure 3-26. *Personal Conversation*

Notice the commands that the bot supports are shown in the compose box when the app loads. Let's test the bot!

Select the MentionMe command, or manually type mentionme in the compose box, and then press enter.

After a few seconds, you should see the bot responding to the user you are signed in with what is shown in Figure 3-27.

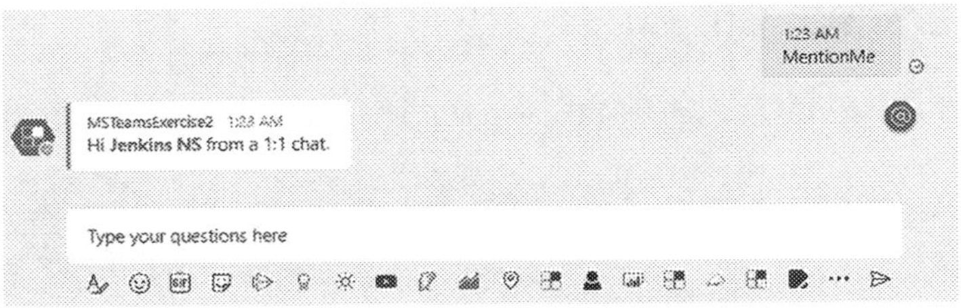

Figure 3-27. *Personal Conversation response*

We have a working personal bot that is responding when it is mentioned.

Testing in the Channel

Using the app bar navigation menu, select the More added apps button. Click and open Conversation bot, then click Add to the team link referred to in Figure 3-25.

Select the channel to install; here I have selected my existing Conversation Bot>Conversation Channel. Then click the "Set up a bot" button and set up the bot to the channel as shown in Figure 3-28.

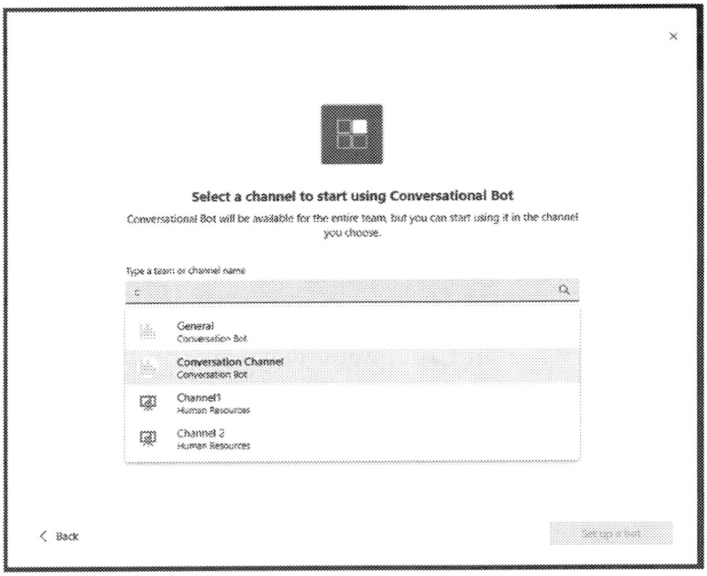

Figure 3-28. *Team Channel setup*

Navigate to an existing channel "Conversation Channel" in a team.

From the channels Conversations tab, type @Conversational Bot the bot (Figure 3-29).

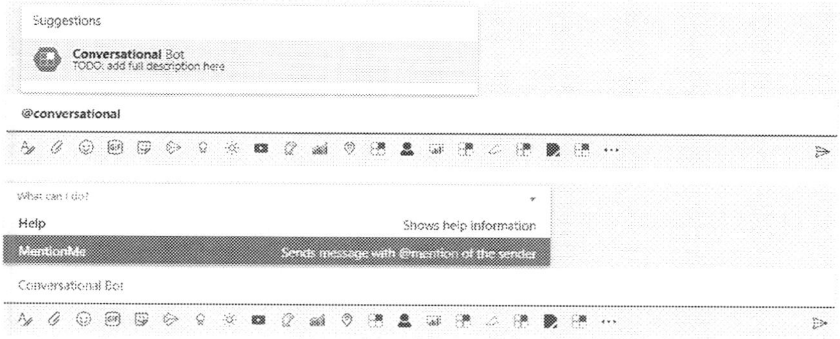

Figure 3-29. *Team Channel bot*

Select the MentionMe command, or manually type mentionme in the compose box, and then press enter.

After a few seconds, you should see the bot responding to the user and the channel conversation message. See Figure 3-30.

Figure 3-30. *Team Channel response*

Now, we have a working Team bot that is responding when it is mentioned.

Exercise 2 - Reply to Messages with Adaptive Cards

In this exercise, you will update the bot to respond to unknown messages using an Adaptive Card. The card's single action will trigger the bot to respond to the existing message with a new Adaptive Card and respond using message reactions.

Cards are actionable snippets of content that you can add to a conversation through a bot, a connector, or app. Using text, graphics, and buttons, cards allow you to communicate with an audience.

What Are Adaptive Cards?

Adaptive Cards are an open card exchange format enabling developers to exchange UI content in a common and consistent way. Adaptive Cards are a way to show and interact with data in a clear and consistent way. You'll often see Adaptive Cards being used by bots and notifications to allow a rich display of information in chats and operating system notifications.

You can use Adaptive Cards to display rich text with graphics, provide buttons to allow people to interact with the chat or notification, display dynamic information, collect feedback, and even use them to create interactive forms.

Adaptive Cards support two teams' components:

- Bots
- Messaging Extension

Also, Adaptive Cards support three action types:

- Action.OpenUrl
- Action.Submit
- Action.ShowCard

Microsoft Teams App Studio allows you to create Adaptive Cards for Teams with json, c#, and nodejs. See Figure 3-31.

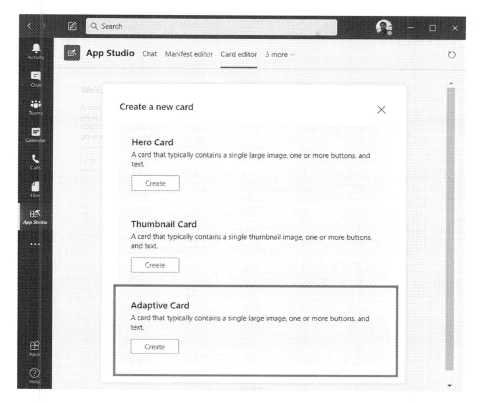

Figure 3-31. *Create Adaptive Cards*

You can also modify the Adaptive Card Action.Submit payload to support the existing Bot Framework actions using a Microsoft Teams property in the data object of Action.Submit.

Figure 3-32 is an example of an Adaptive Card.

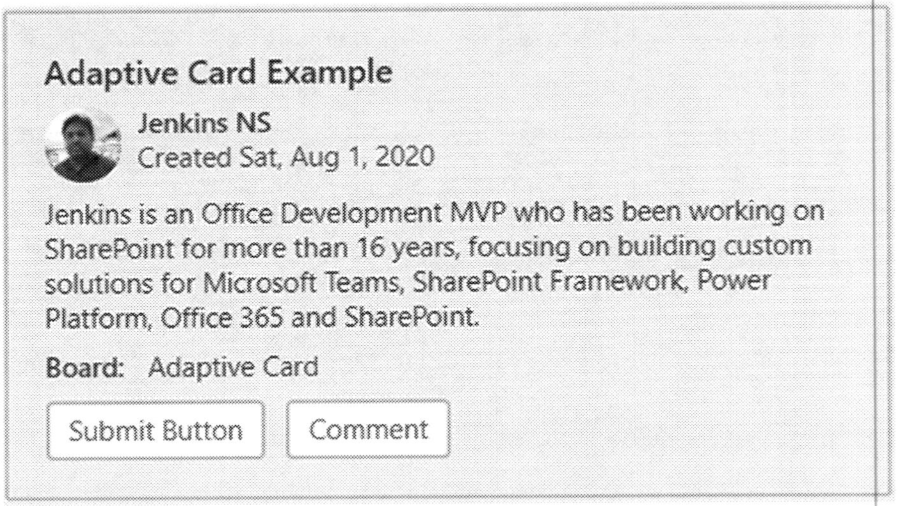

Adaptive Card Example

Jenkins NS
Created Sat, Aug 1, 2020

Jenkins is an Office Development MVP who has been working on SharePoint for more than 16 years, focusing on building custom solutions for Microsoft Teams, SharePoint Framework, Power Platform, Office 365 and SharePoint.

Board: Adaptive Card

| Submit Button | Comment |

Figure 3-32. *Example Adaptive Card*

You will update the existing Teams conversation bot app with Adaptive Cards.

- Navigate to ./src/app/conversationalbotBot folder and create a new file called "ResponseCard.json"

- Copy and paste the code given below:

```
{
"$schema": "http://adaptivecards.io/schemas/adaptive-card.json",
    "type": "AdaptiveCard",
    "version": "1.0",
    "body": [{
            "type": "Container",
            "items": [{
                "type": "TextBlock",
                "text": "My adaptive card response",
                "weight": "bolder",
                "size": "large"
            }]
        },
```

```
    {
        "type": "Container",
        "items": [{
            "type": "TextBlock",
            "text": "Now you have learned to receive response
            from bot by using adaptive card.
",
            "wrap": true
        }]
    }
],
"actions": [{
    "type": "Action.OpenUrl",
    "title": "My Blog Page",
    "url": "http://jenkinsblogs.com"
}]
}
```

- Navigate to ./src/app/conversationalbotBot folder and create another new file called "ResponseCard.ts".

- Copy and paste the code given below:

```
const ResponseCard = require("./ResponseCard.json");

export default ResponseCard;
```

- Go to ./src/app/conversationalbotBot/Conversationalbot.ts file and add the following code.

- Add the header given below:

```
import ResponseCard from "./ResponseCard";
```

- In the **this.onMessage()** handler in the constructor

- Find the code given below:

```
await context.sendActivity(`I\'m terribly sorry, but my master
hasn\'t trained me to do anything yet...`);
```

- Replace the code given below:

```
const card = CardFactory.adaptiveCard(ResponseCard);
await context.sendActivity({ attachments: [card] });
```

Save and Test the Bot with Adaptive Card

Let's test it:

1. From the command line, navigate to the root folder for the project and execute the following command:

    `gulp ngrok-serve`

2. Ngrok has created the temporary URL e459e9c2beca.ngrok.io that will map to our locally running web server.

3. Then go to the Azure portal and open the Bot Channel registration App. Update the Messaging endpoint using the temporary URL e459e9c2beca.ngrok.io

4. Go to the channel where you installed 'the bot' in the previous section.

5. Delete the conversation app and install again in the channel. (FYI: We can also change the version of the app and update the app.)

6. From the Conversations tab, type @**Conversation Bot** the bot with a random string **Ex:anything** to trigger the else condition.

7. The bot will reply to the message with a card (Figure 3-33).

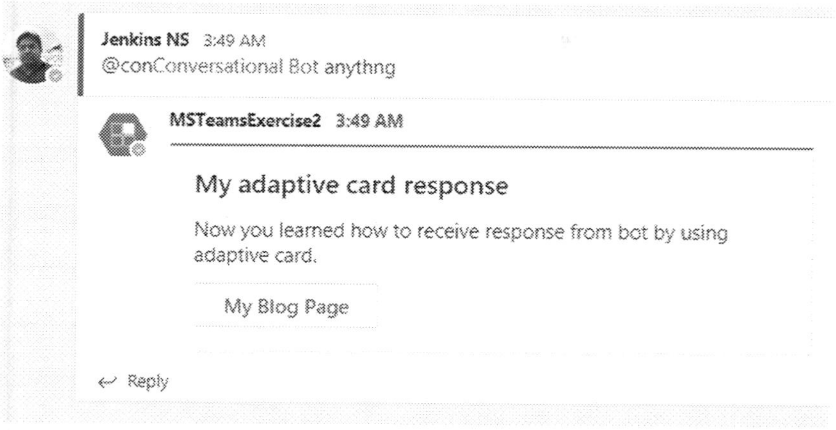

Jenkins NS 3:49 AM
@conConversational Bot anythng

MSTeamsExercise2 3:49 AM

My adaptive card response

Now you learned how to receive response from bot by using adaptive card.

My Blog Page

↩ Reply

Figure 3-33. *Bot with Adaptive Card*

Test the Bot Reacting to Message Reactions

If you would like to change the message or response, go to this.onMessageReaction handler in the `Conversationalbot` class and change it.

In the Microsoft Teams client, go to the channel where you installed the bot in the previous section. From the Conversations tab, find a message from the bot and apply a like reaction to it.

After a few seconds, the bot will reply with a message "That was an interesting reaction" with the reaction clicked (Figure 3-34).

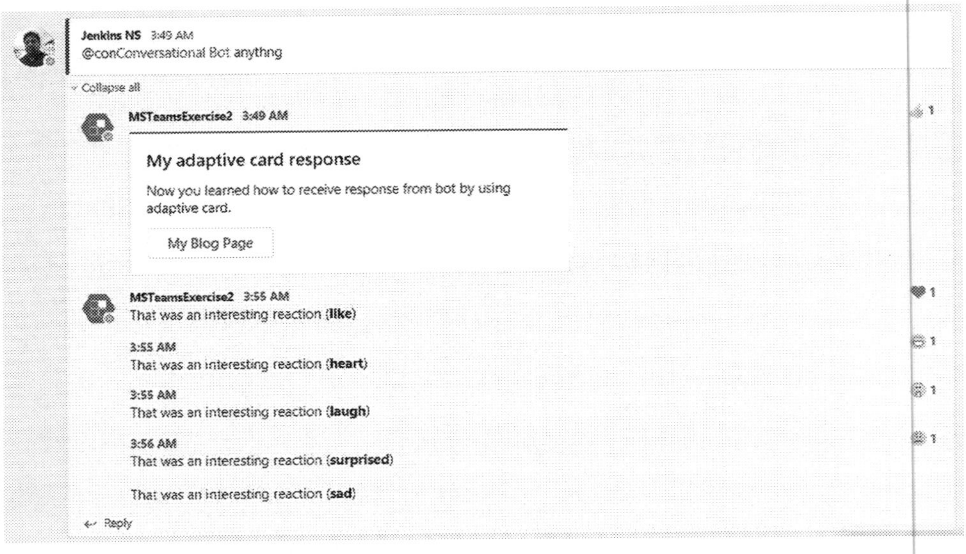

Figure 3-34. *Bot reacting*

In this exercise, you have modified the existing Microsoft Teams conversational bot app to respond to the message using Adaptive Cards and tested the message reactions capabilities.

Exercise 3 - Proactive Messages from Bots

A proactive message is a message that is sent by a bot to start a conversation. You may want your bot to start a conversation for a number of reasons, including the following:

- Welcome messages for personal bot conversations

- Poll responses

- External event notifications

Sending a message to start a new conversation thread is different than sending a message in response to an existing conversation: when your bot starts a new conversation, there is no preexisting conversation to post the message.

Update the Existing Teams App

In this exercise, you will update the existing Teams app to send a proactive message from your bot.

- Go to ResponseCard.json file and add a new action submit button under the actions section.

```
{
        "type": "Action.Submit",
        "title": "Create new thread in this channel",
        "data": { "cardAction": "newconversation" }
}
```

- Navigate ./src/app/conversationalbotBot/Conversationalbot.ts file and add the following code.

- Include "ChannelInfo, TeamsChannelData, ConversationParameters, teamsGetChannelId, Activity, BotFrameworkAdapter, ConversationReference, ConversationResourceResponse" objects reference to the existing botbuilder package:

- i.e.

```
import { StatePropertyAccessor, CardFactory, TurnContext,
MemoryStorage,
    ConversationState, ActivityTypes, TeamsActivityHandler,
    MessageFactory,
    ChannelInfo, TeamsChannelData, ConversationParameters,
    teamsGetChannelId,
  Activity, BotFrameworkAdapter, ConversationReference,
  ConversationResourceResponse
} from "botbuilder";
```

- In the **this.onMessage()** handler in the constructor, add the code given below to add an if statement before the switch statement "switch (context.activity.type) {...}" to handle the new conversation request.

```
if (context.activity.value) {
   switch (context.activity.value.cardAction) {
       case "newconversation":
          const channelId = teamsGetChannelId(context.activity);
          const message = MessageFactory.text("New thread or
          conversation created by bot");
           const newConversation = await this.createConversationI
           nChannel(context, channelId, message);
              break;
          }
       } else {
```

- Then add one closed brace after the switch statement:

```
}
```

- Then add the createConversationInChannel() method that will
  create the new conversation. Add the following method to the
  Conversationalbot class:

```
private async createConversationInChannel(context: TurnContext,
teamsChannelId: string, message: Partial<Activity>):
Promise<[ConversationReference, string]> {
   // create parameters for the new conversation
   const conversationParameters = <ConversationParameters>{
              isGroup: true,
              channelData: <TeamsChannelData>{
                 channel: <ChannelInfo>{
                    id: teamsChannelId
                 }
              },
              activity: message
          };
```

```
// get a reference to the bot adapter & create a connection to
the Teams API
const adapter = <BotFrameworkAdapter>context.adapter;
const connectorClient = adapter.createConnectorClient(context.
activity.serviceUrl);
// create a new conversation and get a reference to it
const conversationResourceResponse:
ConversationResourceResponse = await connectorClient.
conversations.createConversation(conversationParameters);
const conversationReference = <ConversationReference>TurnConte
xt.getConversationReference(context.activity);
conversationReference.conversation.id =
conversationResourceResponse.id;

return [conversationReference, conversationResourceResponse.
activityId];
}
```

- Now, we have completed the coding for proactive message sending.

Save and Test the Bot to Create New Thread/Message

Open the command line, navigate to the root folder for the project, and execute the following command:

```
gulp ngrok-serve
```

- Ngrok has created the temporary URL d23aadf72a73.ngrok.io that will map to our locally running web server.

- Then go to the Azure portal and open the Bot Channel registration App. Update the Messaging endpoint using the temporary URL d23aadf72a73.ngrok.io

- Go to the channel where you installed 'the bot' in the previous section.

- Delete the conversation app and install again in the channel.

- From the Conversations tab, @**Conversation Bot** the bot with a random string **Ex:anything** to trigger the else condition.

- The bot will reply to the message with a card (Figure 3-35).

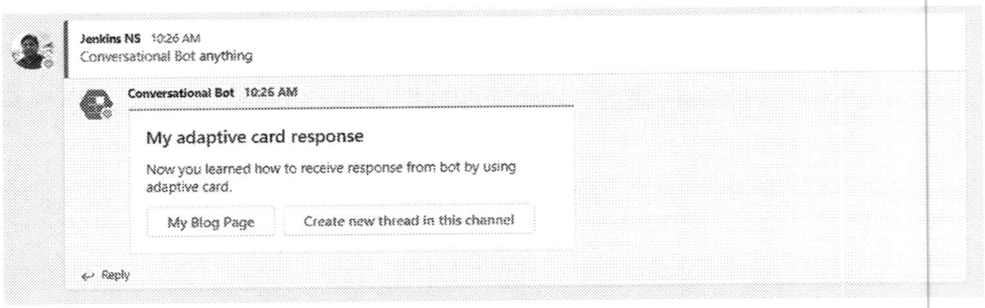

Figure 3-35. *Bot adaptive message*

- Click the "Create new thread in this channel" button.

- After a few seconds, it creates a new conversation created by the bot that appears in the channel (Figure 3-36).

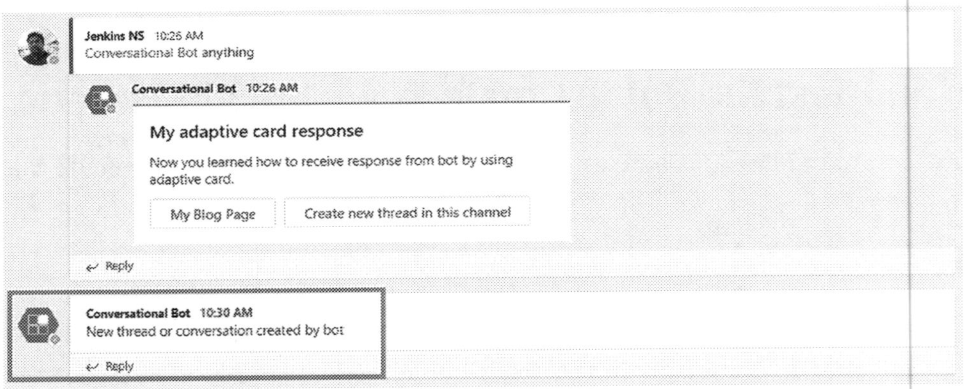

Figure 3-36. *New thread message*

- In this exercise, you will modify the existing Microsoft Teams conversation bot to send a proactive message from your bot, while clicking "Create new thread in this channel" button.

Conclusion

In this chapter, you have learned various features of conversational bots and how to create and add bots to Microsoft Teams using Yeoman generator (yo teams). It also covered how to use Adaptive Cards, action buttons, and send proactive messages from the bot.

You have now learned how to create conversation bots using Yeoman generator for Microsoft Teams. Along with this you will start learning different options and features of Microsoft Teams apps in our upcoming chapters.

CHAPTER 4

Messaging Extension and Action Comments

Messaging extensions are a great way to invoke custom code right in the Teams client. This opens up the possibility of users interacting with your application right in the context of their conversations without having to leave Teams and post the information using Adaptive Cards or Hero Cards or Messages.

In this chapter, you will learn about various features of Messaging extensions as we explain how to create Messaging extensions and command actions with examples to guide users. Messaging extensions that let people share content with channels, communicate expressively, and share collaborative experiences, along with the messaging extensions action command, allow users to search data from APIs using modal pop up, then process their data and send it back to the Teams channel conversation area to share collaborative experiences.

Overview of Messaging Extension

Messaging extensions enable users to execute search commands or action commands from external systems. A messaging extension consists of your hosted web services and defined in the manifest.json file where your web service can be invoked from in the Microsoft Teams. You will also need to register your web service as a bot in the Bot Framework for messaging schema and secure communication protocol.

Microsoft Teams client is able to extend the out-of-the-box capabilities and integrate with your existing line of business applications. So that will help leverage your existing knowledge and make gains in integration line of business applications. It will also reduce the workload for users moving between applications.

© Jenkins NS 2021
J. NS, *Building Solutions with Microsoft Teams*, https://doi.org/10.1007/978-1-4842-6476-8_4

Here are the types of messaging extension commands:

1. Action commands messaging extension

2. Search commands messaging extension

3. Link Unfurling URL with messaging extension

The type of messaging extension command defines the UI elements and interaction flows available to your web service. Some interactions, like authentication and configuration, are available for both types of commands. See Figure 4-1.

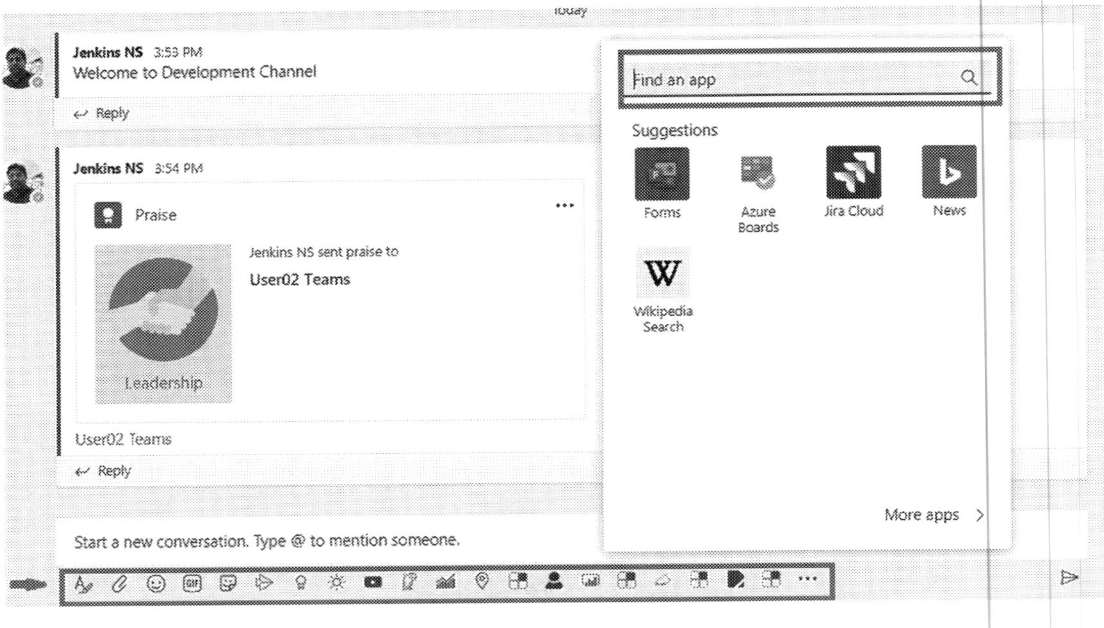

Figure 4-1. *Compose Extensions*

Messaging extensions appear along the bottom of the compose box. A few are built in, such as Emoji, Giphy, and Sticker. Choose the More Options (···) button to see other messaging extensions, including those you add from the app gallery or upload yourself.

Compose Extensions

Compose extensions allow users to query and share rich cards in conversations. Message extensions are available when you are creating a chat message - either a new conversation or when replying to an existing message. Message extensions assist you in searching and inserting content into the chat message you are composing.

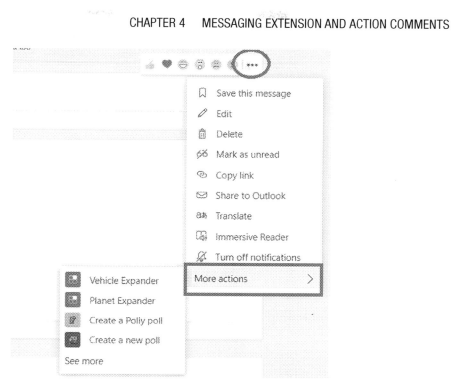

Figure 4-2. *Actionable message*

With Actionable messages (Figure 4-2), you can add rich content to your connector cards. When designing the implementation of Actionable messages, it was key that the solution was both scalable and reliable, while taking into consideration the future growth of services.

Messaging Extensions are a special kind of Microsoft Teams application that is supported by the Bot Framework v4.

How Would You Use Messaging Extensions?

Messaging extensions help with the following:

- Handle work items and bugs

- Customer support tickets

- Usage charts and reports

- Images and media content

- Sales opportunities and leads

Microsoft Teams Messaging Extensions

Messaging extensions allow users to search using web service via button events and initiate actions from the compose message area from an external system. You also use a command box or search directly from the message. Then you can display the results using Adaptive Cards or Hero Cards or messages (Figure 4-3).

Figure 4-3. *Messaging extension Search*

Cards are actionable snippets of content that you can add to a conversation through a bot, connector, or app. Using text, graphics, and buttons, cards allow you to communicate with an audience. A card is a user-interface container for short or related pieces of information. Cards can have multiple properties and attachments. Cards can include buttons that can trigger card actions. See Figure 4-4.

Supported Card Types for Messaging Extensions									
Adaptive card	Hero card	List card	Office 365 connector card	Receipt card	Signin card	OAuth card	Thumbnail card	Carousel collection	List collection
✔	✔	✖	✔	✔	✖	✔	✔	✔	✔

Figure 4-4. *Messaging extension cards*

You can find additional information on how to use cards here: `https://docs.microsoft.com/en-us/microsoftteams/platform/task-modules-and-cards/cards/cards-reference`

How Messaging Extensions Work

Messaging extensions are registered in your custom Microsoft Teams app's manifest that specifies where the extension can be invoked from in the Microsoft Teams client. The three locations that can invoke a messaging extension include the following:

1. **command box**: this is the area at the top of the Microsoft Teams client

2. **compose message box**: this is the area at the bottom of a 1:1 or group chat and at the bottom of the Conversations tab in a channel

3. **message's "More Actions" menu**: the **More Actions** menu item is accessible from the ... when you hover over a message in a conversation

Messaging extensions are implemented as web services registered as a bot using the Bot Framework. When a messaging extension is invoked, Microsoft Teams will call your web service via the Bot Framework's messaging schema and secure communication protocol.

Before creating your command, you will need to decide:

- Where can the action command be triggered from?

- How will the task module be created?

- Will the final message or card be sent to the channel from a bot, or will the message or card be inserted into the compose message area for the user to submit?

Create a Command Using App Studio

Let's do a quick example. The following steps assume you have already created a messaging extension.

1. From the Microsoft Teams client, open App Studio and select the Manifest Editor tab.

2. If you have already created your app package in App Studio, choose it from the list. If not, you can import an existing app package.

3. Click the Add button in the Command section.

4. Choose Allow users to trigger actions in external services while inside of Teams.

5. If you want to use a static set of parameters to create your task module, select that option. Otherwise, choose to Fetch a dynamic set of parameters from your bot.

6. Add a Command Id and a Title.

7. Select where you want your action command to be triggered from.

8. If you're using parameters for your task module, add the first one.

9. Click Save. See Figure 4-5.

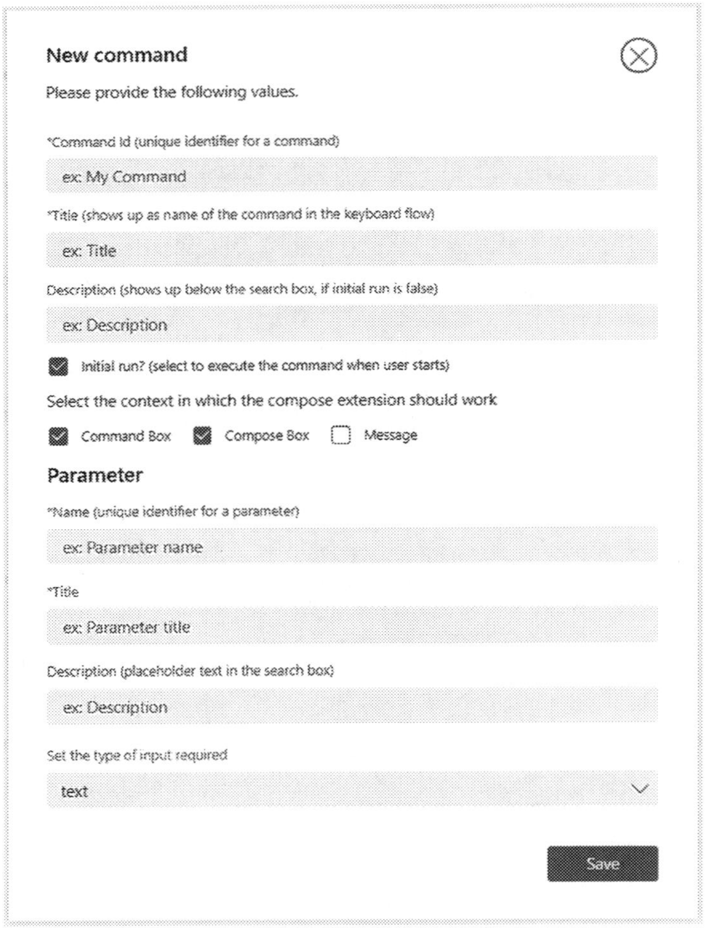

Figure 4-5. *New Command*

If you need to add more parameters, click the Add button in the Parameters section to add them.

Action Command Messaging Extensions

Action commands allow you to present your users with a modal pop up to collect or display information (Figure 4-6).

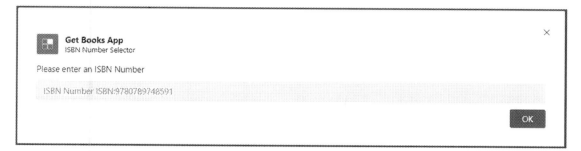

Figure 4-6. *Collect information from User*

When they submit the form, your web service can respond by inserting a message into the conversation directly, or by inserting a message into the compose message area and allowing the user to submit the message. You can even chain multiple forms together for more complex workflows. See Figure 4-7.

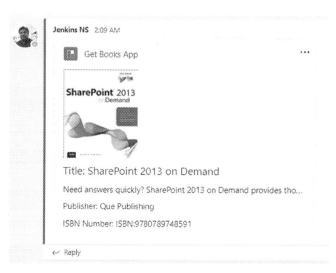

Figure 4-7. *Respond to User*

They can be triggered from the compose message area, the command box, or from a message. When invoked from a message, the initial JSON payload sent to your bot will include the entire message it was invoked from.

Search Command Messaging Extensions

Search commands allow your users to search an external system for information, then insert the results of the search into a message. In the most basic search command flow, the initial invoke message will include the search string the user submitted. You will respond with a list of cards and card previews. The Teams client will render the card previews in a list for the end user to select from. When the user selects a card, the full-size card will be inserted into the compose message area.

They can be triggered from the compose message area or the command box. Unlike action commands, they cannot be triggered from a message. See Figure 4-8.

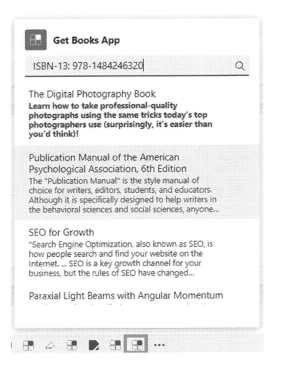

Figure 4-8. *Search command query*

Link Unfurling Messaging Extensions

You also have the option to invoke your service when a URL is pasted in the compose message area. This functionality, known as link unfurling, allows you to subscribe to receive an invoke when URLs containing a domain are pasted into the compose message area. Your web service can "unfurl" the URL into a detailed card, providing more information than the standard website preview card. You can even add buttons to allow your users to immediately act without leaving the Microsoft Teams client.

Exercise 1 - Create an Action Command Messaging Extension

In this exercise, you will learn how to create and add a new messaging extension to a Microsoft Teams app and interact with it from the Microsoft Teams client.

Before starting the exercise, verify your environment. In this exercise, I am using the tools mentioned below, installed in my environment:

- Node.js - v10.16.0

- NPM - 6.9.0

- Gulp

  - CLI version: 2.3.0

  - Local version: 4.0.2

- Yeomen Generator of MS Teams - 2.14.0

- Visual Studio Code

and

- Microsoft Azure Subscription

- Office 365 Subscription

The following steps are to be followed to create a new Microsoft Teams bot app for your Microsoft Team client:

1. Register the bot with Microsoft Azure's Bot Framework

2. Bot Channel Registration

3. Enable the Microsoft Teams channel for the bot

4. Retrieve the bot app ID and password

5. Create action command message extension MS Teams app using Yeoman generator

6. Test the action command message extension app

Register the Bot with Microsoft Azure's Bot Framework

Open a browser and navigate to the Azure portal (`https://portal.azure.com/`. Sign in using your **username@tenantname.onmicrosoft.com** that was used from the Azure subscription.

Click Create resource and Enter **bot** in the **Search the marketplace** input box and select **Bot Channels Registration** from the list of resources returned. Then select **Create** on the next page to start the process of registering a new bot resource (Figure 4-9).

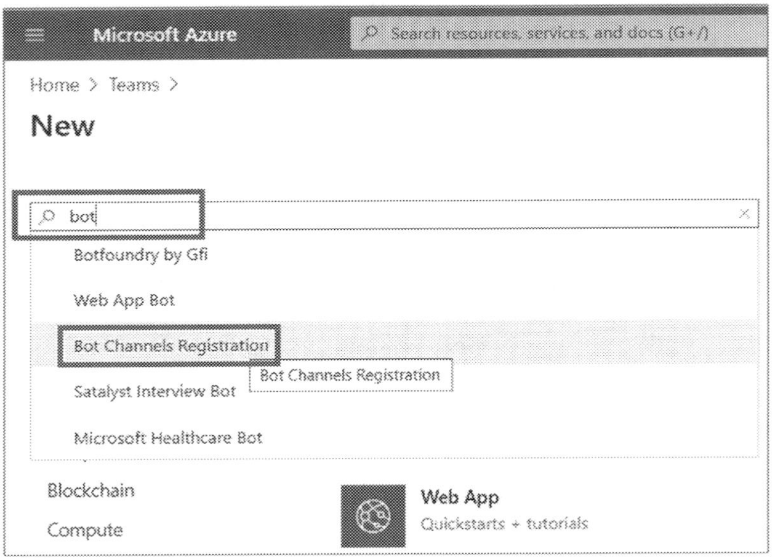

Figure 4-9. *Search Bot Channel Registration*

In the **Bot Channels Registration** Page, click to initiate create Bot Channels Registration (Figure 4-10).

Figure 4-10. *Bot Channel Registration*

In the **Bot Channels Registration blade** (Figure 4-11), enter the following values and then select **Create**:

- Bot handle: Enter a globally unique name for the bot.

    - **Ex:** messagingExtensionCh4

- Subscription: Select the subscription you selected previously when creating the resource group.

- Resource group: Select the resource group you created previously - Ex: Teams

- Location: Select your preferred Azure region.

- Pricing tier: Select a preferred pricing tier; the F0 tier is free.

- Messaging endpoint: `https://REPLACE_THIS.ngrok.io/api/messages`

    The bot registration needs to know the endpoint of the web service where the bot is implemented. This will change each time you start the ngrok utility used in previous exercises.

- Application Insights: Off

- Microsoft App ID and password: Auto create App ID and password

Bot Channels Registration

Bot Service

Bot handle * ⓘ

```
messagingExtensionCh4                          ✓
```

Subscription *

```
Visual Studio Enterprise                       ∨
```

Resource group *

```
Teams                                          ∨
```

Create new

Location *

```
East US                                        ∨
```

Pricing tier (View full pricing details)

```
F0 (10K Premium Messages)                      ∨
```

Messaging endpoint

```
https://REPLACE_THIS.ngrok.io/api/mess...      ✓
```

Application Insights ⓘ

```
On        Off
```

Microsoft App ID and password ⓘ   >
Auto create App ID and password

```
Create        Automation options
```

Figure 4-11. *Bot Channel Registration Form*

Azure will start to provision the new resource. This will take a moment or two. Once it is finished, navigate to the bot resource in the resource group. See Figure 4-12.

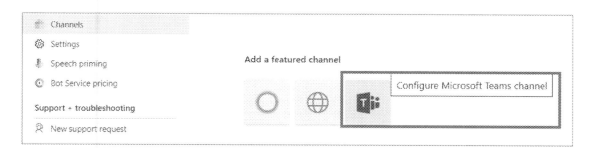

Figure 4-12. *Bot Created*

Enable the Microsoft Teams Channel for the Bot

For the bot to interact with Microsoft Teams, you must enable the Teams channel.

- From the bot resource in Azure, select **Channels** in the left-hand navigation.

- On the **Connect to channels** pane, select the **Microsoft Teams channel**, then select **Save** to confirm the action (Figure 4-13).

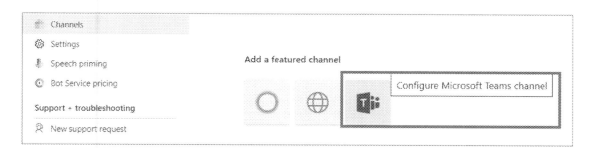

Figure 4-13. *Select Teams Channel*

- Agree to the Terms of Service

Once this process is complete, you should see both the Web Chat and Microsoft Teams listed in your enabled channels (Figure 4-14).

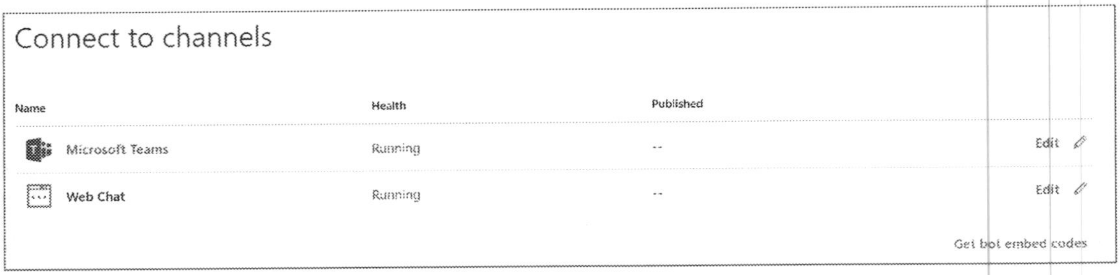

Figure 4-14. *Connect to channels*

Retrieve the Bot App Id and Password

When Azure creates the bot, it also registers a new Azure AD app for the bot. You need to generate this new bot app as a secret and copy the app's credentials.

Select **Settings** from the left-hand navigation. Scroll down to the Microsoft App ID section.

Copy the ID of the bot as you'll need it later (Figure 4-15).

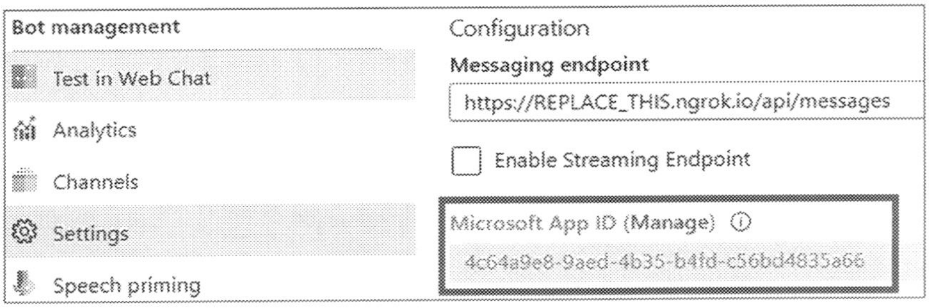

Figure 4-15. *App ID*

Create a Client Secret for the App

Click **Manage** link to navigate to the **Azure AD app**.

For the daemon app to run without user involvement, it will sign into Azure AD with an application ID and either a certificate or a secret. In this exercise, you will use a secret.

Select **Certificates & Secrets** from the left-hand navigation panel.

Select the **New client secret** button under the Client secrets section.

When prompted, give the secret a description and select one of the expiration duration options provided: for example, Never and select **Add** (Figure 4-16).

Note   Copy the new client secret value. You won't be able to retrieve it after you perform another operation or leave this blade.

Client secrets

A secret string that the application uses to prove its identity when requesting a token. Also can be referred to as application password.

+ New client secret

Description	Expires	Value
No description	8/9/2025	rlg***************
MessagingExtension	12/31/2299	5Z_SZ.0tU7cGOWmeciKH3pm3yFg5YOzc-

Figure 4-16. App Client Secret

The Certificate & Secrets page will display the new secret. It's important you copy this value as it's only shown this one time; if you leave the page and come back, it will only show as a masked value.

Copy and store the value of the secret value as you will need it later.

Create Microsoft Teams App Using Yeoman Generator

In this section, you will create a new Messaging Extension Teams app using Yeoman generator (yo teams).

In this exercise I am using REST API (Google Books API) to get information about the books based on ISBN numbers and send it to a channel conversation.

- To create a new Messaging extension app project

- Create a new project directory in your favorite location

- Open command prompt

- Create a new folder "messagingExtensionCh4"

- Navigate to a newly created directory

- Run the Yeoman generator for Microsoft Teams by running the following command: **yo teams** (Figure 4-17).

```
C:\Jenkins\JPower4\Book\MSTeamsBook\messagingExtensionCh4>yo teams
```

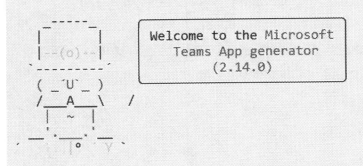

```
                          Welcome to the Microsoft
    |--(o)--|               Teams App generator
                                 (2.14.0)
     ( _`U`_ )
    /___A___\   /
     |   ~   |
```

? What is your solution name? (messaging-extension-ch-4)

Figure 4-17. yo teams

Yeoman will launch and ask you a series of questions (Figure 4-18). Answer the questions with the following values:

- What is your solution name? Messaging-Extension

- Where do you want to place the files? Use the current folder

- Title of your Microsoft Teams App project? Messaging Extension Example

- Your (company) name? (max 32 characters) JPOWER4

- Which manifest version would you like to use? v1.6

- Enter your Microsoft Partner ID, if you have one? (Leave blank to skip)

- What features do you want to add to your project? A Message Extension Command

- The URL where you will host this solution? https://messagingextension.azurewebsites.net

- Would you like show a loading indicator when your app/tab loads? No

- Would you like to include Test framework and initial tests? No

- Would you like to use Azure Applications Insights for telemetry? No

- Where is your message extension hosted? In a new bot

- What is the Microsoft App ID for the bot used by the Message Extension? 4c64a9e8-9aed-4b35-b4fd-c56bd4835a66

- What type of messaging extension command? Action based messaging extension

- What context do you want your action to work from? The compose box, The command box, Conversation messages

- How would you like to collect information from the user for your action? Using an Adaptive Card

- Do you need configuration or authorization when collecting information? No

- Would you like a Settings option for the messaging extension? No

- What is the name of your Message Extension command? GetBooks

- Describe your Message Extension command? Get Books from google API

```
? What is your solution name? Messaging-Extension
? Where do you want to place the files? Use the current folder
? Title of your Microsoft Teams App project? Messaging Extension Example
? Your (company) name? (max 32 characters) JPOWER4
? Which manifest version would you like to use? v1.6
? Enter your Microsoft Partner ID, if you have one? (Leave blank to skip)
? What features do you want to add to your project? A Message Extension Command
? The URL where you will host this solution? https://messagingextension.azurewebsites.net
? Would you like show a loading indicator when your app/tab loads? No
? Would you like to include Test framework and initial tests? No
? Would you like to use Azure Applications Insights for telemetry? No
? Where is your message extension hosted? In a new bot
? What is the Microsoft App ID for the bot used by the Message Extension?  4c64a9e8-9aed-4b35-b4fd-c56bd4835a66
? What type of messaging extension command? Action based messaging extension
? What context do you want your action to work from? The compose box, The command box, Conversation messages
? How would you like to collect information from the user for your action? Using an Adaptive Card
? Do you need configuration or authorization when collecting information? No
? Would you like a Settings option for the messaging extension? No
? What is the name of your Message Extension command? GetBooks
? Describe your Message Extension command? Get Books from google API
   create package.json
   force  yo.rc.json
```

Figure 4-18. *Answer Yeoman questionnaire*

Note   Most of the answers to these questions can be changed after creating the project. For example, the URL where the project will be hosted isn't important at the time of creating or testing the project.

Open Visual Studio Code using **code .** in the command prompt (Figure 4-19).

Figure 4-19. *Visual studio code OOB*

- Open the .env file ➤ and add the *MICROSOFT_APP_PASSWORD copied from the new client secret value*

  MICROSOFT_APP_ID=4c64a9e8-9aed-4b35-b4fd-c56bd4835a66
  MICROSOFT_APP_PASSWORD=_5Z_S2.0tU7cGOWmec1KH3pm3yFg5YOzc-

Step 1: First update the Manifest.json file for message extension commands.

- Navigate to ./src/manifest/manifest.json file and replace the name and description section.

  ```
  "name": {
      "short": "Get Books App",
      "full": "To get books using ISBN number"
  },
  "description": {
      "short": "Messaging extension Teams App to get books",
  ```

```
    "full": "Messaging extension Teams App to get books using ISBN
    number"
},
```

- And update the "commands" section under "composeExtensions" title to "Get Books"

```
"commands": [{
            "id": "getBooksMessageExtension",
            "title": "Get Books",
            "description": "Add a clever description here",
```

Step 2: Request user to give ISBN number to get more details.

- Navigate to ./src/app/ getBooksMessageExtension/ getBooksMessageExtension.ts

- Go to "onFetchTask" method and replace the value section, to get input from user.

```
value: {
                title: "ISBN Number Selector",
                card: CardFactory.adaptiveCard({
                    $schema: "http://adaptivecards.io/schemas/
                    adaptive-card.json",
                    type: "AdaptiveCard",
                    version: "1.0",
                    body: [
                        {
                            type: "TextBlock",
                            text: "Please enter an ISBN Number"
                        },
                        {
                            type: "Input.Text",
                            id: "isbn",
                        placeholder: "ISBN Number
                        ISBN:9780789748591",
                            style: "email"
```

```
                },
            ],
            actions: [
                {
                    type: "Action.Submit",
                    title: "OK",
                    data: { id: "unique-id" }
                }
            ]
        })
    }
```

Step 3: Respond to User

- Go to "onSubmitAction" method to replace the code below

  - This Submit request will call google API (*https://www.googleapis.com/books/v1/volumes?q=ISBN-Number*) based on the ISBN number and respond to the user with the first Book detail:

    - Title

    - Description

    - Book Cover

    - Publisher

    - ISBN Number (for reference)

```
const request = require("request");
    const isbnnumber = value.data.isbn;
    const url = "https://www.googleapis.com/books/v1/
    volumes?q=" + isbnnumber + "&limit=1&offset=0";
    let title: string = "";
    let description: string = "";
    let publisher: string = "";
    let imageurl: string = "";
    let messagingExtensionResult;
    return new Promise<MessagingExtensionResult>((resolve,
    reject) => {
```

```
request(url, {json: true}, (err, res, body) => {
    if (err) {
        return;
    }
    const data = body;
    if (data.items) {
        const item = data.items[0];
        title = item.volumeInfo.title;
        description = item.volumeInfo.description;
        publisher = item.volumeInfo.publisher;
        imageurl = item.volumeInfo.imageLinks.thumbnail;
    }
    const card = CardFactory.adaptiveCard(
        {
            type: "AdaptiveCard",
            body: [
                {
                    type: "Image",
                    url: imageurl
                },
                {
                    type: "TextBlock",
                    size: "Large",
                    text: "Title: " + title
                },
                {
                    type: "TextBlock",
                    size: "Medium",
                    text: description
                },
                {
                    type: "TextBlock",
                    size: "Medium",
                    text: "Publisher: " + publisher
                },
```

```
                                 {
                                         type: "TextBlock",
                                         size: "Medium",
                                         text: "ISBN Number: " + isbnnumber
                                 }
                         ],
                         $schema: "http://adaptivecards.io/schemas/
                         adaptive-card.json",
                         version: "1.0"
                 });
             messagingExtensionResult = {
                 type: "result",
                 attachmentLayout: "list",
                 attachments: [card]
             };
             resolve(messagingExtensionResult);
         });
     });
```

This method will first load the Books and then it loads the Adaptive Card for the modal. Finally, it returns an object of type *MessagingExtensionResult* that defines the task module, implemented using an Adaptive Card, to the Bot Framework. The Bot Framework will communicate with Microsoft Teams to display the card.

At this point, the first part of the action command is complete, which will prompt the user to enter the ISBN number with the messaging extension triggered. The second part of the messaging extension is to use the entered ISBN number to reply to the message that triggered the extension with the book's details or, if the extension is triggered from the compose box, it will add the book's details to a new message.

- *File ➤ Save All* to save the changes

- At this point, your messaging extension is ready to be tested!

Test the Messaging Extension

Open the command Prompt, navigate to the project folder, and execute the following command:

```
gulp ngrok-serve
```

This gulp task will run many other tasks that are displayed within the command-line console. The ngrok-serve task builds your project and starts a local web server (http://localhost:3007). It then starts ngrok with a random subdomain that creates a secure URL to your local webserver.

In development, testing can be done using the tool ngrok that creates a secure rotatable URL to your local HTTP webserver. Ngrok is included as a dependency within the project so there is nothing to set up or configure. See Figure 4-20.

```
[02:33:08] Finished 'build' after 5.83 s
[02:33:08] Starting 'nodemon'...
[02:33:08] Finished 'nodemon' after 23 ms
[02:33:08] Starting 'watch'...
[02:33:08] HOSTNAME: 841c87a33afc.ngrok.io
[tslint-plugin] Starting linter in separate process...
[tslint-plugin] Linting complete.
[tslint-plugin] Linting complete.
  msteams Initializing Microsoft Teams Express hosted App... +0ms
  msteams Creating a new bot instance at /api/messages +0ms
  msteams Found 1 MessagingExtension(s) on the Bot object +5ms
  msteams Adding Messaging extension: getBooksMessageExtension +4ms
  msteams Server running on 3007 +402ms
```

Figure 4-20. *Gulp ngrokserve execution*

Ngrok has created the temporary URL 841c87a33afc.ngrok.io that will map to our locally running web server.

Then go to the Azure portal and open the Bot Channel registration App. Update the Messaging endpoint using the temporary URL 841c87a33afc.ngrok.io (see Figure 4-21).

Bot management	Configuration
▦ Test in Web Chat	**Messaging endpoint** https://841c87a33afc.ngrok.io/api/messages
ᕟ Analytics	☐ Enable Streaming Endpoint
▦ Channels	

Figure 4-21. *Messaging endpoint with ngrok url*

Note   The free version of ngrok will create a new URL each time you restart the web server. Make sure you update the Messaging endpoint of your URL each time you restart the web server when you are testing the app.

Install the Messaging Extension in Microsoft Teams

Now let's install the app in Microsoft Teams. In the browser, navigate to https://teams. microsoft.com and sign in with the credentials of a Work and School account.

Microsoft Teams is available for use as a web client, desktop client, and mobile client.

Using the app bar navigation menu, select the More added apps button. Then select More apps followed by Upload a custom app and then Upload for me or my teams (Figure 4-22).

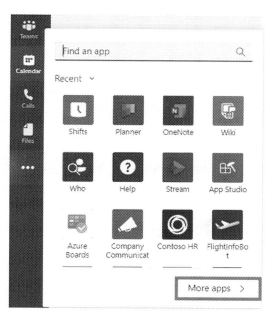

Figure 4-22. *Add apps to MS Teams*

In the file dialog that appears, select the Microsoft Teams package in your project. This app package is a ZIP file that can be found in the projects **./package** folder (Figure 4-23).

Figure 4-23. *Upload apps*

After installation, you will be able to see the app in the apps list (Figure 4-24).

Figure 4-24. *Installed apps*

Once the package is uploaded, Microsoft Teams will display a summary of the app (Figure 4-25).

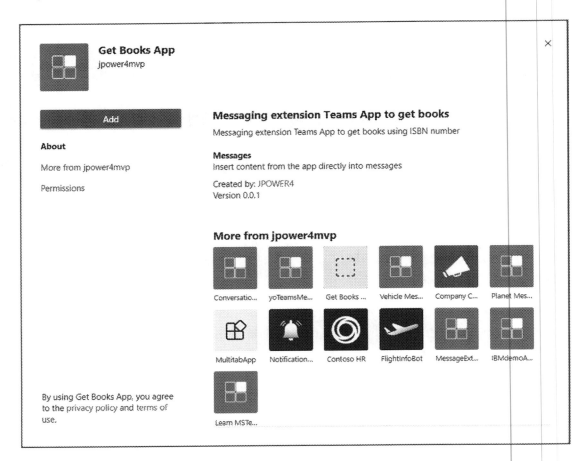

Figure 4-25. *Add the app to teams & channels*

Testing Messaging Extension App from Microsoft Teams Client

- Click the Add button to navigate to chat with the bot to test 1:1 messaging extension.

- Or go to any of your channels and add this app.

- Notice the commands that the messaging extension supports are shown in the compose box when the app loads. Let's test the message extension! See Figure 4-26.

126

Figure 4-26. *Conversation section*

- Click the icon, and it will open the user input modal pop up (Figure 4-27).

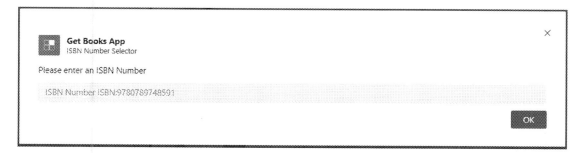

Figure 4-27. *User input modal pop up*

- Enter ISBN Number, Ex: ISBN:9780789748591, it supports any ISBN number.

- After a few seconds, it loads information about the books in the conversation section and you will be able to send this to all your channel users (Figure 4-28).

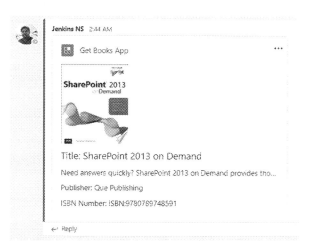

Figure 4-28. *Responded output*

You can also trigger the messaging extension from an existing message in the chat using the ... menu in the upper-right corner of the message. Select Mode actions and then select the Get Books option (Figure 4-29).

Figure 4-29. *Action command*

In this exercise, you have created an action command messaging extension for a custom Microsoft Teams app.

Exercise 2 - Create a Search Command Messaging Extension

In this exercise, you'll learn how to execute a messaging extension search command from an existing message.

In the previous exercise, you created an action messaging extension that enabled a user to add the details of a book to a message. In this section, you will add a search messaging extension to find a specific book.

Update the App's Configuration

First, update the app's manifest to add the new messaging extension. Locate and open the ./src/manifest/manifest.json file.

Next, locate the composeExtensions.commands array. Add the following object to the array to add the search extension:

- Replace type action to query

- Context to "compose"

- Description to "Search for a book"

- Add parameter

After updating, the code looks like this:

```
"commands": [{
        "id": "getBooksMessageExtension",
        "title": "Get Books",
        "description": "Search for a Book",
        "initialRun": true,
        "type": "query",
        "context": [
            "compose"
        ],
        "parameters": [{
            "name": "searchKeyword",
            "description": "Enter ISBN number to search",
            "title": "ISBN Number"
        }],

        "fetchTask": true
    }]
```

Update Messaging Extension Code

Then locate the GetBooksMessageExtension.ts file ./src/app/
GetBooksMessageExtension/ GetBooksMessageExtension.ts

Update the import statement for the botbuilder package to include the object
MessagingExtensionAttachment

```
import { TurnContext, CardFactory, MessagingExtensionQuery,
MessagingExtensionResult, MessagingExtensionAttachment} from "botbuilder";
```

Next, add the following method "*onQuery*" to the **GetBooksMessageExtension** class

```
public async onQuery(context: TurnContext, query: MessagingExtensionQuery):
Promise<MessagingExtensionResult> {
        let isbnnumber = "ISBN:9780789748591";
        if (query && query.parameters && query.parameters[0].name ===
        "searchKeyword" && query.parameters[0].value) {
            isbnnumber = query.parameters[0].value;
        }

        const request = require("request");
        const url = "https://www.googleapis.com/books/v1/volumes?q=" +
        isbnnumber + "&limit=10&offset=0";

        let messagingExtensionResult;
        const attachments: MessagingExtensionAttachment[] = [];

        return new Promise<MessagingExtensionResult>((resolve, reject) => {
            request(url, { json: true }, (err, res, body) => {
                if (err) {
                    return;
                }
                const data = body;

                const searchResultsCards: MessagingExtensionAttachment[] = [];
                data.items.forEach((book) => {
                    searchResultsCards.push(this.getBookResultCard(book));
                });

                messagingExtensionResult = {
                    type: "result",
                    attachmentLayout: "list",
                    attachments: searchResultsCards
                };

                resolve(messagingExtensionResult);
            });
        });

    }
```

130

This method will first get the search keyword from the query sent to the bot from Microsoft Teams. It then will retrieve books based on the query from the Google Books API.

Next it will then take the query results, convert them to cards, and add them to the MessagingExtensionResult returned to the Bot Framework and ultimately to Microsoft Teams.

Then add the private method given below to the same class to bind the Hero Card.

```
private getBookResultCard(selectedBook: any): MessagingExtensionAttachment {
    return CardFactory.heroCard(selectedBook.volumeInfo.title,
    selectedBook.volumeInfo.description);
}
```

- *File ➤ Save All* to save the changes
- At this point, your messaging extension Search command is ready to test!

Save and Test the Messaging Extension Search Command

Here's the process:

- From the command line, navigate to the root folder for the project and execute the following command:

  ```
  gulp ngrok-serve
  ```

- Ngrok has created the temporary URL 956fce259023.ngrok.io that will map to our locally running web server.

- Then go to Azure portal and open the Bot Channel registration App. Update the Messaging endpoint using the temporary URL 956fce259023.ngrok.io

- Go to the channel where you have installed 'the app' in the previous section

- Delete the conversation app and install again in the channel. (FYI: We can also change the version of the app and update the app.)

- Go to Teams ➤ Channel

- Enter the ISBN Number in the search box and wait a few seconds. Microsoft Teams will execute the search and return the results (Figure 4-30).

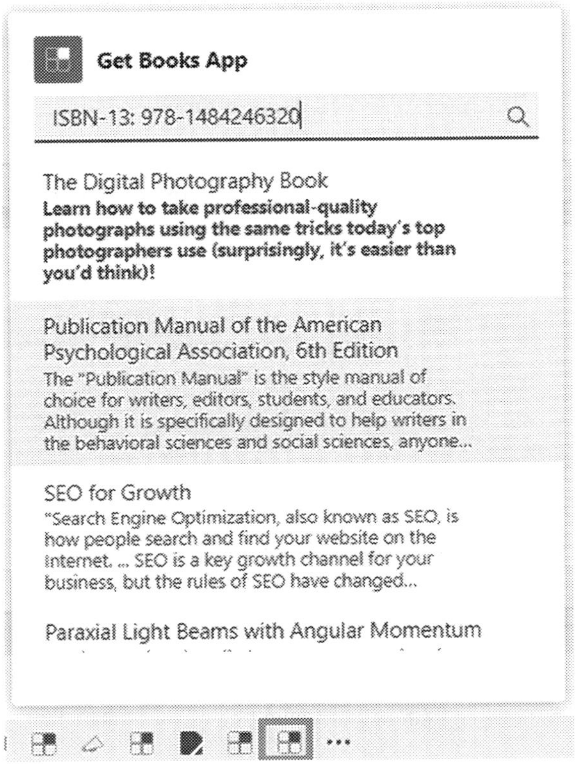

Figure 4-30. *Search command*

In this exercise, you have learned how to execute a messaging extension search command from an existing message.

Exercise 3 - Implement a Link Unfurling Messaging Extension

In this exercise, you will learn how to add a link unfurling to your Microsoft Teams app and how to implement this type of messaging extension.

Update the App's Configuration

First, update the app's manifest to add the new messaging extension. Locate and open the ./src/manifest/manifest.json file.

Next, locate the composeExtensions property. Add the following property after the commands property to add the link unfurling messaging extension.

```
,
    "messageHandlers": [{
        "type": "link",
        "value": {
            "domains": [
                "*. wikipedia.org"
            ]
        }
    }]
```

Next, locate the validDomains property. Add the following domain to the array of valid domains: "*.google.com"

```
"validDomains": [
        "{{HOSTNAME}}",
        "*. wikipedia.org"
    ],
```

Update Messaging Extension Code

Then locate the GetBooksMessageExtension.ts file ./src/app/ GetBooksMessageExtension/ GetBooksMessageExtension.ts

Update the import statement for the botbuilder package to include the object **AppBasedLinkQuery**

```
import {
    TurnContext, CardFactory, MessagingExtensionAttachment,
    MessagingExtensionQuery, MessagingExtensionResult, AppBasedLinkQuery
} from "botbuilder";
```

Next, add the following method "*onQueryLink*" to the **GetBooksMessageExtension** class

```
public async onQueryLink(context: TurnContext, query: AppBasedLinkQuery):
Promise<MessagingExtensionResult> {

        let messagingExtensionResult;
        const attachments: MessagingExtensionAttachment[] = [];
        const url: any = query.url;
        const attachment = CardFactory.thumbnailCard(
            "Link unfurling", url, ["http://jenkinsblogs.com/wp-content/
            uploads/2018/04/cropped-icon.png"]);

        messagingExtensionResult = {
            attachmentLayout: "list",
            type: "result",
            attachments: [attachment]
        };

        return messagingExtensionResult;
    }
```

This method is called by the Bot Framework when a URL matching the domain is listed in the app's manifest and return a MessagingExtensionResult object that contains the updated thumbnail card matching the URL to the existing message.

- **File ➤ Save All** to save the changes
- At this point, your messaging extension link unfurling is ready to test!

Save and Test the Messaging Extension Link Unfurling

Now it's time to test:

- From the command line, navigate to the root folder for the project and execute the following command:

  ```
  gulp ngrok-serve
  ```

- Ngrok has created the temporary URL f95c9feee129.ngrok.io that it will map to our locally running web server.

- Then go to the Azure portal and open the Bot Channel registration App. Update the Messaging endpoint using the temporary URL f95c9feee129.ngrok.io

- Go to the channel where you have installed 'the app' in the previous section

- Delete the conversation app and install again in the channel. (FYI: We can also change the version of the app and update the app.)

- Go to Teams ➤ Channel

- Copy and paste the URL of one of the wikipedia.org Ex: `https://en.wikipedia.org/wiki/book"` into the compose box. Notice the message has been updated to include the card, which is also included when you send the message (Figure 4-31).

Figure 4-31. *Link unfurling*

In this exercise, you have learned how to add link unfurling to your Microsoft Teams app and how to implement this type of messaging extension.

Conclusion

In this chapter, you have learned various features of messaging extensions and how to create and add messaging extension apps to Microsoft Teams using Yeoman generator (yo teams). It also covered how to use Adaptive Cards and action buttons with action commands, a Hero Card with a search command, and a thumbnail card with link **unfurling** from the app.

You have also learned how to create a messaging extension app using Yeoman generator for Microsoft Teams. Along with this, you will start learning about different options and features of Microsoft Teams apps in our upcoming chapters.

CHAPTER 5

Embedded Web Experiences with Tabs

When you want to integrate large area web content or a dashboard to users, then a tab is the best option in Microsoft Teams. Users can interact with the page and get dynamic data. Conversations within the tab will be posted in the team's channel and promote your tab. Team members can access services, content from the channel, or in a chat from the tab. Teams tabs work directly with tools and data, and have conversations about the tools and data, all within the context of the channel or chat.

In this chapter, you will learn about various features of tabs – it explains how to create tabs for personal, groups, and team contexts with examples to guide users. Tabs are a powerful and easy way for users to engage with your app from Microsoft Teams.

Overview of Tabs

Tabs are always visible at the top of the screen in the channel for team members and everyone can easily access them. Tabs in Microsoft Teams allow you to display rich interactive web content like web pages. This can easily be described as the possibility to add more relevant information to your private chat, group chat, or team channel. You can add tabs in all the three different kinds of conversations: a team, a group chat, or a personal app for an individual user. Tabs are embedded in Microsoft Teams using simple iframes that point to domains declared in the app manifest. You can also easily add specific functionality to your tab based on context.

© Jenkins NS 2021
J. NS, *Building Solutions with Microsoft Teams*, https://doi.org/10.1007/978-1-4842-6476-8_5

There are two types of tabs available in Teams:

- Channel/ Group

  A channel/group tab delivers content to channels and group chats and are a great way to create collaborative spaces around dedicated web-based content.

- Personal

  Personal tabs, along with personally scoped bots, are part of personal apps and are scoped to a single user. They can be pinned to the left navigation bar for easy access.

  A good tab should display the following characteristics:

- Focused functionality

  Tabs work best when they are built to address a specific need. Focus on a small set of tasks or a subset of data that is relevant to the channel the tab is in.

- Reduced chrome

  Avoid creating multiple panels in a tab, adding layers of navigation, or requiring users to scroll both vertically and horizontally in one tab. In other words, try not to have tabs in your tab.

- Integration

  Find ways to notify users about tab activity by posting cards to a conversation.

- Streamlined access

  Make sure you're granting access to the right people at the right time. Keeping your sign-in process simple will avoid creating barriers to contribution and collaboration.

- Personality

  Your tab canvas presents a good opportunity to brand your experience. Incorporate your own logos, colors, and layouts to communicate personality. Your logo is an important part of your identity and a connection with your users. So be sure to include it.

- Place your logo in the left or right corner or along the bottom edge.

- Keep your logo small and unobtrusive.

Tab Layouts

Tabs are canvases that you can use to share content, hold conversations, and host third-party services, all within a team's organic workflow. When you build a tab in Microsoft Teams, it puts your web app front and center where it is easily accessible from key conversations.

The tab can be arranged as a list, a grid, columns, or a single canvas, whatever works best for your application.

Single Canvas

This is one large area where work gets done. OneNote and Wiki follow this pattern. If you have an app that doesn't separate content into smaller components, this would be a good fit. See Figure 5-1.

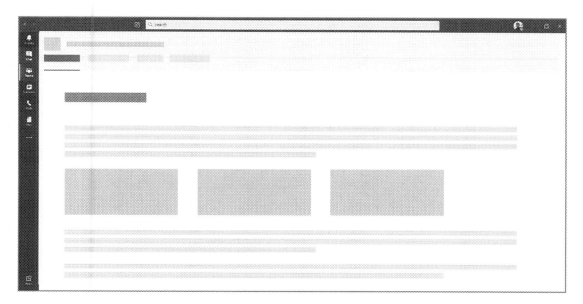

Figure 5-1. *Single Canvas Layout*

Column

Columns are great for workflows that move an item from one column to another to indicate a new status. Consider supporting drag and drop for those scenarios. We recommend using dialogs or inline expansion for detail views. See Figure 5-2.

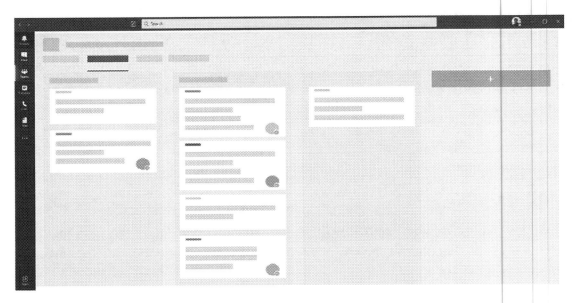

Figure 5-2. *Column Canvas Layout*

List

Lists are great for sorting and filtering large quantities of data and for keeping the most important things at the top. It is helpful to use sortable columns. Actions can be added to each list item under the ellipsis menu. See Figure 5-3.

Figure 5-3. *List Canvas Layout*

Grid

Grids are useful for showing elements that are highly visual. It helps to include a filter or search control at the top (Figure 5-4).

Figure 5-4. *Grid Canvas Layout*

Microsoft Teams Personal Tab

A custom tab is declared in the app manifest of your app package. For each web page that you need to include as a tab in your app, you define a URL and a scope.

Microsoft Teams supports two different type of tabs:

- Static Tabs
- Configurable Tabs

A static tab can only use a personal scope whereas a configurable tab can use the team or 'group chat' scopes. *Static tabs* give a private area for individual users, where the user does not share information with the rest of the team.

Defining a Personal Tab

A personal app is a Teams application with a personal scope. As an app developer, you have the option to provide a version of your app that focuses on interactions with a single user, a personal tab providing an embedded web experience. Personal apps enable users to view their select content in one place.

A custom tab is declared in the app manifest of your app package. For each web page you need to include as a tab in your app, you define a URL and a scope. Whether you choose to expose your tab within the channel/group or personal scope, you will need to present an 'IFramed' HTML content page in your tab. For personal tabs, the content URL is set directly in your manifest by the 'contentUrl' property in the 'staticTabs' array. Your tab's content will be the same for all users.

Creating a Static Tab

To create a static tab, you need to have some web content that you want to expose within Teams. This content should be the same for all users. You need to create a 'manfiest.json' file to represent your Static Tab. Start with the basic template described below, and then add the specific section for creating a static tab.

Below is a personal tab manifest example:

```
"staticTabs": [
    {
        "entityId": "default-data",
```

```
      "name": "My Personal Tab",
      "contentUrl": "https://{{HOSTNAME}}/myPersonalTab/",
      "scopes": [
        "personal"
      ]
    }
  ]
```

Name	Description
entityId	This is a unique identifier for your tab.
Name	The display name of your page as you want it to appear in Teams.
contentUrl	This is the URL that is rendered and shown as the content of your tab.
websiteUrl	Alternative URL, when your contentUrl is rendered, an icon is shown at the top of the page with a 'go to website' link. You can specify a different URL for this link, if you want to direct the user to an alternative experience.
Scopes	Defines where the tab is to be shown in the Teams client. Note: Static tabs support only the personal scope.

The displayed content for personal tabs is the same for all users and is configured in the 'staticTabs' array. You may declare up to sixteen personal tabs in an app.

Note   Personal tabs for mobile clients are currently available in developer preview.

Microsoft Teams Channel or Group Tab

A channel or group tab delivers content to channels and group chats and are a great way to create collaborative spaces around dedicated web-based content. Configurable tabs for channel and 'Group chat', these tabs contain a configuration page in addition to the main content page. You need to create an additional configuration page that allows your users to configure your content page URL, by using URL query string parameters to load the appropriate content for that context. This is because your channel or group tab can be added to multiple different teams or group chats. On each subsequent install, your users will be able to configure the tab allowing you to tailor the experience as needed. When users add a tab or configure a tab, a URL is being associated with the tab that is presented in the Teams UI. Configuring a tab is simply adding additional parameters to that URL.

For example, when you add the Azure DevOps board tab, the configuration page allows you to choose which board the tab will load. The configuration page URL is specified by the configurationUrl property in the configurableTabs array in your app manifest.

Mobile Clients

Your channel or group tab appears on Teams mobile clients, and for that the *setSettings*() method configuration must have a value for the *websiteUrl* property.

Creating Configurable Tabs

Channel or 'group chat' is added in the *configurableTabs* array. You may declare only one channel or 'group chat' in the configurableTabs array. If you need content that changes based on different users or changing circumstances, then you need a Configurable Tab.

Below is a channel/group tab manifest example:

```
"configurableTabs": [
    {
      "configurationUrl": "https://{{HOSTNAME}}/myConfigurableTab/
      config.html",
      "canUpdateConfiguration": true,
        "scopes": [
        "team",
        "groupchat"
      ]
    }
  ],
```

Name	Description
configurationUrl	https:// URL to configuration page.
canUpdateConfiguration	A value indicating whether an instance of the tab's configuration can be updated by the user after creation. Default: true (Boolean)
Scopes	Configurable tabs support only the team and groupchat scopes. (Array of enum)

Note   You can have a maximum of one channel or group tab and up to sixteen personal tabs per app.

Implement Authentication in a Custom Tab

Tabs in Teams are represented as 'Iframes'; therefore some sacrifices must be made. If it is authentication, then the application cannot navigate to a third-party provider without setting up permissions correctly.

Microsoft Teams Authentication Flow for Tabs

OAuth 2.0 is an open standard for authentication and authorization used by Azure AD and many other identity providers. A basic understanding of OAuth 2.0 is a prerequisite for working with authentication in Teams. Authentication flow for tabs and bots are a little different because tabs are very similar to websites so they can use OAuth 2.0 directly; bots are not and must do a few things differently, but the core concepts are identical. See Figure 5-5.

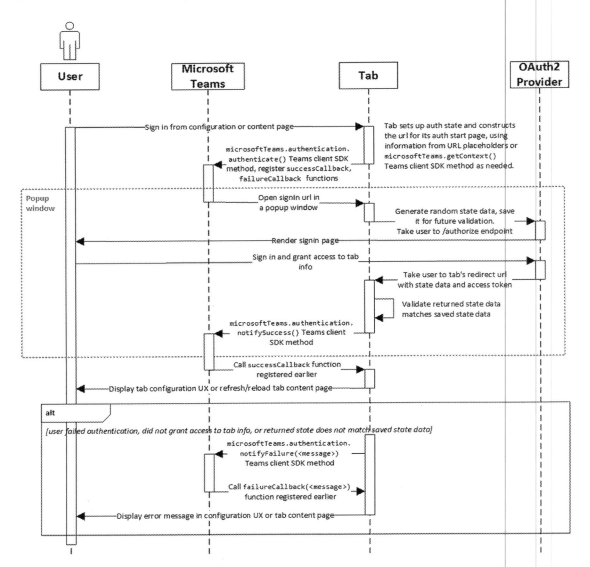

Figure 5-5. *MSTeams authentication flow for tabs*

- The user interacts with the content on the tab configuration or content page, commonly a button labeled "*Sign in*" or "*Log in*."

- The tab constructs the URL for its auth start page, optionally using information from URL placeholders or by calling the *microsoftTeams.getContext()* Teams client SDK method to streamline the authentication experience for the user.

- The tab then calls the *microsoftTeams.authentication.authenticate()* method and registers the *successCallback* and *failureCallback* functions.

- Teams opens the start page in an iframe in a pop-up window. The start page generates random state data, saves it for future validation, and redirects to the identity provider's /authorize endpoint such as `https://login.microsoftonline.com/<tenant ID>/oauth2/` authorize for Azure AD. Replace <tenant id> with your own tenant id (*context.tid*).

- Like other applications auth flows in Teams, the start page must be on a domain that is in its valid Domains list, and on the same domain as the post-login redirect page.

- IMPORTANT: The OAuth 2.0 implicit grant flow calls for a state parameter in the authentication request, which contains unique session data to prevent a cross-site request forgery attack. The examples below use a randomly generated GUID for the state data.

- On the provider's site, the user signs in and is granted access to the tab.

- The provider takes the user to the tab's OAuth 2.0 redirect page with an access token.

- The tab checks that the returned state value matches what was saved earlier, and calls *microsoftTeams.authentication.notifySuccess()*, which in turn calls the *successCallback* function registered in step 3.

- Teams closes the pop-up window.

- The tab either displays the configuration UI or refreshes or reloads the tabs content, depending on where the user started from.

Treat Tab Context as Hints

Although the tab context provides useful information regarding the user, don't use this information to authenticate the user whether you get it as URL parameters to your tab content URL or by calling the *microsoftTeams.getContext()* function in the Microsoft

Teams client SDK. A malicious actor could invoke your tab content URL with its own parameters, and a web page impersonating Microsoft Teams could load your tab content URL in an iframe and return its own data to the *getContext()* function. You should treat the identity-related information in the tab context simply as hints and validate them before use.

Using Azure AD Authentication

There are many services that you may wish to consume inside your Teams app, and most of those services require authentication and authorization to get access to the service; services include Facebook, Twitter, and Teams. Users of Teams have user profile information stored in Azure Active Directory (Azure AD) using Microsoft Graph and this section will focus on authentication using Azure AD to get access to this information.

OAuth 2.0 is an open standard for authentication used by Azure AD and many other service providers. Understanding OAuth 2.0 is a prerequisite for working with authentication in Teams and Azure AD. The examples given below use the OAuth 2.0 Implicit Grant flow with the goal of eventually reading the user's profile information from Azure AD and Microsoft Graph.

Using Silent Authentication

Silent authentication in Azure Active Directory (Azure AD) minimizes the number of times a user needs to enter their login credentials by silently refreshing the authentication token.

?The ADAL.js library creates a hidden iframe for OAuth 2.0 implicit grant flow, but it specifies prompt=none so that Azure AD never shows the login page. If user interaction is required because the user needs to log in or grant access to the application, Azure AD will immediately return an error of ADAL.js and then reports to your app. At this point your app can show a login button if needed.

Note   Currently, silent authentication works only for tabs. It does not work when signing in from a bot.

Using Single Sign-On Authentication

Users 'sign in' to Microsoft Teams via their work, school, or Microsoft accounts. You can take advantage of this by allowing a single sign-on to authorize your Microsoft Teams tab on desktop or mobile clients. Thus, if a user consents to use your app, they don't have to consent again on another device; they will be signed in automatically.

Apps That Require Additional Microsoft Graph Scopes

Current implementation for SSO only grants consent for user-level permissions: email, profile, offline_access, OpenId not for other APIs, such as User.Read or Mail.Read.

Here are some enabling workarounds:

- Tenant Admin Consent

- Asking for additional consent using the Auth API

Exercise 1 - Create a Custom Microsoft Teams Personal Tab

Microsoft Teams Developer Platform helps you to extend your teams with your line of business (LOB) application and services seamlessly into the Microsoft Teams. It also enables you to distribute your custom apps to your organization or public users if you developed generic feature apps.

Before starting the exercise, verify your environment. In this exercise, I am using the tools mentioned below, installed in my environment:

- Node.js - v10.16.0

- NPM - 6.9.0

- Gulp

  - CLI version: 2.3.0

  - Local version: 4.0.2

- Yeomen Generator of MS Teams - 2.14.0

- Visual Studio Code

and

- Microsoft Azure Subscription

- Office 365 Subscription

In this exercise, you will create a new Microsoft Teams personal tab by using the Microsoft Teams Yeoman generator Visual Studio Code and App Studio.

Create Personal Tab Using Yeoman Generator

In this section, you will create a new personal app Teams app using a Yeoman generator (yo teams). This exercise will guide you on how to create a custom personal tab.

To create a new personal tab app project, create a new project directory in your favorite location (Figure 5-6):

1. Open command prompt

2. Create a new folder "personaltabCh5"

3. Navigate to a newly created directory and run the Yeoman generator for Microsoft Teams by running the following command:

   yo teams

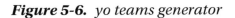

Figure 5-6. *yo teams generator*

Yeoman will launch and ask you a series of questions. Answer the questions with the following values (Figure 5-7):

- What is your solution name? Personaltab

- Where do you want to place the files? Use the current folder

- Title of your Microsoft Teams App project? Personal Tab

- Your (company) name? (max 32 characters) JPOWER4

- Which manifest version would you like to use? v1.6

- Enter your Microsoft Partner ID, if you have one? (Leave blank to skip)

- What features do you want to add to your project? A Tab

- The URL where you will host this solution? `https://personaltab.azurewebsites.net`

- Would you like show a loading indicator when your app/tab loads? No

- Would you like to include Test framework and initial tests? No

- Would you like to use Azure Applications Insights for telemetry? No

- Default Tab name? (max 16 characters) My Tab

- What kind of Tab would you like to create? Personal (static)

- Do you require Azure AD Single-Sign-On support for the tab? No

```
? What is your solution name? Personaltab
? Where do you want to place the files? Use the current folder
? Title of your Microsoft Teams App project? Personal Tab
? Your (company) name? (max 32 characters) JPOWER4
? Which manifest version would you like to use? v1.6
? Enter your Microsoft Partner ID, if you have one? (Leave blank to skip)
? What features do you want to add to your project? A Tab
? The URL where you will host this solution? https://personaltab.azurewebsites.net
? Would you like show a loading indicator when your app/tab loads? No
? Would you like to include Test framework and initial tests? No
? Would you like to use Azure Applications Insights for telemetry? No
? Default Tab name? (max 16 characters) My Tab
? What kind of Tab would you like to create? Personal (static)
? Do you require Azure AD Single-Sign-On support for the tab? No
```

Figure 5-7. *Answer Yeoman questionnaire*

Note   Most of the answers to these questions can be changed after creating the project. For example, the URL where the project will be hosted is not important at the time of creating or testing the project.

Open Visual Studio Code using **code .** in the command prompt (Figure 5-8).

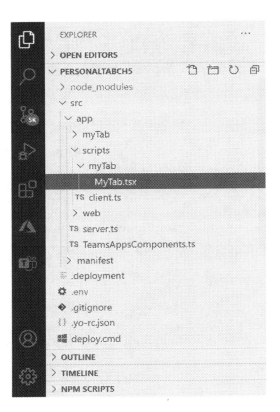

Figure 5-8. *Visual studio code*

Step 1: First update Manifest.json file for the personal tab scope:

- Navigate to ./src/manifest/manifest.json file and replace name and description section as per your tab Line of Business.

- Find "staticTabs": section and replace entityid - default-data to 'personaldata'.

Step 2: Update react component MyTab.tsx (response to user)

- Navigate to ./src/app/scripts/MyTab/MyTab.tsx

- Find export interface IMyTabState and define userEmailID typed variable

```
export interface IMyTabState extends ITeamsBaseComponentState {

    entityId?: string;
    userEmailID?: string;
}
```

- Go to public async componentWillMount() method and get user email Id from tab context.

```
this.setState({
                entityId: context.entityId,
                userEmailID: context.upn
            });
```

- Then go to render method to render user information.

```
replace <Text content={this.state.entityId} /> to
User Email ID: <Text content={this.state.userEmailID} />
```

This component will display to the user the email id and sample button. This is the TypeScript React-based class for your Tab. Locate the render() method and add the user line of business.

To add more React fluent UI controls (**@fluentui/react-northstar**), refer to the control library section in App Studio – control Library tab. This tab is a showcase of the Microsoft Teams UI Controls library.

Below are the available React libraries in the control library:

- **msteams-ui-styles-core** - The core CSS styles of UI components. Independent of any UI framework.

- **msteams-ui-icons-core** - The core set of Teams icons. Independent of any UI framework.

- **msteams-ui**-components-react - The React binding library. It depends on msteams-ui-styles-core and React.

- **msteams-ui-icons-react** - The React binding library for the set of Teams icons. It depends on msteams-ui-icons-core and React.

Go to Teams ➤ App Studio (Figure 5-9).

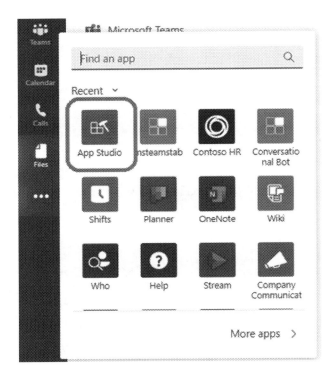

Figure 5-9. *App Studio*

It will open App Studio; navigate to the control library tab and get sample code for your development using the control library from App Studio (Figure 5-10).

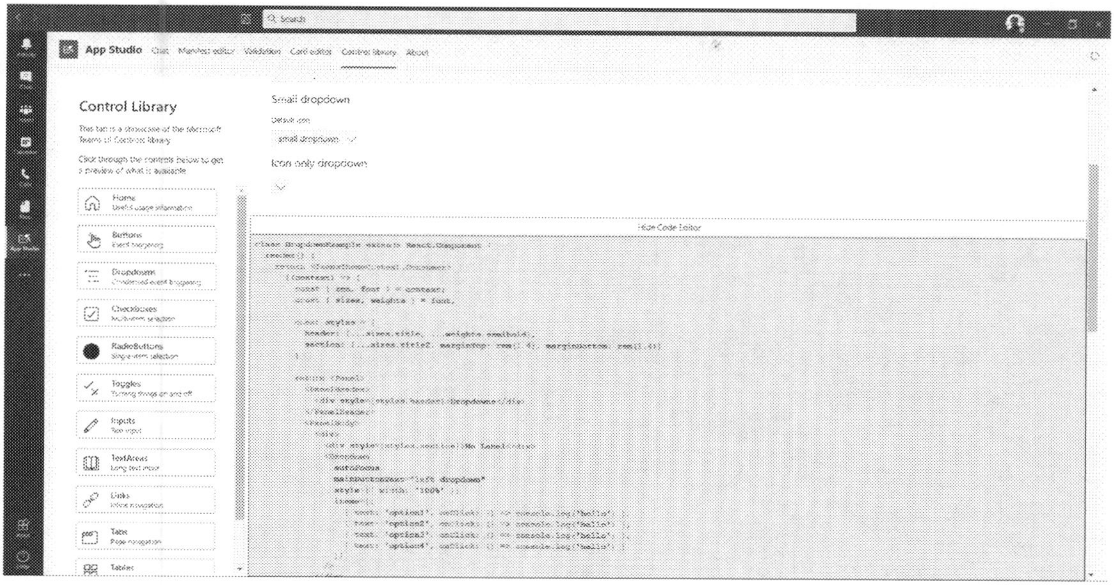

Figure 5-10. *App Studio control library*

- **File ➤ Save All** to save the changes

At this point, your personal tab is ready to be tested!

Run Your Personal Tab Locally

Open the command Prompt to navigate to the project folder and execute the following command; to run your tab, you use the **gulp serve** command.

```
gulp serve
```

This will build and start a local web server for you to test your app. The command will also rebuild the application whenever you save a file in your project.

You should now be able to browse *http://localhost:3007/MyTab/index.html* to ensure that your tab is rendering. See Figure 5-11.

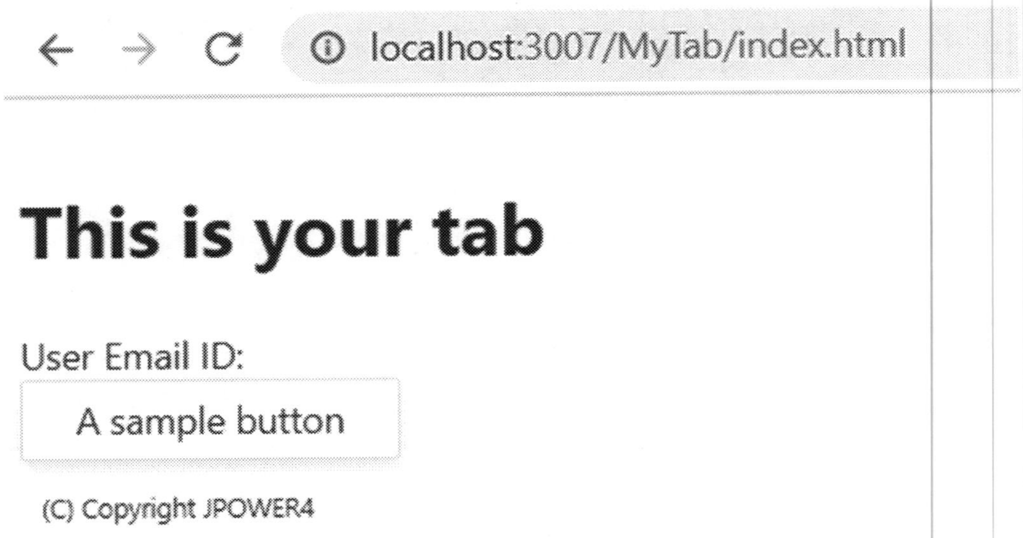
localhost:3007/MyTab/index.html
This is your tab
User Email ID:
A sample button
(C) Copyright JPOWER4

Figure 5-11. *Personal tab Localhost rendering*

Test the Personal Tab in Teams

Open the command Prompt, navigate to the project folder, and execute the following command:

```
gulp ngrok-serve
```

This gulp task will run many other tasks that are displayed within the command-line console. The ngrok-serve task builds your project and starts a local web server (`http://localhost:3007`). It then starts ngrok with a random subdomain that creates a secure URL to your local webserver.

In development, testing can be done using the tool ngrok that creates a secure rotatable URL to your local HTTP webserver. Ngrok is included as a dependency within the project so there is nothing to set up or configure (Figure 5-12).

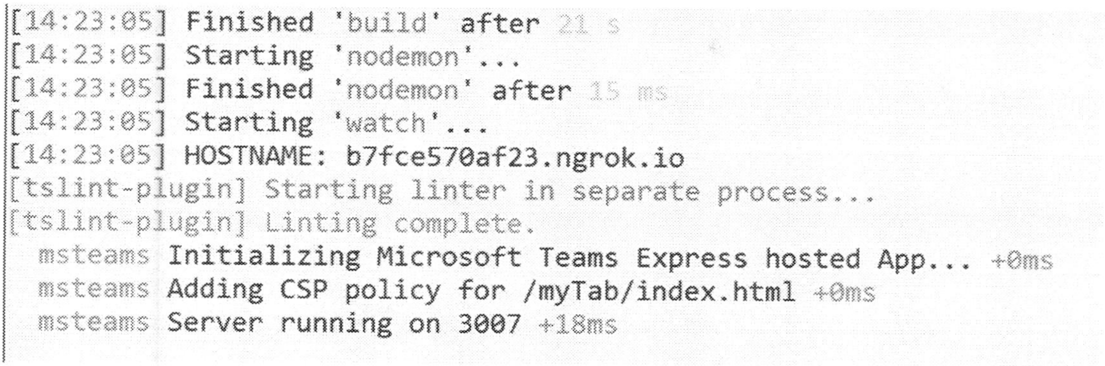

```
[14:23:05] Finished 'build' after 21 s
[14:23:05] Starting 'nodemon'...
[14:23:05] Finished 'nodemon' after 15 ms
[14:23:05] Starting 'watch'...
[14:23:05] HOSTNAME: b7fce570af23.ngrok.io
[tslint-plugin] Starting linter in separate process...
[tslint-plugin] Linting complete.
  msteams Initializing Microsoft Teams Express hosted App... +0ms
  msteams Adding CSP policy for /myTab/index.html +0ms
  msteams Server running on 3007 +18ms
```

Figure 5-12. *Gulp ngrok serve execution*

Ngrok has created the temporary URL b7fce570af23.ngrok.io that will map to our locally running web server.

Install the Personal Tab in Microsoft Teams

Now let's install the app in Microsoft Teams. In the browser, navigate to `https://teams.microsoft.com` and sign in with the credentials of a Work and School account.

Microsoft Teams is available for use as a web client, desktop client, and mobile client. Using the app bar navigation menu, select the More added apps button. Then select More apps followed by Upload a custom app and then Upload for me or my teams (Figure 5-13).

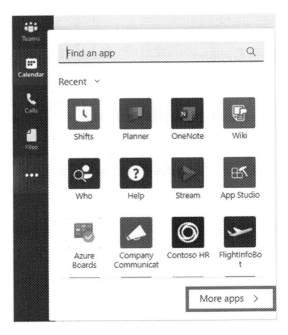

Figure 5-13. *Add apps to MS Teams*

In the file dialog that appears, select the Microsoft Teams package in your project. This app package is a ZIP file that can be found in the projects **./package** folder (Figure 5-14).

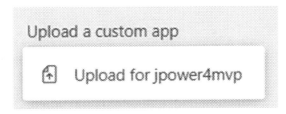

Figure 5-14. *Upload apps*

After installation, you will be able to see the app in the apps list (Figure 5-15).

Personal Tab
JPOWER4

This exercise will guide you on how to create a custom personal tab

Figure 5-15. *Personal apps installed*

Click the app, and Microsoft Teams will display a summary of the app (Figure 5-16).

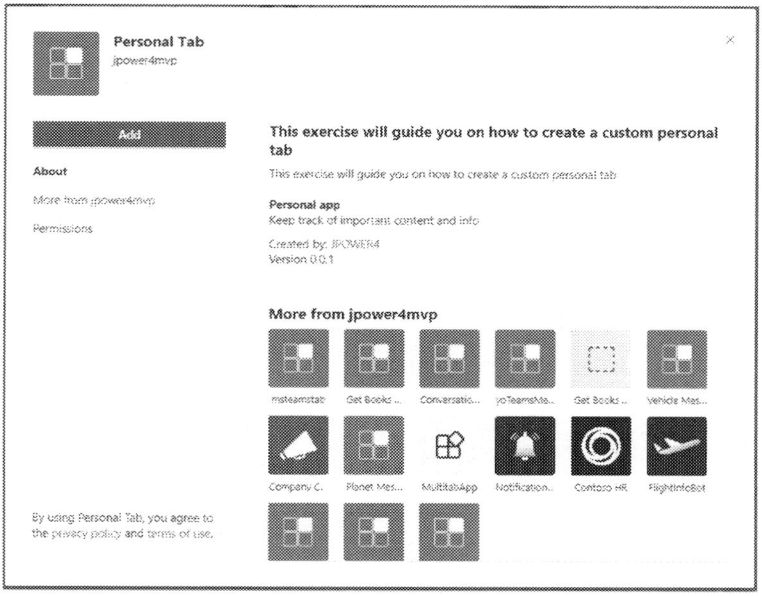

Personal Tab
jpower4mvp

Add

About

More from jpower4mvp

Permissions

This exercise will guide you on how to create a custom personal tab

This exercise will guide you on how to create a custom personal tab

Personal app
Keep track of important content and info

Created by: JPOWER4
Version 0.0.1

More from jpower4mvp

msteamstab   Get Books ...   Conversatio...   yoTeamsMe...   Get Books ...   Vehicle Mes...

Company C.   Planet Mes...   MultitabApp   Notification...   Contoso HR   FlightInfoBot

By using Personal Tab, you agree to the privacy policy and terms of use.

Figure 5-16. *Add the personal tab*

Install Personal Tab App in Teams

- Click the Add button to navigate to the personal tab to test.

- Also, you can pin the personal tab in far-left navigation bar permanently.

- Or select the ... menu and choose your app from the list (Figure 5-17).

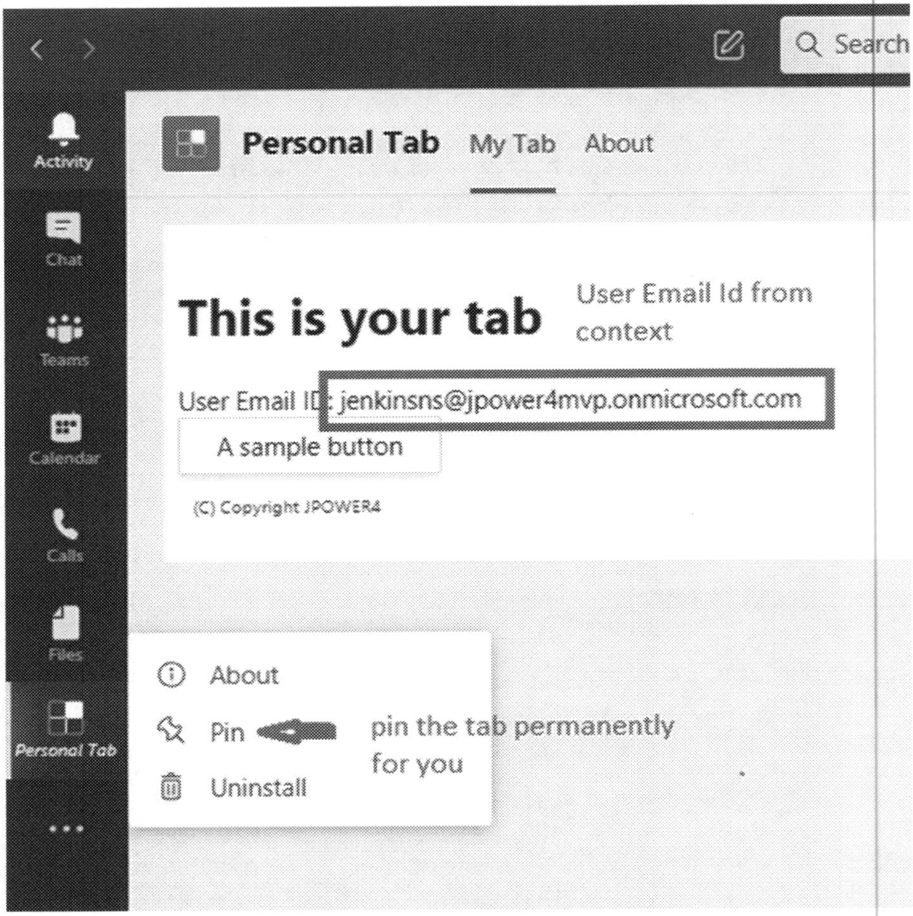

Figure 5-17. *Personal tab output*

In this exercise, you have created a personal tab for a custom Microsoft Teams app.

Exercise 2 - Create a Custom Microsoft Teams Channel or Group Tab

In this exercise, you will create a new configurable tab for a Teams app using a Yeoman generator (yo teams). This exercise will guide you on how to create a custom tab for a channel or group chat.

To create a new configurable tab app project, create a new project directory in your favorite location.

1. Open the command prompt and create a new folder "configurabletabCh5"

2. Navigate to a newly created directory

3. Run the Yeoman generator for Microsoft Teams by running the following command:

   ```
   yo teams
   ```

4. Modify the solution name if you want. I have changed it to "ConfigurableTab" (Figure 5-18).

```
C:\Jenkins\JPower4\Book\MSTeamsBook\configurabletabCh5>yo teams
```

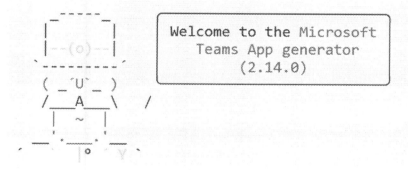

```
? What is your solution name? ConfigurableTab
```

Figure 5-18. *yo teams for configurable tab*

Yeoman will launch and ask you a series of questions. Answer the questions with the following values (Figure 5-19):

- What is your solution name? ConfigurableTab

- Where do you want to place the files? Use the current folder

- Title of your Microsoft Teams App project? configurabletabCh5

- Your (company) name? (max 32 characters) JPOWER4

- Which manifest version would you like to use? v1.6

- Enter your Microsoft Partner ID, if you have one? (Leave blank to skip)

- What features do you want to add to your project? A Tab

- The URL where you will host this solution? `https://configurabletab.azurewebsites.net`

- Would you like show a loading indicator when your app/tab loads? No

- Would you like to include Test framework and initial tests? No

- Would you like to use Azure Applications Insights for telemetry? No

- Default Tab name? (max 16 characters) My Team Tab

- What kind of Tab would you like to create? Configurable

- What scopes do you intend to use for your Tab? **In a Team, In a group chat** (I have selected both team and group chat)

- Do you require Azure AD Single-Sign-On support for the tab? No

- Do you want this tab to be available in SharePoint Online? No

```
? What is your solution name? ConfigurableTab
? Where do you want to place the files? Use the current folder
? Title of your Microsoft Teams App project? configurabletabCh5
? Your (company) name? (max 32 characters) JPOWER4
? Which manifest version would you like to use? v1.6
? Enter your Microsoft Partner ID, if you have one? (Leave blank to skip)
? What features do you want to add to your project? A Tab
? The URL where you will host this solution? https://configurabletab.azurewebsites.net
? Would you like show a loading indicator when your app/tab loads? No
? Would you like to include Test framework and initial tests? No
? Would you like to use Azure Applications Insights for telemetry? No
? Default Tab name? (max 16 characters) My Team Tab
? What kind of Tab would you like to create? Configurable
? What scopes do you intend to use for your Tab? In a Team, In a group chat
? Do you require Azure AD Single-Sign-On support for the tab? No
? Do you want this tab to be available in SharePoint Online? No
  create package.json
```

Figure 5-19. *Answer Yeoman questionnaire*

Note   Most of the answers to these questions can be changed after creating the project. For example, the URL where the project will be hosted is not important at the time of creating or testing the project

162

Open Visual Studio Code using **code .** in the command prompt (Figure 5-20).

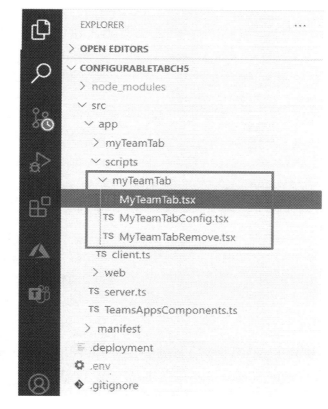

Figure 5-20. *Visual studio code OOB*

The configurable tab project shows three files: MyTeamTab, config, and Remove react components.

- MyTeamTab.tsx – Implementation of the custom tab content page

- MyTeamTabconfig.tsx – Implementation of the My Team Tab configuration page

- MyTeamTabRemove.tsx - Implementation of the My Team Tab remove page

Step 1: Update the Manifest.json file to configure the configurable tab:

- Navigate to ./src/manifest/manifest.json file and replace the name and description section as per your tab Line of Business.

```
"configurableTabs": [{
        "configurationUrl": "https://{{HOSTNAME}}/myTeamTab/
        config.html",
        "canUpdateConfiguration": true,
        "scopes": [
            "team",
            "groupchat"
        ]
    }],
```

Step 2: Update the react component MyTeamTab.tsx (custom tab content page to respond to user):

- In your project, navigate to /src/app/scripts/MyTeamTab/ MyTeamTab.tsx file

- Find the export interface IMyTeamTabState and define **useremail, TeamID, Teamname, ChannelID, ChannelName** typed variables.

```
export interface IMyTeamTabState extends ITeamsBaseComponentState
{
    entityId?: string;
    useremail?: string;
    TeamID?: string;
    TeamName?: string;
    ChannelID?: string;
    ChannelName?: string;
}
```

- Go to public async componentWillMount() method and get user email Id, teams, and channel details from the tab context.

```
this.setState({
                    entityId: context.entityId,
                    useremail: context.upn,
```

```
                TeamID: context.teamId,
               TeamName: context.teamName,
ChannelID: context.channelId, ChannelName: context.channelName

                });
```

- Then go to the render method to render user information and find these:

  ```
  "<div><Text content={this.state.entityId} /></div>"
  ```

- Add the code given below next to this statement mentioned above

  ```
  <div>User Email ID : <Text content={this.state.useremail} /></div>
          <div>Team ID : <Text content={this.state.TeamID} /></div>
          <div>Team Name : <Text content={this.state.TeamName} />
          </div>
          <div>Chanel ID : <Text content={this.state.ChannelID} />
          </div>
          <div>Channel Name : <Text content={this.state.ChannelName}
          /></div>
  ```

This component will display the user email id, team and channel information, and sample button. This is the TypeScript React-based class for your tab. Locate the render() method and add a user line of business logic.

To add more react fluent UI controls (**@fluentui/react-northstar**), refer to the control library section in App Studio – control Library tab. This tab is a showcase of the Microsoft Teams UI Controls library.

- *File ➤ Save All* to save the changes

- At this point, your configurable tab is ready to be tested!

Run Your Configurable Tab Locally

Open the command Prompt. Navigate to the project folder and execute the following command; to run your tab, you use the **gulp serve** command.

```
gulp serve
```

This will build and start a local web server for you to test your app. The command will also rebuild the application whenever you save a file in your project.

You should now be able to browse to $http://localhost:3007/MyTeamTab$ to ensure that your tab is rendering (Figure 5-21).

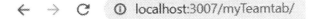

This is your tab

This is not hosted in Microsoft Teams
User Email ID :
Team ID :
Team Name :
Chanel ID :
Channel Name :

A sample button

(C) Copyright JPOWER4

Figure 5-21. Configurable tab localhost execution

Test the Configurable Tab in Teams

Open the command Prompt, navigate to the project folder, and execute the following command:

```
gulp ngrok-serve
```

This gulp task will run many other tasks that are displayed within the command-line console. The ngrok-serve task builds your project and starts a local web server (http://localhost:3007). It then starts ngrok with a random subdomain that creates a secure URL to your local web server.

In development, testing can be done using the tool ngrok that creates a secure rotatable URL to your local HTTP web server. Ngrok is included as a dependency within the project so there is nothing to set up or configure (Figure 5-22).

```
[16:26:13] Finished 'build' after 20 s
[16:26:13] Starting 'nodemon'...
[16:26:13] Finished 'nodemon' after 25 ms
[16:26:13] Starting 'watch'...
[16:26:13] HOSTNAME: ae55b4e27b81.ngrok.io
[tslint-plugin] Linting complete.
  msteams Initializing Microsoft Teams Express hosted App... +0ms
  msteams Adding CSP policy for /myTeamTab/remove.html +0ms
  msteams Adding CSP policy for /myTeamTab/config.html +1ms
  msteams Adding CSP policy for /myTeamTab/index.html +7ms
  msteams Server running on 3007 +26ms
```

Figure 5-22. *Ngrok serve execution*

Ngrok has created the temporary URL b7fce570af23.ngrok.io that will map to our locally running web server.

Install the Configurable Tab in Microsoft Teams

Now let's install the app in Microsoft Teams. In the browser, navigate to `https://teams.microsoft.com` and sign in with the credentials of a Work and School account.

Microsoft Teams is available for use as a web client, desktop client, and mobile client. Using the app bar navigation menu, select the More added apps button. Then select More apps followed by Upload a custom app and then Upload for me or my teams. See Figure 5-23.

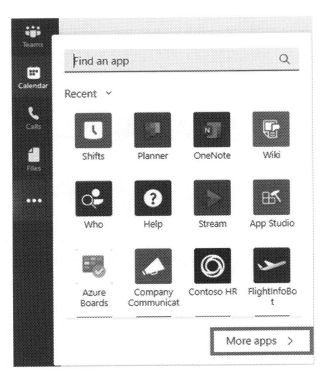

Figure 5-23. *Add apps to MS Teams*

In the file dialog that appears, select the Microsoft Teams package in your project. This app package is a ZIP file that can be found in the projects **./package** folder (Figure 5-24).

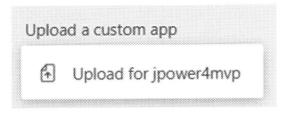

Figure 5-24. *Upload apps*

After installation, you will be able to see the app in the apps list (Figure 5-25).

Figure 5-25. *Installed apps*

Click the app, and Microsoft Teams will display a summary of the app (Figure 5-26).

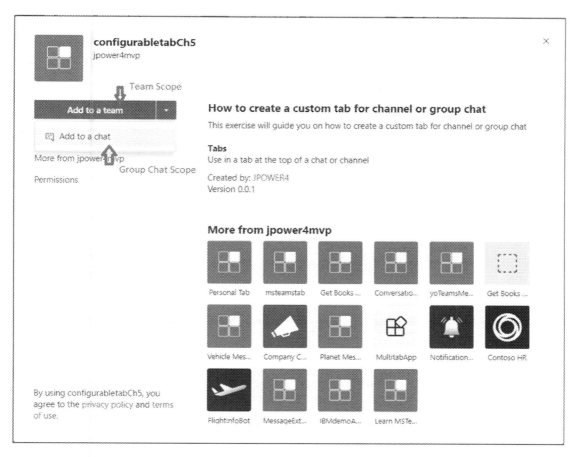

Figure 5-26. *Add the app to team*

Install Configurable Tab in Teams

- Click Add to a team button to navigate to the configuration page to add this tab in Channel.

- Then search and select channel to set up the tab (Figure 5-27).

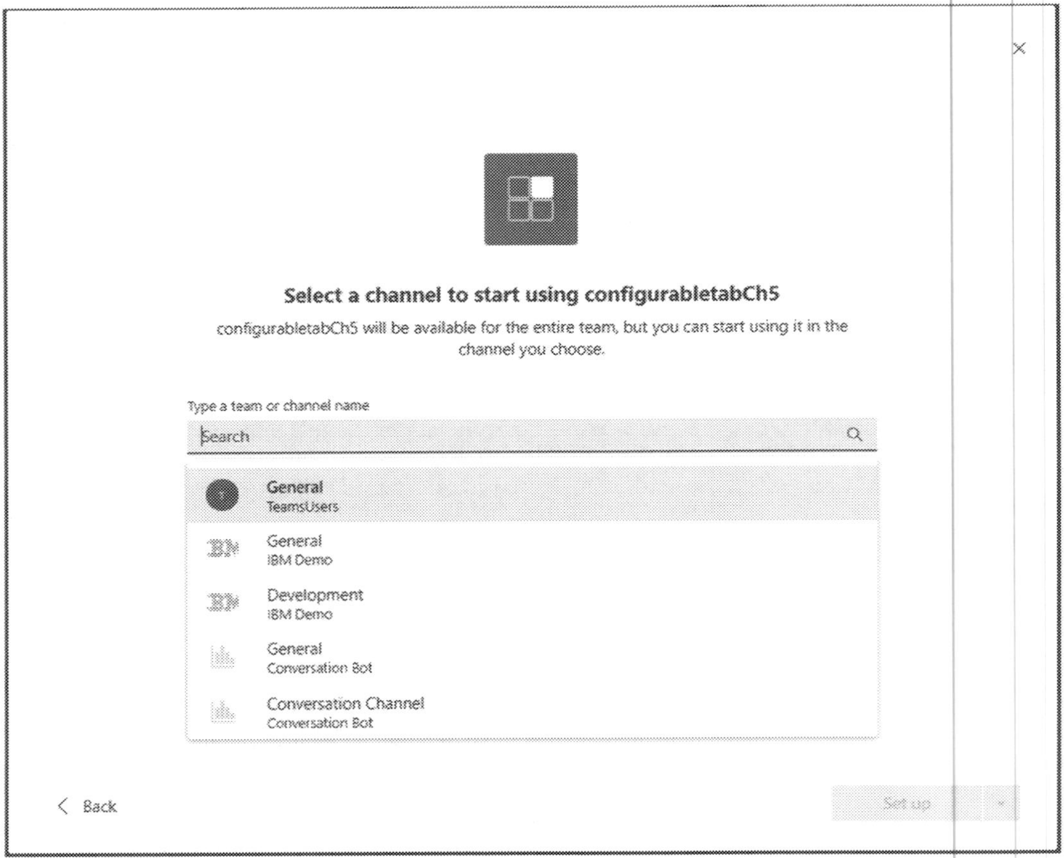

Select a channel to start using configurabletabCh5

configurabletabCh5 will be available for the entire team, but you can start using it in the channel you choose.

Type a team or channel name

Search

General
TeamsUsers

General
IBM Demo

Development
IBM Demo

General
Conversation Bot

Conversation Channel
Conversation Bot

‹ Back

Set up

Figure 5-27. *Select channel team*

- Enter the name for Tab "My Team Tab" and save it (Figure 5-28).

Figure 5-28. *Enter Tab Name*

It will add the tab in the channel and display all information via tab as shown below in Figure 5-29.

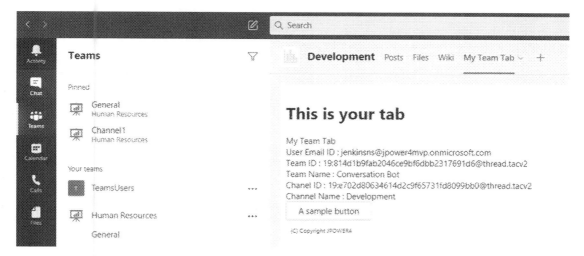

Figure 5-29. *Configurable Tab Name output*

In this exercise, you have created a configurable tab for a custom Microsoft Teams app.

Conclusion

In this chapter, you have learned various features of tabs and how to create and add personal and configurable apps to Microsoft Teams using the Yeoman generator (yo teams). It also covers how to use silent authentication, SSO authentication, and Azure AD authentication from the tab.

You have also learned how to create tabs using the Yeoman generator for Microsoft Teams. Along with this you will start learning different options and features of Microsoft Teams apps in our upcoming chapters.

CHAPTER 6

Collect Input from User Using Task Modules

Task modules are pop-up experience modals so that you can populate HTML with JavaScript content or an Adaptive Card for your custom Microsoft Teams app. Also, you can collect input from users using task modules.

In this chapter, you will learn various features of tasks modules – it explains how to create modals for task modules with examples to guide users. Task modules are a powerful and easy way for users to engage with your app from Microsoft Teams.

Overview of Task Modules

Task modules are pop-up windows to collect input or display information to users from tab or bot teams' apps. Task modules load in iframe-based widgets and supports two types of render options. The first one is to run your custom HTML page with JavaScript scripts, and the second one is an Adaptive Card. Tabs supports both HTML pages and Adaptive Cards, but Bots support only Adaptive Cards. However Task modules build on top of Microsoft Teams Tabs, and they are essentially a tab inside a pop-up window to collect input from users or display videos, forms, or Adaptive Cards.

Task modules can be invoked in three ways:

- Channel or personal tabs

  Using the Microsoft Teams Tabs, you can invoke task modules from buttons, links, or menus on your tab.

- Bots

  Buttons on cards sent from your bot. This is particularly useful when you don't need everyone in a channel to see what you are doing with a bot.

173

© Jenkins NS 2021
J. NS, *Building Solutions with Microsoft Teams*, https://doi.org/10.1007/978-1-4842-6476-8_6

- Outside of Teams from a deep link

  You can also create URLs to invoke a task module from anywhere. This is covered in detail here.

Figure 6-1 shows what a task module looks like.

Figure 6-1. *Tasks Module view*

1. Your app's color icon.

2. Your app's short name.

3. The task module's title specified in the title property of the 'TaskInfo' object.

4. Title of the Adaptive or HTM page.

5. The orange rectangle is where your web page appears if you are loading your own web page using the URL property of the 'TaskInfo' object.

6. The Yellow rectangle; if you are displaying an Adaptive Card via the card property of the 'TaskInfo' object, the padding is added for you.

7. Adaptive Card buttons will render here. If you are using your own page, you must create your own buttons.

Task modules can be invoked from tabs, bots, or deep links and what appears in one can be either HTML or an Adaptive Card, so there is a lot of flexibility in terms of how they are invoked and how to deal with the result of a user's interaction.

Collect User Input with Task Modules in Tabs

Adding a task module to your tab can greatly simplify your experience for any workflows that require data input. Task modules allow you to gather their input in a Teams-aware pop up using HTML with JavaScript and Adaptive Cards.

Using JavaScript and HTML

- Call the Teams client SDK function tasks.startTask() with a TaskInfo object.

- For html and JavaScript task info using URL property:

```
const taskInfo = {
            url: this.appRoot() + `/taskModulesTab/getinfo.html`,
            title: "Custom Form",
            height: 300,
            width: 400
        };
```

- Use the Teams client SDK function tasks.startTask() with an optional submitHandler(err, result) callback function

```
microsoftTeams.tasks.startTask(taskModuleInfo);
```

- In the task module code, after the user completes the entry, call the Teams SDK function tasks.submitTask() with a result object as a parameter. If a submitHandler callback is specified in tasks.startTask(), Teams calls it with the result as a parameter.

```
const submitHandler = (err, result) => {
        this.setState(Object.assign({}, this.state, {
            name: `Name : ${result.name}`,
        }));
};
```

- If there is an error when invoking tasks.startTask(), the submitHandler function is called with an err string instead.

```
microsoftTeams.tasks.startTask(taskInfo, submitHandler);
```

- You can also specify a completionBotId when calling teams.startTask() - in that case the result is sent to the bot instead.

Keyboard and Accessibility Guidelines

As discussed in a previous section, Task modules allow you to gather user input in a pop-up bind with HTML or Adaptive Cards; that is, Task modules render in a HTML page or Adaptive Card. While using HTML-based task modules, it is your responsibility to handle all keyboard events, but Adaptive Cards handle the keyboard events using an out-of-the-box feature.

Task modules HTML files are available under the project folder:

```
Ex: ...\taskModulesTab\src\app\web\taskModulesTab\index.html
```

To render the tomnoddies app within your HTML page:

```
taskModulesTab.TaskModulesTab.render(document.getElementById('app'), {});
```

In the HTML page we are using JavaScript to handle the events and return data to the user tab app. The code below initializes Microsoft teams, handles the escape key, and validates the input form in the HTML page.

```
<script>
      microsoftTeams.initialize();

   //- Handle the Esc key
   document.onkeyup = function(event) {
       if ((event.key === 27) || (event.key === "Escape")) {
           microsoftTeams.tasks.submitTask(null);
//- this will return an err object to the completionHandler()
           }
      }

      function validateForm() {
          let customerInfo = {
              name: document.forms["customerForm"]["name"].value,
              email: document.forms["customerForm"]["email"].value,
              designation: document.forms["customerForm"]["designation"].
              value
          }

          microsoftTeams.tasks.submitTask(customerInfo, "");
          return true;
      }
  </script>
```

Then Microsoft Teams will ensure that the keyboard navigation works properly from the task module header into your HTML and vice versa.

Using Adaptive Card

The second option is an Adaptive Card to collect input from task modules in teams. To do this, follow the steps below.

- Call the Teams client SDK function tasks.startTask() with a TaskInfo object and TaskInfo.card containing the JSON for the Adaptive Card to show in the task module pop up.

- For Adaptive Cards using card.

```
const taskModuleInfo = {
            title: "Custom Form",
            card: adaptiveCard,
            width: 500,
            height: 500
        };
```

- If a submitHandler callback is specified in tasks.startTask(), Teams calls it with an err string if there is an error when invoking tasks. startTask() or if the user closes the task module pop up using the X at the upper right.

```
microsoftTeams.tasks.startTask(taskInfo, submitHandler);
```

- If the user presses an Action.Submit button, then its data object is returned as the value of result.

```
"actions": [{
        "type": "Action.Submit",
        "title": "Submit"
    }]
```

Task Info Object

The taskInfo object contains properties that tell Microsoft Teams about the task module. This object includes the following properties:

```
microsoftTeams.tasks.startTask(taskInfo, Callback);

const taskInfo = {
            url: this.appRoot() + `/taskModulesTab/getinfo.html`,
            title: "Custom Form",
            height: 300,
            width: 400,
        failbackurl:    "",
        card: "adaptivecardjosnobj"
        };
```

- **title** (string): Task Module Title

- **height & width** (number | string): Task module pop-up modal height and width dimensions or predefined sizes (small, medium, or large). The named sizes are predefined percentages of the available space to display the task module. For the width, they are 20%, 50%, and 60% while the height values are 20%, 50%, and 60%.

url (string): The URL is task module html page path and it is loaded as an <iframe> inside the task module and the URL domain should add in the validDomains array section in the manifest package file

- **failbackUrl** (string): If a Teams client does not support the task module feature, then this URL is opened in a browser tab.

- **card**: If you are not using an HTML page for task modules, then add the card object or an Adaptive Card bot card attachment, If you are using a task module from a bot, then HTML won't support it, and you must have a user card.

- **completionBotId** (string): While using a bot, you are required to specify the bot APP ID to send the result of the user interaction with the task module.

Deep Links in Task Modules

Task modules can be invoked using buttons and other types of user actions within Microsoft Teams. Another way to invoke a task module is with a deep link. Deep links are URLs that contain specific values that Microsoft Teams uses to invoke the task module.

The format for a deep link is as follows:

```
https://teams.microsoft.com/l/task/<APP_ID>?url=<TaskInfo.url>
&height=<TaskInfo.height>&width=<TaskInfo.width>&title=<TaskInfo.title>
```

- Deep link Syntax for JavaScript and HTML

  ```
  https://teams.microsoft.com/l/task/APP_ID?url=<TaskInfo.
  url>&height=<TaskInfo.height>&width=<TaskInfo.
  width>&title=<TaskInfo.title>&completionBotId=BOT_APP_ID
  ```

- Deep link Syntax for Adaptive Cards

  ```
  https://teams.microsoft.com/l/task/APP_ID?card=<TaskInfo.
  card>&height=<TaskInfo.height>&width=<TaskInfo.
  width>&title=<TaskInfo.title>&completionBotId=BOT_APP_ID
  ```

Let's look at each of these values:

- **<APP_ID>:** This is the ID of the custom Microsoft Teams app. The app ID, a GUID, can be found in the app's **manifest.json** file.

- **<TASKINFO.*>:** The additional properties in the query string of the URL map to specific properties on the **taskInfo** object.

The deep link can be used from anywhere, including the conversations within Microsoft Teams channels or in external applications.

Bots Using Task Modules

Task modules can be triggered from bots buttons on Adaptive Cards and Bot Framework Cards like Hero Card or Thumbnail Card or Office 365 connector. Task modules give a rich user experience and multiple conversation steps must track on the bot state and allow the user to interrupt or cancel the flow. Bots only support Adaptive Card task modules.

There are two ways of invoking task modules:

- A new kind of invoke message task/fetch

  This is the new way to invoke card action for a Bot Frameworks card (Action.Submit) with a task/fetch the task modules modal pop-up card dynamically from your bot.

- Deep link URLs

  Deep link URLs support open URL card action for a Bot Framework card (Action.OpenUrl). With deep link URLs, the task module URL is avoiding a server round trip relative to task/fetch.

Deep link syntax with bot ID:

```
https://teams.microsoft.com/l/task/APP_ID?card/url=<TaskInfo.card>
&height=<TaskInfo.height>&width=<TaskInfo.width>&title=<TaskInfo.
title>&completionBotId=BOT_APP_ID
```

Based on the implementation, we need to modify the card/url and fallbackUrl.

Invoking a Task Module via Task/Fetch

When a user clicks the button, it invokes card action (Action.Submit) and invokes the message that is sent to the bot. Then the HTTP response object invokes the message using the task Info Object and displays to the task module.

Submitting the Result of a Task Module

When the user completes the task module and clicks the submit button, the result back to the bot is like the way it works with tabs, but there are a few differences with HTML and Adaptive Cards.

HTML/JavaScript and Adaptive Card

In HTML it validates using JavaScript what the user has entered, and it calls the submit task function. If you want to close the task module without any parameters but remember that always required to pass parameters for task modules invoke from tabs. To handle submitHandler function without error, pass an object or string. Then teams will invoke submitHandler: function and error will be null, and result will be object or string you passed to submitTask function.

In the Adaptive Card it sent to the bot using a task/submit message when the user clicked the submit button (Action.Submit). An Adaptive Card can handle data easily from task modules compared to HTML.

The Flexibility of Task/Submit

You have several options when responding to the task/submit message:

- Teams will display the value in a pop-up message box.

```
{
  "task": {
    "type": "message",
    "value": "Message text"
```

```
    }
  }
```

- Allows you to "chain" sequences of Adaptive Cards together in a wizard/multi-step experience.

```
{
  "task": {
    "type": "continue",
    "value": <TaskInfo object>
  }
}
```

Bot Framework Card Actions vs. Adaptive Card Action. Submit Actions

We have two card actions: Bot Framework card actions and Adaptive Card Action.Submit action as well as a small difference while using the schema. The following syntax shows the difference.

First the Bot Framework card action:

```
{
  "type": "invoke",
  "title": "Buy",
  "value": {
    "type": "task/fetch",
    <...>
  }
}
```

Now the Adaptive Card Action.Submit action:

```
{
  "type": "Action.Submit",
  "id": "btnBuy",
```

```
"title": "Buy",
"data": {
  <...>,
  "msteams": {
    "type": "task/fetch"
  }
}
}
```

Task modules can be invoked from Microsoft Teams bots using buttons on Adaptive Cards and Bot Framework cards. In exercise 5, you will learn how to use task modules with bots in Microsoft Teams.

Exercise 1 - Send Data to Task Modules

The Microsoft Teams Developer Platform helps you to extend your teams with your line of business (LOB) application and services seamlessly into the Microsoft Teams. It also enables you to distribute your custom apps to your organization or public users if you developed generic feature apps.

Before starting the exercise, verify your environment. In this exercise, I am using the tools mentioned below, which are installed in my environment:

- Node.js - v10.16.0

- NPM - 6.9.0

- Gulp

  - CLI version: 2.3.0

  - Local version: 4.0.2

- Yeomen Generator of MS Teams - 2.14.0

- Visual Studio Code

and

- Microsoft Azure Subscription

- Office 365 Subscription

In this exercise, you will learn the basics of task modules in Microsoft Teams and how to send input to task modules, that is, from the tab to get a video ID from the user and send it to a standard HTML page that accepts the ID of a video on YouTube.

When the task module is invoked, it will display the video using the YouTube embedded player. This task module will get the video ID from the query string, but it will not return any information back to the tab.

In this exercise, you will create a new Microsoft Teams personal tab for Task modules by using the Microsoft Teams Yeoman generator, Visual Studio Code, and App Studio.

Create Microsoft Teams Task Modules App

In this section, you will create a task modules app for tab using Yeoman generator (yo teams). This exercise will guide you on how to create a custom task module from a tab.

To create a new task module tab app project:

- Create a new project directory in your favorite location.

- Open the command prompt.

- Create a new folder "taskModulesTab."

- Navigate to a newly created directory.

- Run the Yeoman generator for Microsoft Teams by running the following command: **yo teams** (refer to Figure 6-2).

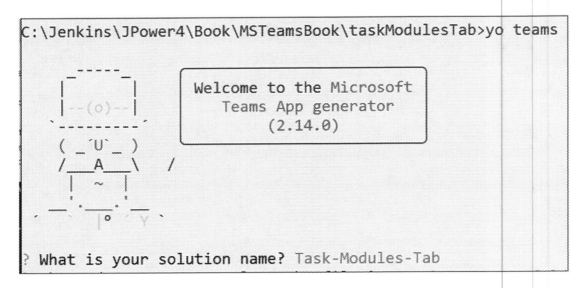

Figure 6-2. *yo teams generator*

Yeoman will launch and ask you a series of questions. Answer the questions with the following values (Figure 6-3):

- What is your solution name? Task-Modules-Tab

- Where do you want to place the files? Use the current folder

- Title of your Microsoft Teams App project? Task Modules Tab

- Your (company) name? (max 32 characters) JPOWER4

- Which manifest version would you like to use? v1.6

- Enter your Microsoft Partner ID, if you have one? (Leave blank to skip)

- What features do you want to add to your project? A Tab

- The URL where you will host this solution? `https://taskmodulestab.azurewe`

- bsites.net

- Would you like show a loading indicator when your app/tab loads? No

- Would you like to include Test framework and initial tests? No

- Would you like to use Azure Applications Insights for telemetry? No

- Default Tab name? (max 16 characters) Task Modules

- What kind of Tab would you like to create? Configurable

- What scopes do you intend to use for your Tab? In a Team

- Do you require Azure AD Single-Sign-On support for the tab? No

- Do you want this tab to be available in SharePoint Online? No

```
? What is your solution name? Task-Modules-Tab
? Where do you want to place the files? Use the current folder
? Title of your Microsoft Teams App project? Task Modules Tab
? Your (company) name? (max 32 characters) JPOWER4
? Which manifest version would you like to use? v1.6
? Enter your Microsoft Partner ID, if you have one? (Leave blank to skip)
? What features do you want to add to your project? A Tab
? The URL where you will host this solution? https://taskmodulestab.azurewebsites.net
? Would you like show a loading indicator when your app/tab loads? No
? Would you like to include Test framework and initial tests? No
? Would you like to use Azure Applications Insights for telemetry? No
? Default Tab name? (max 16 characters) Task Modules
? What kind of Tab would you like to create? Configurable
? What scopes do you intend to use for your Tab? In a Team
? Do you require Azure AD Single-Sign-On support for the tab? No
? Do you want this tab to be available in SharePoint Online? No
```

Figure 6-3. *Answer Yeoman questionnaire*

Note   Most of the answers to these questions can be changed after creating the project. For example, the URL where the project will be hosted is not important at the time of creating or testing the project.

- The first step is to install the fluent UI library, and for that execute the following command in the command line from the root folder of the project:

  npm i @fluentui/react

- Open Visual Studio Code using **Code .** in the command prompt (Figure 6-4).

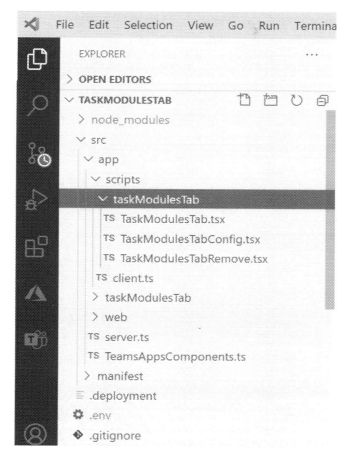

Figure 6-4. *Visual studio code*

- Locate and open the file that contains the React component used in the project. **..\src\app\scripts\taskModulesTab\TaskModulesTab. tsx**

- Add the import statement below in the **TaskModulesTab.tsx** file to use the Textfield control from a fluent UI.

```
import { TextField, ITextFieldStyles } from "@fluentui/react";
```

- Update the state of the component to a property for a new item.

- Add a new property youTubeVideoId in the interface ITaskModulesTabState to define the state.

```
export interface ITaskModulesTabState extends
ITeamsBaseComponentState {
    entityId?: string;
    youTubeVideoId?: string;
}
```

- Locate componentWillMount() method to initiate the youTubeVideoId property.

  - youTubeVideoId: "eSJ-dVp83ks"

- After it is added, it looks like the statement given below:

```
this.setState({
            entityId: context.entityId,
            youTubeVideoId: "eSJ-dVp83ks"
        });
```

- Then locate the render() method and replace the flex tag with the return statement to the following code. The render() method return statement will now display as shown below.

```
return (
        <Provider theme={this.state.theme}>
            <Flex column gap="gap.smaller">
                <Header>Task Module Demo</Header>
                <TextField label="Enter your youtube Video
                ID" value={this.state.youTubeVideoId}
                styles={narrowTextFieldStyles}
                onChange={(event, value) => { this.setState({
                youTubeVideoId: String(value) }); }} />
                <Button content="Show Video" primary
                onClick={this.onShowVideo}></Button>
            </Flex>
        </Provider>
    );
```

- Add style for 'Textfield', locate public render() method, and add the code below as the first line of the render method.

```
const narrowTextFieldStyles: Partial<ITextFieldStyles> = {
fieldGroup: { width: 250 } };
```

- The next step is to add the onShowVideo method. Add the following method to the TaskModulesTab class. This method will handle the task module functionality to open the YouTube video based on the YouTube video ID.

```
private onShowVideo = (event: React.MouseEvent<HTMLButtonElement>):
void => {
     const taskModuleInfo = {
         title: "YouTube Player",
         url: this.appRoot() + `/taskModulesTab/player.
         html?vid=${this.state.youTubeVideoId}`,
         width: 1000,
         height: 700
     };
     microsoftTeams.tasks.startTask(taskModuleInfo);
 }
```

- This code will create a new taskModuleInfo object with the details of the task module. It will then launch the task module. This task module doesn't reply with anything but displays information, so we don't need to implement the callback.

- Add the following utility method approot() to get the hostname:

```
private appRoot(): string {
     if (typeof window === "undefined") {
         return "https://{{HOSTNAME}}";
     } else {
     return window.location.protocol + "//" + window.location.
     host;
     }
 }
```

- Locate and create a file "player.html" under .\src\app\web\ taskModulesTab

- Then add the below code to player.html

```html
<!DOCTYPE html>
<html lang="en">

<head>
    <title>YouTube Player Task Module</title>
    <style>
        #embed-container iframe {
            position: absolute;
            top: 0;
            left: 0;
            width: 95%;
            height: 95%;
            padding-left: 20px;
            padding-right: 20px;
            padding-top: 10px;
            padding-bottom: 10px;
            border-style: none;
        }
    </style>
</head>

<body>
    <div id="embed-container"></div>
    <script>
        function getUrlParameter(name) {
            name = name.replace(/[\[]/, '\\[').replace(/[\]]/, '\\]');
            var regex = new RegExp('[\\?&]' + name + '=([^&#]*)');
            var results = regex.exec(location.search);
            return results === null ? '' :
            decodeURIComponent(results[1].replace(/\+/g, ' '));
        };
```

```
    var element = document.createElement("iframe");
    element.src = "https://www.youtube.com/embed/" +
    getUrlParameter("vid");
    element.width = "1000";
    element.height = "700";
    element.frameborder = "0";
    element.allow = "autoplay; encrypted-media";
    element.allowfullscreen = "";

    document.getElementById("embed-container").
    appendChild(element);
  </script>
 </body>

</html>
```

The video player task module will use the YouTube embedded player to show the specified video. The video will be defined in the query string when the player.html file is loaded. Implement the <iframe> embedded video player by adding the following JavaScript before closing the </body> tag in the player.html file:

Test the Video Player Task Module

From the command line, navigate to the root folder for the project and execute the following command:

```
gulp ngrok-serve
```

This gulp task will run many other tasks that are displayed within the command-line console. The ngrok-serve task builds your project and starts a local web server (http:// localhost:3007). It then starts ngrok with a random subdomain that creates a secure URL to your local webserver.

In development, testing can be done using the tool ngrok, which creates a secure rotatable URL to your local HTTP webserver. Ngrok is included as a dependency within the project so there is nothing to set up or configure (Figure 6-5).

```
C:\Jenkins\JPower4\Book\MSTeamsBook\taskModulesTab>gulp ngrok-serve
[13:21:23] Using gulpfile C:\Jenkins\JPower4\Book\MSTeamsBook\taskModulesTab\gulpfile.js
[13:21:23] Starting 'ngrok-serve'...
[13:21:23] Starting 'start-ngrok'...
[13:21:23] [NGROK] starting ngrok...
[13:21:26] [NGROK] Url: https://efd13006d296.ngrok.io
[13:21:26] [NGROK] You have been assigned a random ngrok URL that will only be available fo
e Teams manifest next time you run this command.
[13:21:26] [NGROK] HOSTNAME: efd13006d296.ngrok.io
[13:21:26] Finished 'start-ngrok' after 2.6 s
```

Figure 6-5. *Gulp ngrok serve execution*

Note   The free version of ngrok will create a new URL each time you restart the
web server. Make sure you delete and install the app each time you restart the web
server when you are testing the app.

Install the Task Module Tab in Microsoft Teams

Now let's install the app in Microsoft Teams. In the browser, navigate to https://teams.
microsoft.com and sign in with the credentials of a Work and School account.

Microsoft Teams is available for use as a web client, desktop client, and mobile client.

Using the app bar navigation menu, select the More added apps button. Then select
More apps followed by Upload a custom app and then Upload for me or my teams
(Figure 6-6).

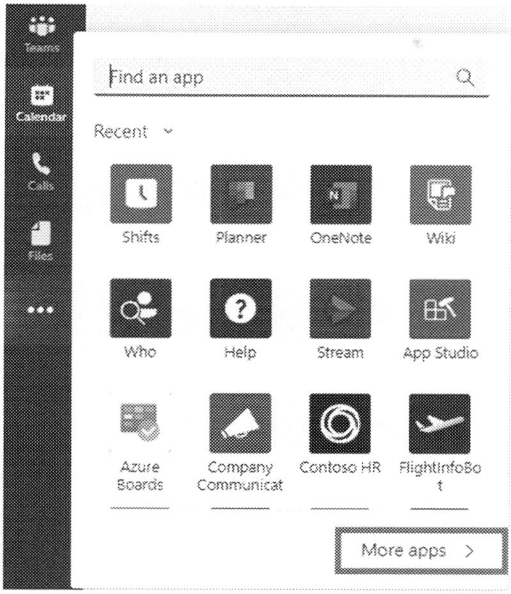

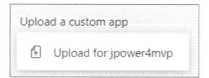

Figure 6-6. *Add apps to MS Teams*

In the file dialog that appears, select the Microsoft Teams package in your project. This app package is a ZIP file that can be found in the projects **./package** folder (Figure 6-7).

Figure 6-7. *Upload apps*

After installation, you will be able to see the app in the apps list (Figure 6-8).

Figure 6-8. *Apps installed*

Go to any one of your teams ➤ channel

Then Click + button to add a new tab in your channel (Figure 6-9).

Figure 6-9. *Add tabs*

Search and find the "Task Modules Tab" app and select it as shown in Figure 6-10.

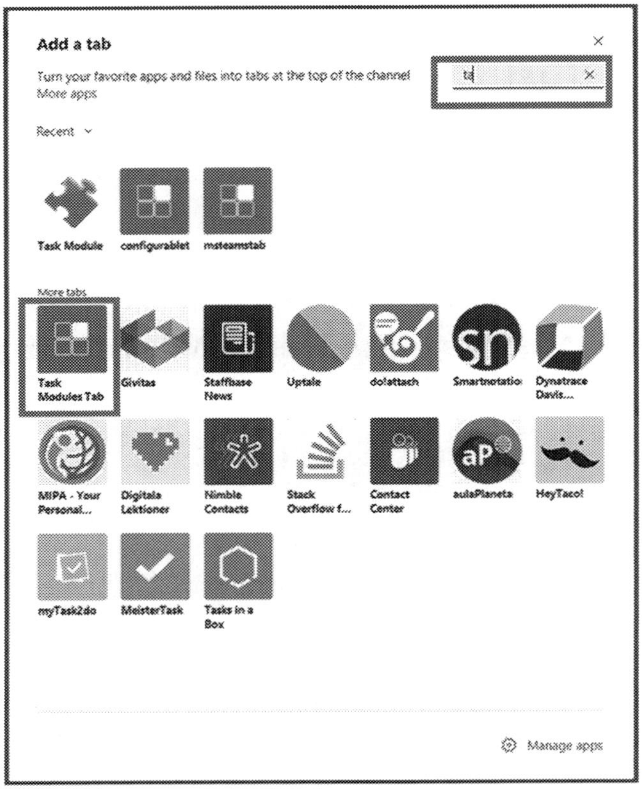

Figure 6-10. *Select the tab*

It will open a new window and show all details about this app, and then Click **Add** button to configure your tab (Figure 6-11).

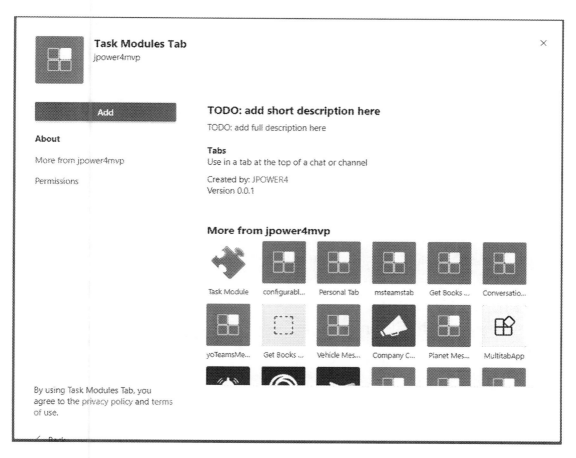

Figure 6-11. *Add the tab in teams*

Then give the name of the tab and click the save button (Figure 6-12).

Figure 6-12. *Configure your tab*

It will create the tab and display with an input control and button to show the video. See Figure 6-13.

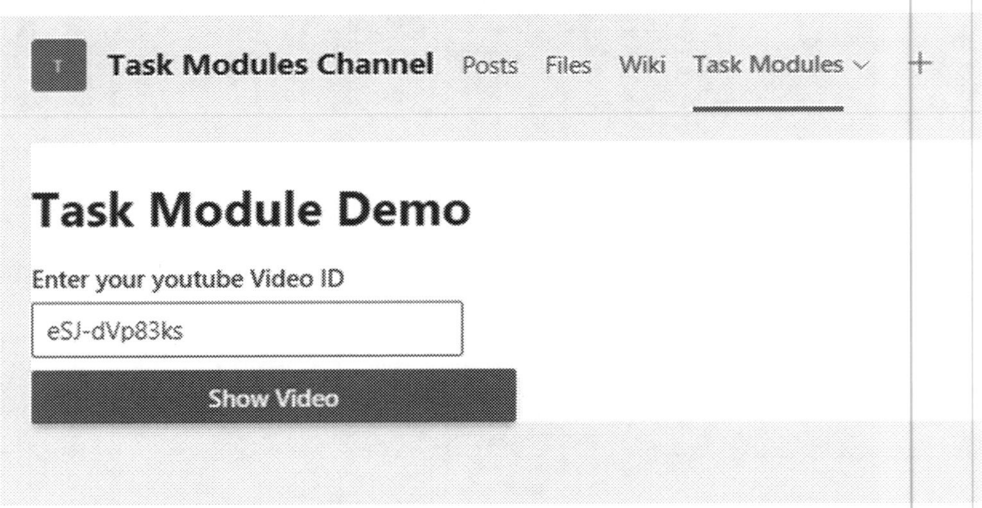

Figure 6-13. *Tasks Module Demo*

Click the show video button (Figure 6-14).

It will open a modal window and show the video (Figure 6-14).

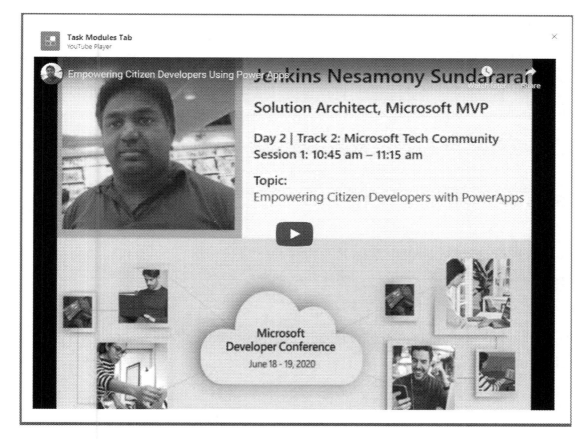

Figure 6-14. *Tasks Module youtube video output*

Now the user can change the video loaded in the player task module by updating the video ID in the Text box.

For that, enter your new YouTube video id in the text box and test again (Figure 6-15).

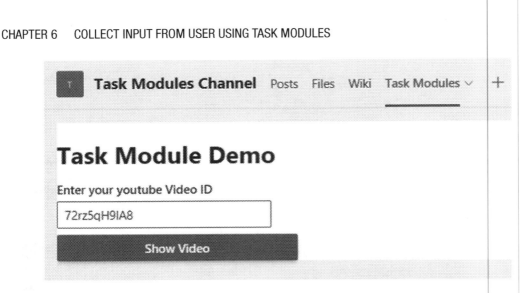

Figure 6-15. *New Video ID*

Click the show video button.

It will open a modal window and show the new video (Figure 6-16).

Figure 6-16. *Tasks Module new YouTube video output*

In this exercise, you have learned the basics of task modules in Microsoft Teams and how to send data from a custom Teams tab to a task module.

Exercise 2 - Collect User Input with Task Modules

In this exercise, you will learn the basics of task modules in Microsoft Teams and how to collect user input from a task module and process from a tab. This task module is implemented using React, the same way custom tabs are implemented using the Yeoman generator for Microsoft Teams. This task module enables you to collect user input from users and submit it and when the user submits their inputs, it will use the callback to close and submit the user input back to the tab.

In this exercise, you will use the Microsoft Teams app project with the Yeoman generator in the previous exercise, which contains a tab from the previous exercise in this chapter. You will update the project to add a new task module that is used to collect data from the user.

Add Code to the Project

Locate and open the file that contains the React component used in the project ..\src\app\scripts\taskModulesTab\TaskModulesTab.tsx

To update the state of the component to properties for new items, add a new properties name, email, and designation in interface ITaskModulesTabState to define the state:

```
export interface ITaskModulesTabState extends ITeamsBaseComponentState {
    entityId?: string;
    youTubeVideoId?: string;
    name?: string;
    email?: string;
    designation?: string;
}
```

Then locate the render() method and add the code below next to the **Showvideo** button tag.

```
<Button content="Get information" primary onClick={this.
ongetEmployeeInfo}></Button>
        <Text>{this.state.name}</Text>
        <Text>{this.state.email}</Text>
        <Text>{this.state.designation}</Text>
```

Then add a private method ongetEmployeeInfo to handle the task module and add the following method to the TaskModulesTab class.

```
private ongetEmployeeInfo = (event: React.MouseEvent<HTMLButtonElement>):
void => {
const taskInfo = {
            url: this.appRoot() + `/taskModulesTab/getinfo.html`,
            title: "Custom Form",
            height: 300,
            width: 400,
        };

    const submitHandler = (err, result) => {
            this.setState(Object.assign({}, this.state, {
                name: `Name : ${result.name}`,
                email: `Email ID : ${result.email}`,
                designation: `Designation : ${result.designation}`
            }));

        };

        microsoftTeams.tasks.startTask(taskInfo, submitHandler);
}
```

This code will create a new task Info object with the details of the task module. It will then launch the task module. This task module does reply to user inputs to the tab, so that it can implement a submit Handler for callback. From the submit handler callback handle is the result to process the user input.

Locate and create a file "getinfo.html" under .\src\app\web\taskModulesTab.

Then add the code given below to getinfo.html:

```html
<!DOCTYPE html>
<html lang="en">
<head>
    <style>
        body {
            margin: 4px;
            padding-left: 4px;
            padding-right: 4px;
        }

        html,
        body,
        div.surface,
        div.panel {
            height: 100%;
            margin: 0;
        }

        div.panel {
            padding: 15px;
        }
    </style>
    <title>Microsoft Teams Task Module Tester - Custom Form</title>
    <script src="https://unpkg.com/@microsoft/teams-js@1.3.7/dist/
    MicrosoftTeams.min.js" integrity="sha384-glExfvkpce98dO2oN+diZ/
    Luv/5qrZJiOvWCeR8ng/ZxlhpvBgHKeVFRURrh+NEC" crossorigin="anonymous"></
    script>
</head>

<body class="theme-light">
    <script>
        microsoftTeams.initialize();
```

```
    //- Handle the Esc key
    document.onkeyup = function(event) {
        if ((event.key === 27) || (event.key === "Escape")) {
            microsoftTeams.tasks.submitTask(null); //- this will return
            an err object to the completionHandler()
        }
    }

    function validateForm() {
        let customerInfo = {
            name: document.forms["customerForm"]["name"].value,
            email: document.forms["customerForm"]["email"].value,
            designation: document.forms["customerForm"]["designation"].
            value
        }

        microsoftTeams.tasks.submitTask(customerInfo, "");
        return true;
    }
</script>
<div class="surface">
    <div class="panel">
        <div class="font-semibold font-title">Enter employee
        information:</div>
        <form method="POST" id="customerForm" action="/register"
        onSubmit="return validateForm()">
            <div>
                <table>
                    <tr>
                        <td><label for="name">Enter the Name :
                        </label></td>
                        <td><input class="form-control input-field"
                        id="name" type="text" placeholder="Full Name"
                        name="name" tabindex="1" autofocus></td>
                    </tr>
```

```
    <tr>
        <td><label for="email">Enter the Email ID :
        </label></td>
        <td><input class="form-control input-field"
        id="email" type="email" placeholder="name@
        email.com" name="email" tabindex="2"></td>
    </tr>
    <tr>
        <td><label for="designation">Enter the
        Designation: </label></td>
        <td><input class="form-control input-
        field" id="designation" type="text "
        placeholder="designation" name="designation"
        tabindex="3" </td>
    </tr>
    <tr style="text-align: center;">
        <td colspan="2"><button class="btn button-
        primary " type="submit " tabindex="5 ">Submit</
        button></td>
    </tr>
    </table>
    </form>
    </div>
</div>
</body>

</html>
```

In the code given above, I have added three textboxes - name, email, and designation and added a submit button to send data back to the tab. You can add your own styles to make the app look prettier.

Test the Collect Input Task Module

If you have not stopped the gulp ngrok-serve execution, then save the code and go to Teams and refresh the tab. It will add the 'get Information' button (Figure 6-17).

Figure 6-17. *Refresh the App*

If you have stopped the gulp ngrok-serve execution, then follow the same steps used for exercise 1 testing and redeploy the app.

- Click Get Information button.

- It opens a modal pop-up window to collect information using the task module. See Figure 6-18.

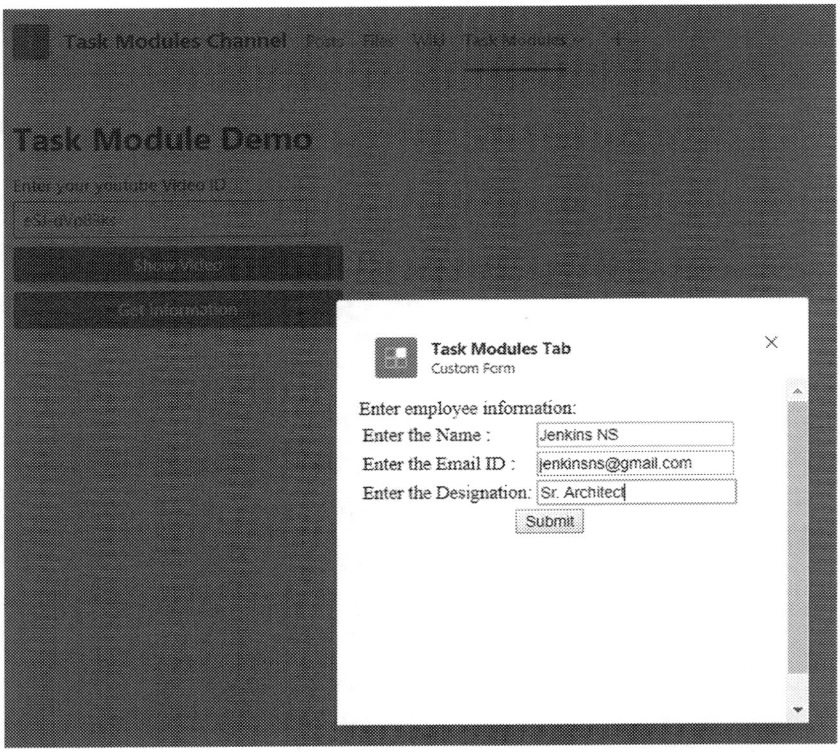

Figure 6-18. *Task Module Custom Form to collect input*

Enter the name, email id, and designation and submit the form. It will send the data to the tab and display it to the user; using this data you will be able to process any functionality based on your LOB. See Figure 6-19.

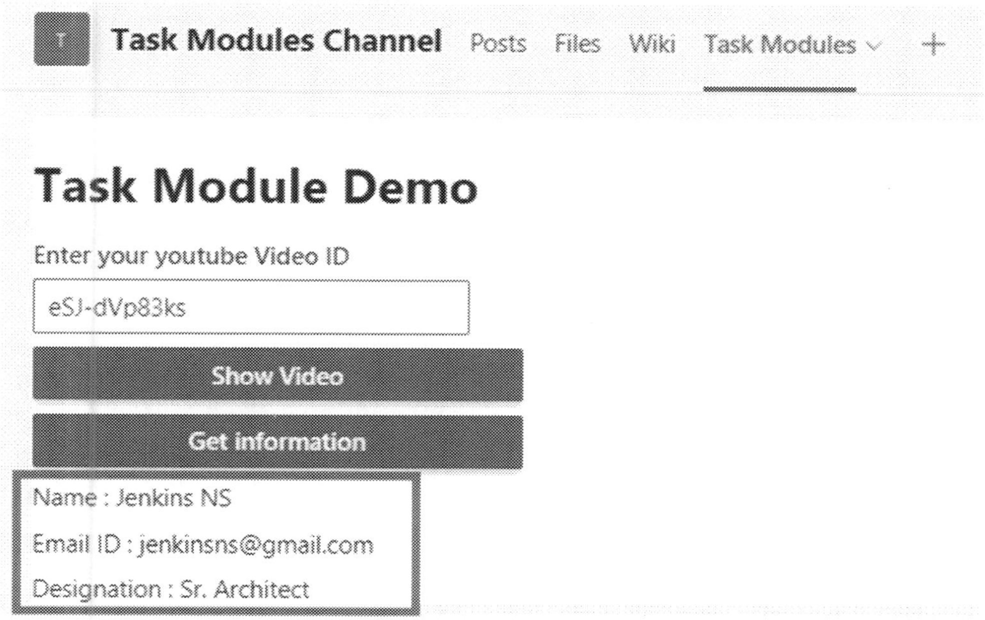

Figure 6-19. *Task Module Custom Form to collect input*

In this exercise, you have learned the basics of task modules in Microsoft Teams and how to collect user input and send it back to the custom Teams tab for processing the functionality by using a task module.

Exercise 3 - Using Adaptive Cards

In this exercise, you will learn how to use Adaptive Cards in a custom task module in a custom Microsoft Teams app. This task module is implemented using React, the same way custom tabs are implemented using the Yeoman generator for Microsoft Teams. This task module enables you to collect user input from the user and submit it; when the user submits their input, it will use the callback to close and submit the user input back to the tab. Here I am implementing the same exercise 2 functionality using an Adaptive Card.

In this exercise you will use the Microsoft Teams app project with the Yeoman generator, which contains a tab from the previous exercise in this chapter. You will update the project to add a new task module that is used to collect data from the user.

Add Code to the Project

Locate and open the file that contains the React component used in the project: ..\src\app\scripts\taskModulesTab\TaskModulesTab.tsx

Then locate the render() method and add the code below next to the **Get information** button tag.

```
<Button content="Get information (AdaptiveCard)" primary onClick={this.
onGetAdaptiveCard}></Button>
```

Then add a private method onGetAdaptiveCard to handle the task module. Add the following method to the TaskModulesTab class:

```
private onGetAdaptiveCard = (event: React.MouseEvent<HTMLButtonElement>):
void => {
      // load adaptive card
      const adaptiveCard: any = require("./customform.json");
      const taskModuleInfo = {
          title: "Custom Form",
          card: adaptiveCard,
          width: 500,
          height: 500
      };
      const submitHandler = (err: string, result: any): void => {
          this.setState(Object.assign({}, this.state, {
              name: `Name : ${result.name}`,
              email: `Email ID : ${result.email}`,
              designation: `Designation : ${result.designation}`
          }));

      };
      microsoftTeams.tasks.startTask(taskModuleInfo, submitHandler);
}
```

This code will create a new task Info object with the details of the task module. It will then launch the task module using an Adaptive Card. This task module does reply to user inputs to the tab, so that it implements the submit Handler for callback. From the submit handler callback, handle the result from the Adaptive Card to process the user input.

Locate and create a file "customform.json" under .\src\app\scripts\taskModulesTab. Then add the code below to customform.json:

```
{
    "$schema": "http://adaptivecards.io/schemas/adaptive-card.json",
    "type": "AdaptiveCard",
    "version": "1.0",
    "body": [{
            "type": "Container",
            "items": [{
                "type": "TextBlock",
                "text": "Custom Form",
                "weight": "bolder",
                "size": "extraLarge"
            }]
        },
        {
            "type": "Container",

            "items": [{
                    "type": "TextBlock",
                    "text": "Enter your name",
                    "weight": "bolder",
                    "size": "medium"
                },
                {
                    "type": "Input.Text",
                    "id": "name",
                    "value": ""
                },
                {
                    "type": "TextBlock",
                    "text": "Enter your Email",
```

```
                        "weight": "bolder",
                        "size": "medium"
                },
                {
                        "type": "Input.Text",
                        "id": "email",
                        "value": ""
                },
                {
                        "type": "TextBlock",
                        "text": "Enter your Designation",
                        "weight": "bolder",
                        "size": "medium"
                },
                {
                        "type": "Input.Text",
                        "id": "designation",
                        "value": ""
                }
            ]
        }
    ],
    "actions": [{
            "type": "Action.Submit",
            "title": "Submit"
    }]
}
```

In the above Adaptive Card code, I have added three textboxes - name, email, and designation and added one submit action to send data back to the tab.

Test the Collect Input Task Module

If you have not stopped the gulp ngrok-serve execution, then save the code and go to Teams and refresh the tab (Figure 6-20).

Figure 6-20. *Refresh the app for new changes*

If you have stopped the gulp ngrok-serve execution, then follow the same steps used for exercise 1 testing and redeploy the app.

Click "Get Information(AdaptiveCard)" button

It will open a modal pop-up window to collect information using an Adaptive Card and task module (Figure 6-21).

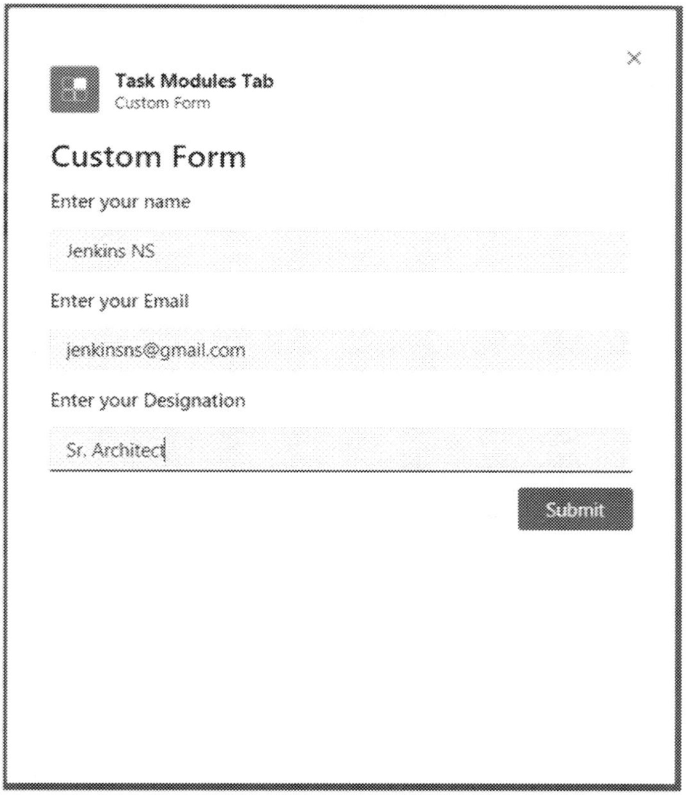

Figure 6-21. *Task module Adaptive Card*

Enter the name, email id, and designation and submit the Adaptive Card. It will send it to the tab and display it to the user; using this data, you will be able to process any functionality. See Figure 6-22.

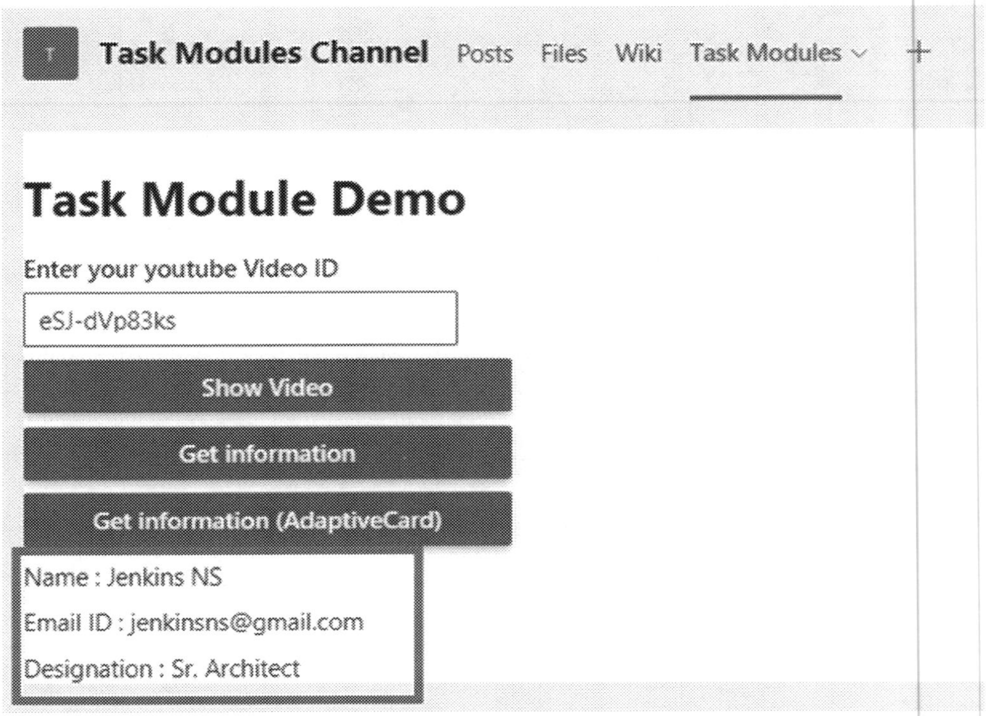

Figure 6-22. *Task module Adaptive Card output*

In this exercise, you have learned the basics of task modules in Microsoft Teams and how to collect user input using and Adaptive Card and sending it back to the custom Teams tab for processing the functionality using a task module.

Exercise 4 - Deep Links in Task

Task modules can be invoked by selecting a button in the Microsoft Teams experience or using a deep link. Deep links allow you to trigger a task module invocation from outside of teams, or within teams from a conversation.

The format for a deep link is as follows:

```
https://teams.microsoft.com/l/task/<APP_ID>?url=<TaskInfo.
url>&height=<TaskInfo.height>&width=<TaskInfo.width>&title=<TaskInfo.title>
```

Consider if you want to open a task module from a conversation that will display the following video **Getting started with Microsoft Teams development.**

As you have learned in exercise 1, the URL to display the video in the player task module will be the following:

```
https://{{REPLACE_WITH_YOUR_NGROK_URL}}/ taskModulesTab/player.
html?vid=eSJ-dVp83ks
```

The deep link to launch the video player task module will be the following (assuming your custom Microsoft Teams app's ID is 3fc49350-e11d-11ea-ac20-5fbc213e7a43):

To find App ID -> go to .env file and copy the APPLICATION_ID

Replace the ngrok-serve url - `https://`**`1f81e0623b36`**`.ngrok.io/`

```
https://teams.microsoft.com/l/task/3fc49350-e11d-11ea-ac20-5fbc213e7a43?url
=https://1f81e0623b36.ngrok.io/taskModulesTab/player.html?vid=eSJ-dVp83ks&h
eight=700&width=1000&title=Youtube Player
```

In Microsoft teams, go to a channel, select the Conversations tab, and select the Format button in the message dialog. See Figure 6-23.

Figure 6-23. *Conversation Format button*

Enter a message to post to the channel. Select some of the text and use the Link feature to add the deep **link** to the message (Figure 6-24).

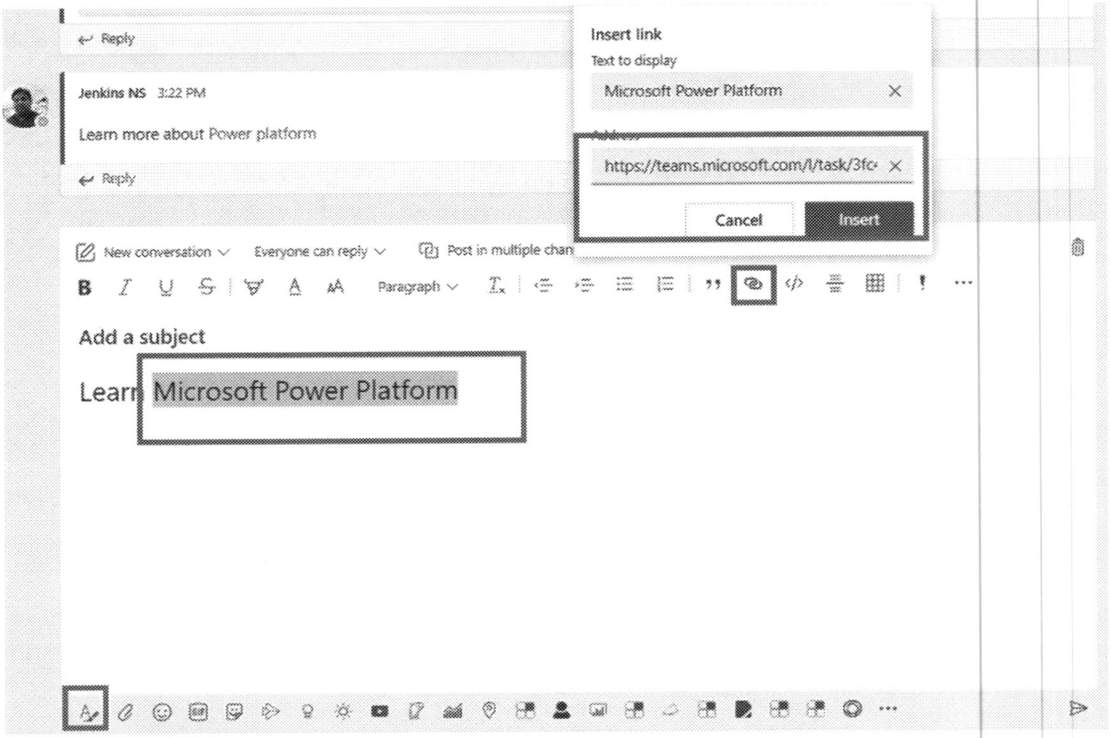

Figure 6-24. Conversation with deep link

Now, select the link to see the task module open without having to trigger it from the custom tab (Figure 6-25).

Figure 6-25. Task module deep link

Anyone from your team/channel can click the link and access the task module from the conversation.

In this exercise, you have learned how to invoke task modules from anywhere within Microsoft Teams using deep links.

Exercise 5 - Using Task Modules with Bots

In this exercise, you will learn to create and add task modules to a Microsoft Teams app and interact with it from the Microsoft Teams client. The following steps are to be followed to create a new Microsoft Teams bot app for your Microsoft Team client.

- Register the bot with Microsoft Azure's Bot Framework

- Bot Channel Registration

- Enable the Microsoft Teams channel for the bot

- Retrieve the bot app ID and password

- Create task modules and implement with bots using the Yeoman generator

- Test the task modules with bot's app

Creating your app package and registering your web service with the Bot Framework can be done in any order. Because these two pieces are so intertwined, no matter which order you do them in you will need to return to update the others. Your registration needs the messaging endpoint from your deployed web service, and your web service needs the Id and password created from your registration. Your app manifest also needs that Id to connect Teams to your web service.

Register the Bot with Microsoft Azure's Bot Framework

Open a browser and navigate to the Azure portal (`https://portal.azure.com/`. Sign in using your **username@tenantname.onmicrosoft.com** that was used from the Azure subscription.

Click Create resource and Enter **bot** in the **Search the marketplace** input box and select **Bot Channels Registration** from the list of resources returned. Then select **Create** on the next page to start the process of registering a new bot resource.

In the **Bot Channels Registration** Page, click to initiate create Bot Channels Registration (Figure 6-26).

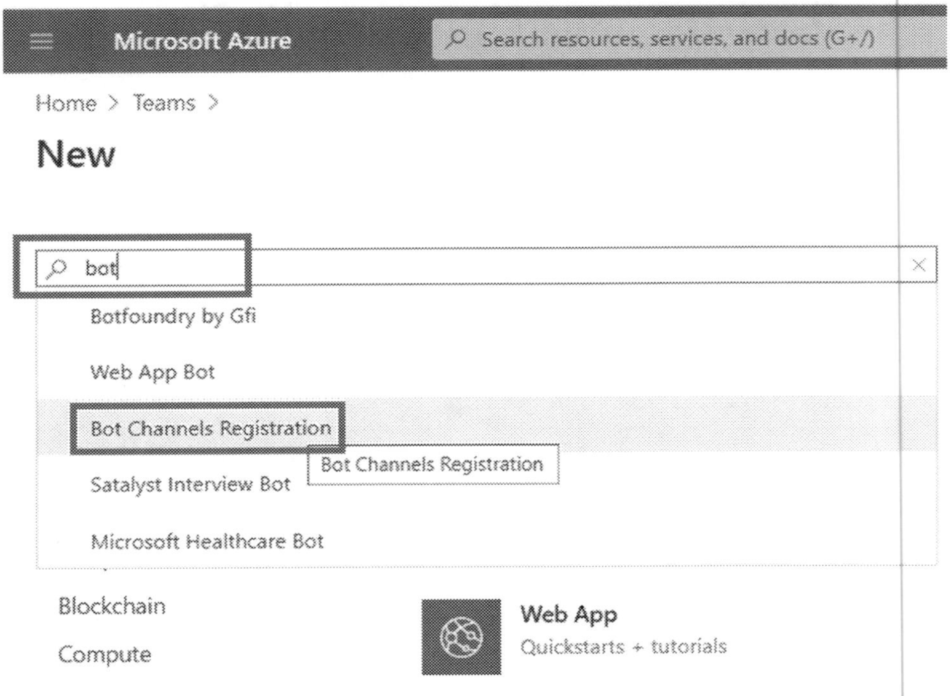

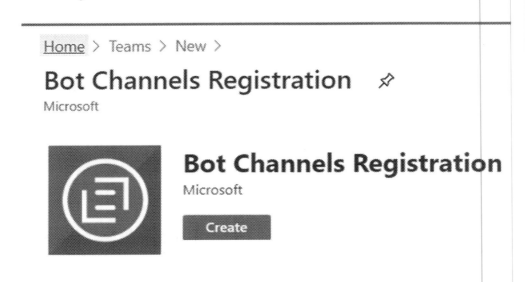

Figure 6-26. *Search Bot Channel Registration*

In the **Bot Channels Registration blade**, enter the following values and then select **Create**. See Figure 6-27.

Figure 6-27. *Bot Channel Registration*

- Bot handle: Enter a globally unique name for the bot:

  - **Ex**:TaskModulesBot

- **Subscription**: Select the subscription you selected previously when creating the resource group

- **Resource group**: Select the resource group you created previously - **Ex:** Teams

- **Location**: Select your preferred Azure region

- **Pricing tier**: Select a preferred pricing tier; the F0 tier is free

- **Messaging endpoint**: `https://REPLACE_THIS.ngrok.io/api/ messages`

- The bot registration needs to know the endpoint of the web service where the bot is implemented. This will change each time you start the ngrok utility used in previous exercises.

- Application Insights: Off

- Microsoft App ID and password: Auto create App ID and password (see Figure 6-28).

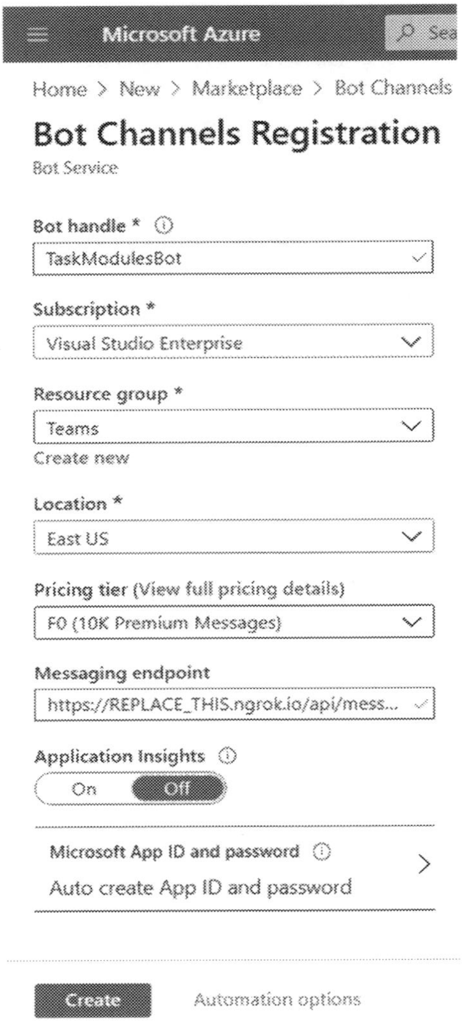

Figure 6-28. *Bot Channel Registration Form*

Azure will start to provision the new resource. This will take a moment or two. Once it is finished, navigate to the bot resource in the resource group (Figure 6-29).

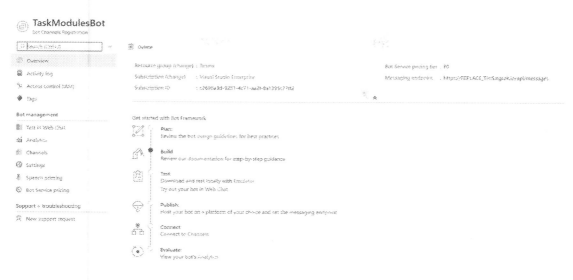

Figure 6-29. *Bot Created*

Enable the Microsoft Teams Channel for the Bot

For the bot to interact with Microsoft Teams, you must enable the Teams channel.

- From the bot resource in Azure, select **Channels** in the left-hand navigation.

- On the **Connect to channels** pane, select the **Microsoft Teams channel**, then select **Save** to confirm the action (Figure 6-30).

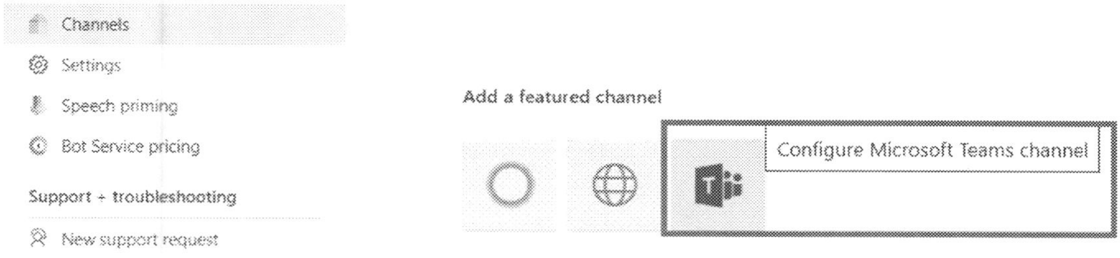

Figure 6-30. *Select Teams Channel*

- Agree to the Terms of Service

Once this process is complete, you should see both the Web Chat and Microsoft Teams listed in your enabled channels (Figure 6-31).

Connect to channels

Name	Health	Published	
Microsoft Teams	Running	..	Edit ✎
Web Chat	Running	..	Edit ✎

Get bot embed codes

Figure 6-31. *Connect to channels*

Retrieve the Bot App Id and Password

When Azure creates the bot, it also registers a new Azure AD app for the bot. You need to generate this new bot app as a secret and copy the app's credentials.

Select **Settings** from the left-hand navigation. Scroll down to the Microsoft App ID section.

Copy the ID of the bot as you'll need it later (Figure 6-32).

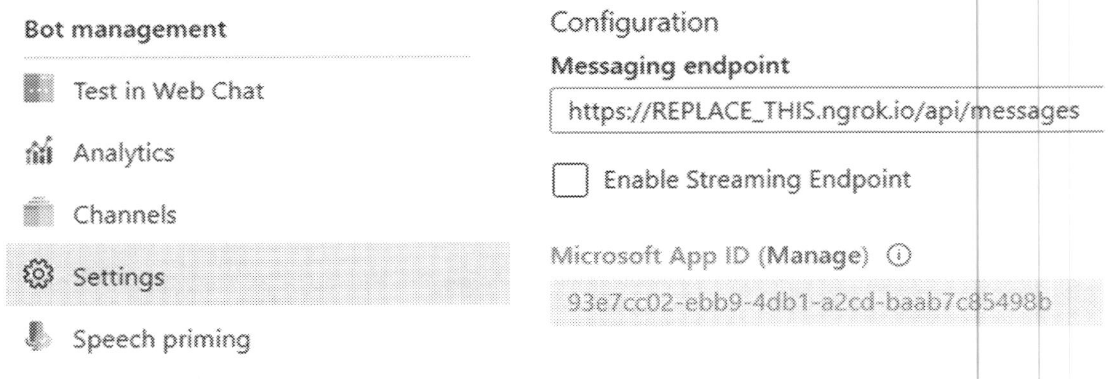

Bot management

- Test in Web Chat
- Analytics
- Channels
- ⚙ Settings
- Speech priming

Configuration

Messaging endpoint

https://REPLACE_THIS.ngrok.io/api/messages

☐ Enable Streaming Endpoint

Microsoft App ID (**Manage**) ⓘ

93e7cc02-ebb9-4db1-a2cd-baab7c85498b

Figure 6-32. *App ID creation*

Create a Client Secret for the App

Click the **Manage** link to navigate to the **Azure AD app.**

For the daemon app to run without user involvement, it will sign into Azure AD with an application ID and either a certificate or a secret. In this exercise, you will use a secret.

Select **Certificates & secrets** from the left-hand navigation panel.

Select the **New client secret** button under the Client secrets section.

When prompted, give the secret a description and select one of the expiration duration options provided; for example: Never and select **Add** (Figure 6-33).

Note   Copy the new client secret value. You won't be able to retrieve it after you perform another operation or leave this blade.

Client secrets

A secret string that the application uses to prove its identity when requesting a token. Also can be referred to as application password

+ New client secret

Description	Expires	Value	
No description	8/18/2025	%m{******************	🗑
TaskModulesBot	12/31/2299	vmT******************	🗑

Figure 6-33. *App Client Secret*

The Certificate & Secrets page will display the new secret. It's important you copy this value as it's only shown this one time; if you leave the page and come back, it will only show as a masked value.

Copy and store the value of the secret value as you will need it later.

Create Microsoft Teams App Using Yeoman Generator

In this section, you will create a new task module with bot Teams app using Yeoman generator (yo teams)

To create a new web part project:

- Create a new project directory in your favorite location

- Open command prompt

- Create a new folder "**taskModuleBot**"

- Navigate to a newly created directory

- Run the Yeoman Generator for Microsoft Teams by running the following command: **yo teams** (Figure 6-34).

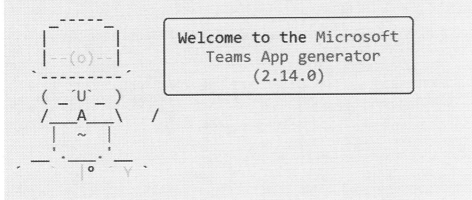

```
C:\Jenkins\JPower4\Book\MSTeamsBook\taskModulesBot>yo teams

        ------
       |        |        ┌──────────────────────────┐
       |--(o)--|         │  Welcome to the Microsoft │
       `--------'        │    Teams App generator    │
                         │         (2.14.0)          │
      ( _`U`_ )          └──────────────────────────┘
      /___A___\   /
       |    ~    |
     __'.___.'__
   `  ·    |  o  ·  Y  `

? What is your solution name? Task-Modules-Bot
```

Figure 6-34. *yo teams*

Yeoman will launch and ask you a series of questions. Answer the questions with the following values (as shown in Figure 6-35):

- What is your solution name? Task-Modules-Bot

- Where do you want to place the files? Use the current folder

- Title of your Microsoft Teams App project? Task Modules Bot

- Your (company) name? (max 32 characters) JPOWER4

- Which manifest version would you like to use? v1.6

- Enter your Microsoft Partner ID, if you have one? (Leave blank to skip)

- What features do you want to add to your project? A bot

- The URL where you will host this solution? `https://taskmodulesbot.azurewebsites.net`

- Would you like show a loading indicator when your app/tab loads? No

- Would you like to include Test framework and initial tests? No

- Would you like to use Azure Applications Insights for telemetry? No

- What type of bot would you like to use? A new Bot Framework bot

- What is the name of your bot? Task Modules Bot

- What is the Microsoft App ID for the bot? It's found in the Bot Framework portal (`https://dev.botframework.com`). 93e7cc02-ebb9-4db1-a

- 2cd-baab7c85498b

- Do you want to add a static tab to your bot? No

- Do you want to support file upload to the bot? No

```
? What is your solution name? Task-Modules-Bot
? Where do you want to place the files? Use the current folder
? Title of your Microsoft Teams App project? Task Modules Bot
? Your (company) name? (max 32 characters) JPOWER4
? Which manifest version would you like to use? v1.6
? Enter your Microsoft Partner ID, if you have one? (Leave blank to skip)
? What features do you want to add to your project? A bot
? The URL where you will host this solution? https://taskmodulesbot.azurewebsites
? Would you like show a loading indicator when your app/tab loads? No
? Would you like to include Test framework and initial tests? No
? Would you like to use Azure Applications Insights for telemetry? No
? What type of bot would you like to use? A new bot Framework bot
? What is the name of your bot? Task Modules Bot
? What is the Microsoft App ID for the bot? It's found in the Bot Framework porta
2cd-baab7c85498b
? Do you want to add a static tab to your bot? No
? Do you want to support file upload to the bot? No
```

Figure 6-35. *Answer Yeoman questionnaire*

Note   Most of the answers to these questions can be changed after creating the project. For example, the URL where the project will be hosted is not important at the time of creating or testing the project.

Open the Visual Studio Code using **code .** in a command prompt (Figure 6-36).

Figure 6-36. *Visual studio code OOB*

- Open .env file ➤ Open and add the MICROSOFT_APP_PASSWORD copied from the new client secret value

  ```
  MICROSOFT_APP_PASSWORD= vmTMorc76SJto2_w6R-2yeD.YJ.F-g8dr_
  ```

Update the Bot Code

Here's the process:

- Go to ./src/app/taskModulesBot/TaskModulesBot.ts file and add the following code.

- At first, add the headers given below:

  ```
  import * as Util from "util";
  const TextEncoder = Util.TextEncoder;
  ```

- Then include TaskModuleResponse, TaskModuleRequest, TaskModuleTaskInfo, object reference to the existing **botbuilder** package:

  ```
  TeamsActivityHandler, TaskModuleResponse, TaskModuleRequest,
  TaskModuleTaskInfo
  } from "botbuilder";
  ```

- Go to taskModulesBot class and find handler **this.onMessage()** within the public constructor(conversationState: ConversationState)

- In the **this.onMessage()** handler, proceed with the following code to handle one-to-one conversation and channel conversation.

- Find the code given below:

```
switch (context.activity.type) {...}
```

- Replace the switch statement code given below:

```
switch (context.activity.type) {
    case ActivityTypes.Message:
      const card = CardFactory.heroCard("Learn Microsoft Power
      Platform", undefined, [
                    {
                    type: "invoke",
                    title: "Empowering Citizen Developers Using
                    Power Apps",
    value: { type: "task/fetch", taskModule: "player", videoId:
    "eSJ-dVp83ks" }
                    }
                    ]);
                    await context.sendActivity({ attachments:
                    [card] });
                default:
                    break;
        }
```

To handle TaskModule taskinfo, add the handleTeamsTaskModuleFetch method in the class. Whenever the user clicks the button, it will call the player.html button as a modal window to show the YouTube video.

```
protected handleTeamsTaskModuleFetch(context: TurnContext, request:
TaskModuleRequest): Promise<TaskModuleResponse> {
        let response: TaskModuleResponse;
        response = {
            task: {
```

```
                type: "continue",
                value: {
                    title: "YouTube Player",
                    url: `https://${process.env.HOSTNAME}/player.
                    html?vid=${request.data.videoId}`,
                    width: 1000,
                    height: 700
                } as TaskModuleTaskInfo
            }
        } as TaskModuleResponse;

        return Promise.resolve(response);
    }
```

Navigate to .src/app/web/ and create a new file **player.html**. Then add the code given below in the player.html file:

```html
<!DOCTYPE html>
<html lang="en">

<head>
    <title>YouTube Player Task Module</title>
    <style>
        #embed-container iframe {
            position: absolute;
            top: 0;
            left: 0;
            width: 95%;
            height: 95%;
            padding-left: 20px;
            padding-right: 20px;
            padding-top: 10px;
            padding-bottom: 10px;
            border-style: none;
        }
    </style>
</head>
```

```
<body>
    <div id="embed-container"></div>
</body>
<script>
    function getUrlParameter(name) {
        name = name.replace(/[\[]/, '\\[').replace(/[\]]/, '\\]');
        var regex = new RegExp('[\\?&]' + name + '=([^&#]*)');
        var results = regex.exec(location.search);
        return results === null ? '' : decodeURIComponent(results[1].
        replace(/\+/g, ' '));
    };

    var element = document.createElement("iframe");
    element.src = "https://www.youtube.com/embed/" +
    getUrlParameter("vid");
    element.width = "1000";
    element.height = "700";
    element.frameborder = "0";
    element.allow = "autoplay; encrypted-media";
    element.allowfullscreen = "";

    document.getElementById("embed-container").appendChild(element);
</script>

</html>
```

- *File ➤ Save All* to save the changes

- At this point, your task module is ready to be tested!

Test the Task Module in the Bot

Open the command Prompt, navigate to the project folder, and execute the following command:

```
gulp ngrok-serve
```

This gulp task will run many other tasks that are displayed within the command-line console. The ngrok-serve task builds your project and starts a local web server (http:// localhost:3007). It then starts ngrok with a random subdomain that creates a secure URL to your local webserver.

In development, testing can be done using the tool ngrok that creates a secure rotatable URL to your local HTTP webserver. Ngrok is included as a dependency within the project so there is nothing to set up or configure (Figure 6-37).

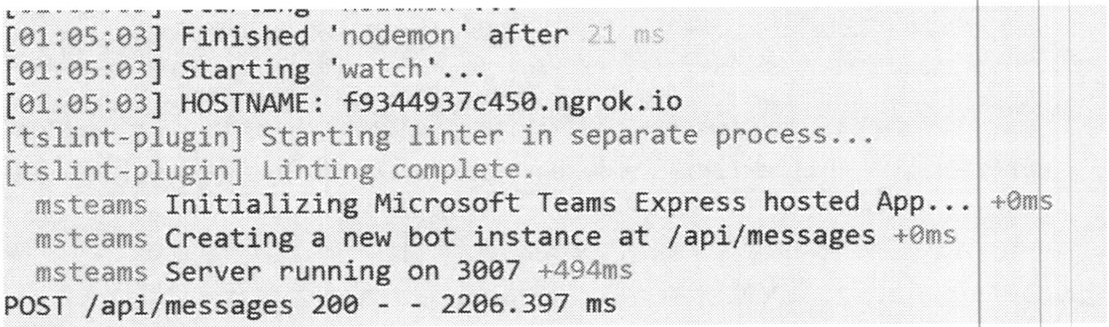

```
[01:05:03] Finished 'nodemon' after 21 ms
[01:05:03] Starting 'watch'...
[01:05:03] HOSTNAME: f9344937c450.ngrok.io
[tslint-plugin] Starting linter in separate process...
[tslint-plugin] Linting complete.
  msteams Initializing Microsoft Teams Express hosted App... +0ms
  msteams Creating a new bot instance at /api/messages +0ms
  msteams Server running on 3007 +494ms
POST /api/messages 200 - - 2206.397 ms
```

Figure 6-37. *Ngrok-serve execution*

Ngrok has created the temporary URL f9344937c450.ngrok.io that will map to our locally running web server.

Then go to the Azure portal and open the Bot Channel registration App. Update the Messaging endpoint using the temporary URL f9344937c450.ngrok.io (Figure 6-38).

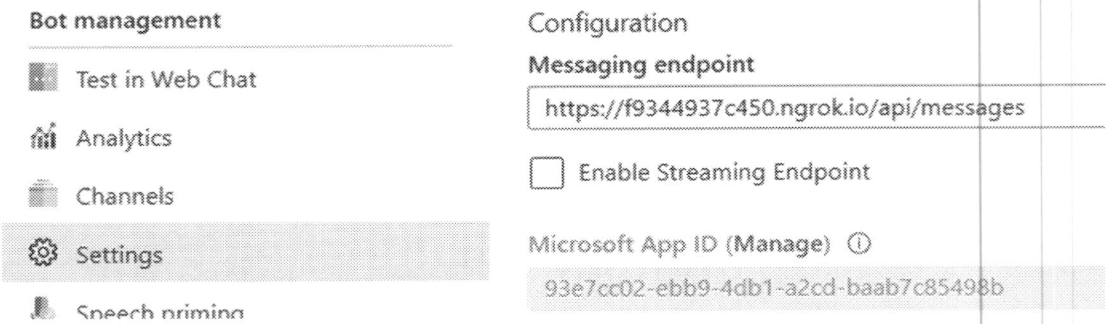

Bot management   Configuration

  ■ Test in Web Chat   **Messaging endpoint**
                                          https://f9344937c450.ngrok.io/api/messages

  📊 Analytics
                                          ☐ Enable Streaming Endpoint
  ▤ Channels

  ⚙ Settings   Microsoft App ID (**Manage**) ⓘ
                                          93e7cc02-ebb9-4db1-a2cd-baab7c85498b
  🐾 Speech priming

Figure 6-38. *Update Messaging Endpoint*

Note   The free version of ngrok will create a new URL each time you restart the web server. Make sure you update the Messaging Endpoint of your URL each time you restart the web server when you are testing the app.

Install the Conversation Bot in Microsoft Teams

Now let's install the app in Microsoft Teams. In the browser, navigate to `https://teams.microsoft.com` and sign in with the credentials of a Work and School account.

Microsoft Teams is available for use as a web client, desktop client, and a mobile client.

Using the app bar navigation menu, select the More added apps button. Then select More apps followed by Upload a custom app and then Upload for me or my teams (Figure 6-39).

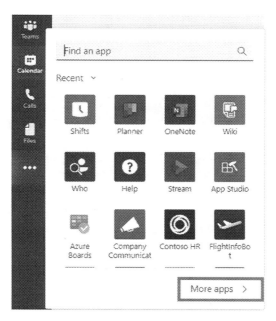

Figure 6-39. *Add apps to MS Teams*

In the file dialog that appears, select the Microsoft Teams package in your project. This app package is a ZIP file that can be found in the projects **./package** folder (Figure 6-40).

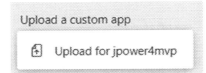

Figure 6-40. *Upload apps*

After installation, you will be able to see the app in the apps list (Figure 6-41).

Figure 6-41. *Installed app*

Once the package is uploaded, Microsoft Teams will display a summary of the app (Figure 6-42).

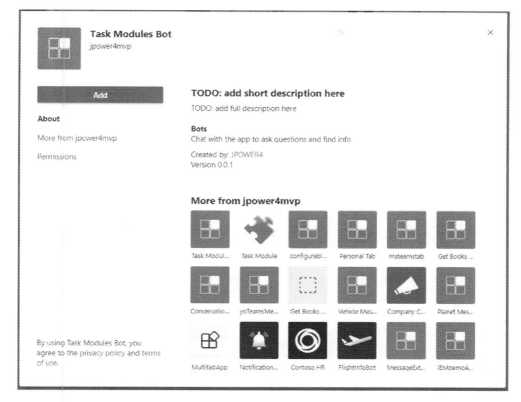

Figure 6-42. *Add the app to chat*

Testing the Task Module as Personal Bot

Here's how to do this testing:

- Click the Add button to navigate to chat with the bot.

- Notice the commands that the bot supports are shown in the compose box when the app loads. Let's test the bot!

- Select the help command, or manually type anything in the compose box, then press enter; I have entered hello.

- After a few seconds, you should see the bot responding with a Hero Card with a button: "Empowering Citizen Developers Using Power Apps".

See Figure 6-43.

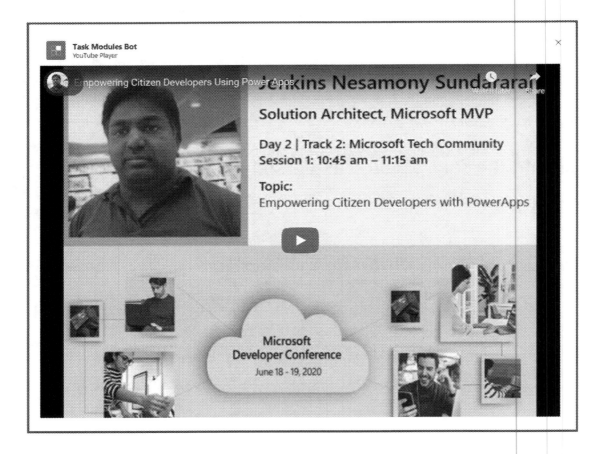

Figure 6-43. *Bot conversation response*

- Then click the button "Empowering Citizen Developers Using Power Apps,"and it will open a modal window and load the player.html file with the YouTube video based on a given video Id.

In this exercise, you have learned how to invoke task modules within Microsoft Teams using Bot.

Conclusion

In this chapter, you have learned various features of task modules with tabs and bots and how to send data to task modules and modal windows, how to collect user input from task modules using HTML with JavaScript and Adaptive Cards, and about task modules that can be invoked by selecting a button in the Microsoft Teams experience or using a deep link.

You have also learned how to create task modules using the Yeoman generator for Microsoft Teams. Along with this, you will start learning different options and features of Microsoft Teams apps in our upcoming chapters.

CHAPTER 7

Connect Web Services to Microsoft Teams with Webhooks

Webhooks and connectors are simple ways to connect your web services to channels and teams inside Microsoft Teams. Outgoing webhooks allow your users to send text messages from a channel to your web services. Connectors allow users to subscribe to receive notifications and messages from your web services. There are two types of connectors available in Microsoft Teams: incoming webhooks and Office 365 connectors. In this chapter you will learn about webhooks and connectors and how to implement them in Microsoft Teams channels.

Overview of Web Services and Webhooks

Web services and webhooks are both performing the same functions, but the execution process is different (refer to Figure 7-1). Webhooks perform a specific function whenever someone or some other application calls on it. They allow inbound data to be received or outbound data to be sent. Web services carry data from one system to another, so the receiving application can store or process the data; you can automate the process using web services or webhooks.

A webhook is also called a web callback or HTTP push API. As seen in Figure 7-1, you can visualize the differences between APIs and webhooks. Webhooks call only once when it is required, but APIs always call and verify the status.

© Jenkins NS 2021
J. NS, *Building Solutions with Microsoft Teams*, https://doi.org/10.1007/978-1-4842-6476-8_7

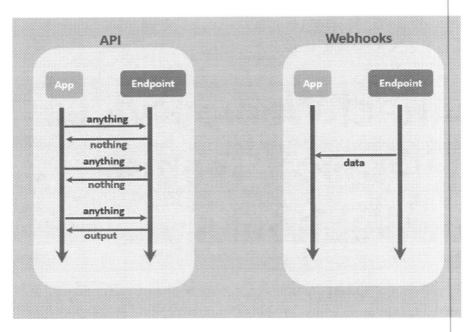

Figure 7-1. *Differences between API and webhooks*

Outgoing Webhooks and Microsoft Teams

In Chapter 3, you learned about conversational bots for which we registered and implemented. Outgoing webhooks provide a simple way to allow users to send messages to your web service without having to go through the full process of creating bots via the Microsoft Bot Framework. Outgoing webhooks post data from Teams to any service accepting a JSON payload. Outgoing webhooks act like a bot once you are registered in Teams. They will be used for listening in channels, @mention, sending notifications services, and the better part of them responds with cards.

Outgoing webhooks support send text messages from a channel to your services. Your web service will have five seconds to send a response to the message as a text or card and outgoing webhooks are not suitable for large amounts of inputs and responses. See Table 7-1.

Table 7-1. *Outgoing Webhook Key Features*

Feature	Description
Scoped Configuration	Outgoing webhooks are scoped at the team level and you need to add the outgoing webhooks for each team you want.
Reactive Messaging	Users must use @mention for the webhook to receive reactive messages and outgoing webhooks support only in public channels.
Standard HTTP message exchange	Standard HTTP message exchange response will appear in the same chain as the original request. Also, it supports rich text, images, cards, and emojis. It won't support card action.
Teams API method support	Outgoing webhooks in Teams only support http post web services and cannot support Teams APIs.

Create a URL on Your App's Server to Accept and Process a POST Request with a JSON Payload

Your web service receives messages from an Azure bot service messaging schema, or a Bot Framework connector enables your service to process the interchange of JSON formatted messages via HTTPS protocols from an Azure bit service API. As mentioned before, outgoing webhooks scope a Team level, like a bot user is required to @mention the name of the outgoing webhooks to invoke in the channel. Outgoing webhooks post data from Teams to any service accepting a JSON payload

Create a Method to Verify the Outgoing Webhook HMAC Token

Always validate the HTTP HMAC Signature included in the request as a header and from your authentication protocol to ensure that your service is receiving calls from your Teams client.

- Microsoft Teams uses standard SHA256 HMAC cryptography. You will need to convert the body to a byte array in UTF8 to generate a HMAC token from the request body of the message.

- When you register the outgoing webhook in Teams, you should compute the hash from the byte array security token provided by Teams and convert the hash to a string using UTF-8 encoding.

- Finally compare the string value with the generated value from the HTTL request.

The following sample code is for your reference to verify and convert the message:

```
const securityToken = process.env.SECURITY_TOKEN;
      if (securityToken && securityToken.length > 0) {
         // There is a configured security token
         const auth = req.headers.authorization;
         const msgBuf = Buffer.from((req as any).rawBody, "utf8");
         const msgHash = "HMAC " + crypto.
            createHmac("sha256", Buffer.from(securityToken as
            string, "base64")).
            update(msgBuf).
            digest("base64");

      if (msgHash === auth) {
```

Create a Method to Send a Success or Failure Response

Standard HTTP message exchange responses will appear in the same chain as the original request. When a user invokes the query, your code will have five seconds to respond to the message, and Microsoft Teams handle the synchronous HTTP request to your service issues before the connection times out and terminates.

Incoming Webhooks and Microsoft Teams

Incoming webhooks are the same as connectors or special types of connectors. Incoming webhooks are the simplest type of connector. Incoming webhooks provide a simple way from an external app to share content in channels and are mostly used as tracking and notification tools. You can choose to send data using an https endpoint from the channel that will accept formatted JSON and receive messages for channels. Incoming webhooks are a quick and easy way to connect a channel to your service. The best example is creating an incoming webhook in your DevOps channel for your application to build, configure, deploy, monitor, and send alerts. Incoming webhooks are messages that you want to POST, typically in a card format. Cards are user-interface containers that contain content and actions related to a single topic and are a way to present message data in a consistent way from incoming webhooks. See Table 7-2.

Table 7-2. *Incoming Webhook Key Features*

Feature	Description
Scoped Configuration	Incoming webhooks are scoped in channel level, as mentioned earlier session in this chapter outgoing webhooks are scoped at the team level.
Secure resource definitions	Incoming webhooks messages are formatted as JSON payloads, and they will prevent the injection of malicious code.
Actionable messaging support	Actionable messaging supports in Teams and Incoming webhooks send messages via cards and only supports Actionable message card format.
Independent HTTPS messaging support	Incoming webhook Send HTTPS POST requests can send messages to Teams using cards.
Markdown support	HTML markup will not support actionable messaging cards, so they always use basic markdowns for all test fields.

You have three options for distributing your incoming webhook:

- Set up an incoming webhook from your channel.

- Add a configuration page and wrap your incoming webhook in a O365 Connector.

- Package and publish your incoming webhook as a Connector and part of your AppSource submission.

Connectors

Connectors are push information from third-party services directly to your Microsoft channels. You can access information posted by connectors from multiple Microsoft 365 channels like Microsoft Teams, Yammer, Outlook, and Microsoft 365 Groups. Connectors allow you to create a custom configuration for your incoming webhook. Then you can distribute the connector to any third party and the app store. Connectors always use cards, but card actions have limitations for Office 365 connectors. Connectors are configured in a channel level but installed in a team level.

For example, find a weather connector that allows users to enter a location and time and receive the weather report about tomorrow's predicted weather.

In Teams we have 150+ connectors available, it is growing daily, and you can also publish it to the Microsoft Store and make it available for everyone. For that you need to register your Connector in the Office 365 developer portal. There are three stages of a review process from Microsoft.

Integrating the Connector Configuration Experience in Teams Client

For users able to complete the connector configuration without leaving a Teams client, Team client embeds your configuration page directly within an iframe.

The steps below should be followed to configure a connector from a Teams client:

- Go to Teams Client.

- Click on your connector to begin the configuration process.

- It will load all connectors.

- You can complete the configuration with web experience.

- The user presses "Save," which triggers a callback in your code.

- Your code will process the save event by retrieving the webhook settings.

Also, you can reuse the configuration or create a separate version to be hosted specifically in Teams, and for that you need control from a code. Microsoft Teams JavaScript SDK gives your code access to APIs to perform common operations like getting the current user/channel/team context and initiating authentication flows.

- Initialize the SDK by calling microsoftTeams.initialize()

- Call microsoftTeams.settings.setValidityState(true)

  - when you want to enable the Save button.

- Register a microsoftTeams.settings.registerOnSaveHandler() event handler, which gets called when the user clicks Save.

- Call microsoftTeams.settings.setSettings() to save the connector settings, and it will help the user to update the existing configuration.

- While reconfiguring you need to Call microsoftTeams.settings. getSettings() to fetch webhook properties, with the parameters below:

    - entityId - Set by your code when calling setSettings().

    - configName - Set by your code when calling setSettings().

    - contentUrl - The URL of the configuration page.

    - webhookUrl - The webhook URL created for this connector.

    - appType - Return values.

    - userObjectId - This is the unique id corresponding to the Office 365 user who initiated setup of the connector.

- Register a microsoftTeams.settings.registerOnRemoveHandler() event handler, which gets called when the user removes your connector.

- registerOnRemoveHandler() event gives your service to perform any clean-up actions.

Including the Connector in Your Manifest

While creating connectors using yo team's generator, it auto-generates the Teams app manifest from the portal. Open the manifest and verify the connectors section.

```
"connectors": [
  {
    "connectorId": "{{CONNECTOR_ID}}",
    "configurationUrl":
 "https://{{HOSTNAME}}/myFirstTeamsConnector/config.html",
    "scopes": [
      "team"
    ]
  }
]
```

Exercise 1 - Create Outgoing Webhooks

The Microsoft Teams Developer Platform helps you to extend your teams with your Line of Business (LOB) application and services seamlessly into the Microsoft Teams. Also, you will be able to distribute your custom apps to your organization or public users if you developed generic feature apps.

Before starting the exercise, verify your environment. In this exercise, I am using the tools mentioned below and installed in my environment:

- Node.js - v10.16.0

- NPM - 6.9.0

- Gulp

  - CLI version: 2.3.0

  - Local version: 4.0.2

- Yeomen Generator of MS Teams - 2.14.0

- Visual Studio Code

and

- Microsoft Azure Subscription

- Office 365 Subscription

- Postman Chrome extension

Build the Webhook

In this exercise, you will learn how to create a web service and register it as an outgoing webhook in Microsoft Teams.

- Open your command prompt, and navigate to a directory where you want to save your work.

- Create a new folder 'OutgoingWebhooks', and change the directory into that folder.

- Run the Yeoman generator for Microsoft Teams by running the following command:

  `yo teams` (Figure 7-2).

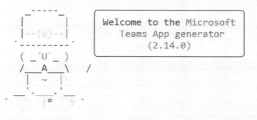

```
C:\Jenkins\JPower4\Book\MSTeamsBook\OutgoingWebhooks>yo teams
```

```
Welcome to the Microsoft
    Teams App generator
         (2.14.0)
```

```
? What is your solution name? (outgoing-webhooks)
```

Figure 7-2. *yo teams generator*

Yeoman will launch and ask you a series of questions. Answer the questions with the following values (Figure 7-3):

- What is your solution name? outgoing-webhooks

- Where do you want to place the files? Use the current folder

- Title of your Microsoft Teams App project? Outgoing WebHooks

- Your (company) name? (max 32 characters) JPOWER4

- Which manifest version would you like to use? v1.6

- Enter your Microsoft Partner ID, if you have one? (Leave blank to skip)

- What features do you want to add to your project? An Outgoing Webhook

- The URL where you will host this solution? `https://outgoingwebhooks.azurewebsites.net`

- Would you like show a loading indicator when your app/tab loads? No

- Would you like to include Test framework and initial tests? No

- Would you like to use Azure Applications Insights for telemetry? No

- What is the name of your outgoing webhook? My Outgoing Webhook

```
? What is your solution name? outgoing-webhooks
? Where do you want to place the files? Use the current folder
? Title of your Microsoft Teams App project? Outgoing WebHooks
? Your (company) name? (max 32 characters) JPOWER4
? Which manifest version would you like to use? v1.6
? Enter your Microsoft Partner ID, if you have one? (Leave blank to skip)
? What features do you want to add to your project? An Outgoing Webhook
? The URL where you will host this solution? https://outgoingwebhooks.azurewebsites.net
? Would you like show a loading indicator when your app/tab loads? No
? Would you like to include Test framework and initial tests? No
? Would you like to use Azure Applications Insights for telemetry? No
? What is the name of your outgoing webhook? My Outgoing Webhook
```

Figure 7-3. *Answer yeoman questionnaire*

Our web service will need one more NPM package to simplify finding data in an array. Execute the following command in the command prompt from the root folder of the project to install the library **Lodash**:

```
npm install lodash -S
```

- The Yeoman generator for Microsoft Teams created a stub web service endpoint for our outgoing webhook.

- Locate and open the file ./src/app/myOutgoingWebhook/ MyOutgoingWebhook.ts. It listens for HTTPS requests at the endpoint **/api/webhook**.

- Find the requestHandler() method in the MyOutgoingWebhook class. The method first checks the HMAC value in the authorization header against the security token that you'll obtain when you add the webhook to a team.

- Locate the following code:

```
message.text = `Echo ${incoming.text}`;
```

- This code simply echoes the string entered in the message back to Microsoft Teams that will be added in a reply to the message that triggered the webhook.

- Update this code to add some real functionality using the planets.json data and Adaptive Card.

Create a new file 'planets.json' in the **./src/app/myOutgoingWebhook** folder and add the following JSON to it. This file will contain an array of planet details:

```
[{
      "id": "1",
      "name": "Mercury",
      "summary": "Mercury is the smallest and innermost planet in the
      Solar System. Its orbit around the Sun takes 87.97 days, the
      shortest of all the planets in the Solar System. It is named after
      the Roman deity Mercury, the messenger of the gods.",
      "solarOrbitYears": 0.24,
      "solarOrbitAvgDistanceKm": 57909050,
      "numSatellites": 0,
      "wikiLink": "https://en.wikipedia.org/wiki/Mercury_(planet)",
      "imageLink": "https://upload.wikimedia.org/wikipedia/commons/d/d9/
      Mercury_in_color_-_Prockter07-edit1.jpg",
      "imageAlt": "NASA/Johns Hopkins University Applied Physics
      Laboratory/Carnegie Institution of Washington [Public domain]"
},
{
      "id": "2",
      "name": "Venus",
      "summary": "Venus is the second planet from the Sun. It is named
      after the Roman goddess of love and beauty. As the second-brightest
      natural object in the night sky after the Moon, Venus can cast
      shadows and, rarely, is visible to the naked eye in broad daylight.
      Venus lies within Earth's orbit, and so never appears to venture
      far from the Sun, setting in the west just after dusk and rising in
      the east a bit before dawn.",
      "solarOrbitYears": 0.62,
      "solarOrbitAvgDistanceKm": 108208000,
      "numSatellites": 0,
      "wikiLink": "https://en.wikipedia.org/wiki/Venus",
      "imageLink": "https://upload.wikimedia.org/wikipedia/commons/e/e5/
      Venus-real_color.jpg",
      "imageAlt": "&quot;Image processing by R. Nunes&quot;, link to
      http://www.astrosurf.com/nunes [Public domain]"

]
```

Next, create a new file **planetDisplayCard.json** in the **./src/app/ myOutgoingWebhook** folder and add the following JSON to it. This file will contain a template of the Adaptive Card and the web service will respond with:

```json
{
    "$schema": "http://adaptivecards.io/schemas/adaptive-card.json",
    "type": "AdaptiveCard",
    "version": "1.0",
    "body": [{
            "id": "cardHeader",
            "type": "Container",
            "items": [{
                "id": "planetName",
                "type": "TextBlock",
                "weight": "bolder",
                "size": "medium"
            }]
        },
        {
            "type": "Container",
            "id": "cardBody",
            "items": [{
                    "id": "planetSummary",
                    "type": "TextBlock",
                    "wrap": true
                },
                {
                    "id": "planetDetails",
                    "type": "ColumnSet",
                    "columns": [{
                            "type": "Column",
                            "width": "100",
                            "items": [{
                                "id": "planetImage",
                                "size": "stretch",
```

```
                "type": "Image"
            }]
        },
        {
            "type": "Column",
            "width": "250",
            "items": [{
                "type": "FactSet",
                "facts": [{
                        "id": "orderFromSun",
                        "title": "Order from the sun:"
                    },
                    {
                        "id": "planetNumSatellites",
                        "title": "Known satellites:"
                    },
                    {
                        "id": "solarOrbitYears",
                        "title": "Solar orbit (*Earth
                        years*):"
                    },
                    {
                        "id": "solarOrbitAvgDistanceKm",
                        "title": "Average distance from the
                        sun (*km*):"
                    }
                ]
            }]
        }
    ]
},
{
    "id": "imageAttribution",
    "type": "TextBlock",
    "size": "medium",
```

```
                    "isSubtle": true,
                    "wrap": true
              }
          ]
      }
  ],
  "actions": [{
      "type": "Action.OpenUrl",
      "title": "Learn more on Wikipedia"
  }]
}
```

Add the following import statement to the **./src/app/MyOutgoingWebhook/
myOutgoingWebhook.t**s file, just after the existing import statements:

```
import { find, sortBy } from "lodash";
```

Add the following method to the **MyOutgoingWebhook** class. The
getPlanetDetailCard() method will load and populate the Adaptive Card template with
details using the provided planet object:

```
private static getPlanetDetailCard(selectedPlanet: any): builder.Attachment {

        // load display card
        const adaptiveCardSource: any = require("./planetDisplayCard.json");

        // update planet fields in display card
        adaptiveCardSource.actions[0].url = selectedPlanet.wikiLink;
        find(adaptiveCardSource.body, { "id": "cardHeader" }).items[0].text
        = selectedPlanet.name;
        const cardBody: any = find(adaptiveCardSource.body, { "id":
        "cardBody" });
        find(cardBody.items, { "id": "planetSummary" }).text =
        selectedPlanet.summary;
        find(cardBody.items, { "id": "imageAttribution" }).text = "*Image
        attribution: " + selectedPlanet.imageAlt + "*";
        const cardDetails: any = find(cardBody.items, { "id":
        "planetDetails" });
        cardDetails.columns[0].items[0].url = selectedPlanet.imageLink;
```

246

```
find(cardDetails.columns[1].items[0].facts, { "id": "orderFromSun"
}).value = selectedPlanet.id;
find(cardDetails.columns[1].items[0].facts, { "id":
"planetNumSatellites" }).value = selectedPlanet.numSatellites;
find(cardDetails.columns[1].items[0].facts, { "id":
"solarOrbitYears" }).value = selectedPlanet.solarOrbitYears;
find(cardDetails.columns[1].items[0].facts, { "id":
"solarOrbitAvgDistanceKm" }).value = Number(selectedPlanet.
solarOrbitAvgDistanceKm).toLocaleString();

// return the adaptive card
return builder.CardFactory.adaptiveCard(adaptiveCardSource);
}
```

Next, add the following method to the **MyOutgoingWebhook** class. The **processAuthenticatedRequest()** method takes the incoming text and uses it to find a planet in the **planets.json** file. If it finds one, it calls the **getPlanetDetailCard()** method to get an Adaptive Card and returns it as an Activity that will be sent back to Microsoft Teams. If a planet isn't found, it just echoes the text back in a reply to the request:

```
private static processAuthenticatedRequest(incomingText: string):
Partial<builder.Activity> {
    const message: Partial<builder.Activity> = {
        type: builder.ActivityTypes.Message
    };

    // load planets
    const planets: any = require("./planets.json");
    // get the selected planet
    const selectedPlanet: any = planets.filter((planet) => (planet.
    name as string).trim().toLowerCase() === incomingText.trim().
    toLowerCase());

    if (!selectedPlanet || !selectedPlanet.length) {
        message.text = `Echo ${incomingText}`;
    } else {
        const adaptiveCard = MyOutgoingWebhook.getPlanetDetailCard(sele
        ctedPlanet[0]);
```

```
        message.type = "result";
        message.attachmentLayout = "list";
        message.attachments = [adaptiveCard];
    }

    return message;
}
```

Add the following **scrubMessage**() method to the **MyOutgoingWebhook** class. A user must @mention an outgoing webhook in order to send a message to it. This method will remove the <at></at> text and any spaces to extract the planet name:

```
private static scrubMessage(incomingText: string): string {
    const cleanMessage = incomingText
        .slice(incomingText.lastIndexOf(">") + 1, incomingText.length)
        .replace(" ", "");
    return cleanMessage;
}
```

Then, update the **requestHandler**() method:

- Locate the following code and change the message declaration from a **const** to **let** as you will change this value.

```
let message: Partial<builder.Activity> = {
            type: builder.ActivityTypes.Message
        };
```

- Locate and replace the following code:

```
message.text = `Echo ${incoming.text}`;
```

with the following code:

```
const scrubbedText = MyOutgoingWebhook.scrubMessage(incoming.text);
            message = MyOutgoingWebhook.processAuthenticatedRe
            quest(scrubbedText);
```

Test the Outgoing Webhook

Here's how to test:

- Add the outgoing webhook to a team in Microsoft Teams. In the browser, navigate to `https://teams.microsoft.com` and sign in with the credentials of a Work and School account.

- Once you are signed in, select a team you want to add the webhook to.

- Click and Select Manage team (Figure 7-4).

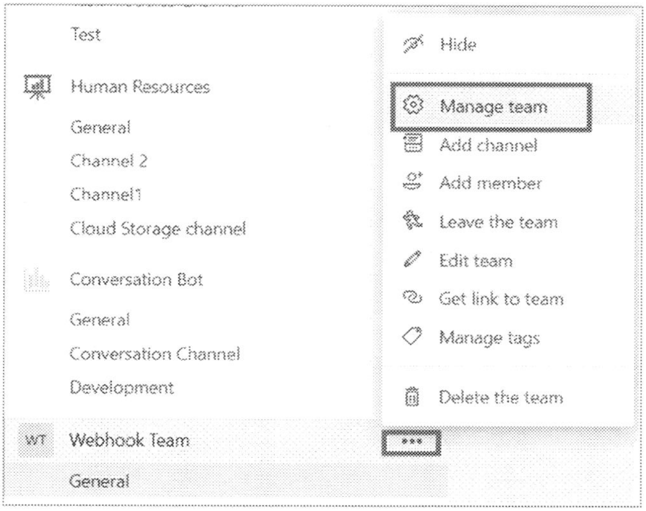

Figure 7-4. *Manage Team*

- Select Apps and Click 'Create an outgoing webhook' in the bottom (Figure 7-5).

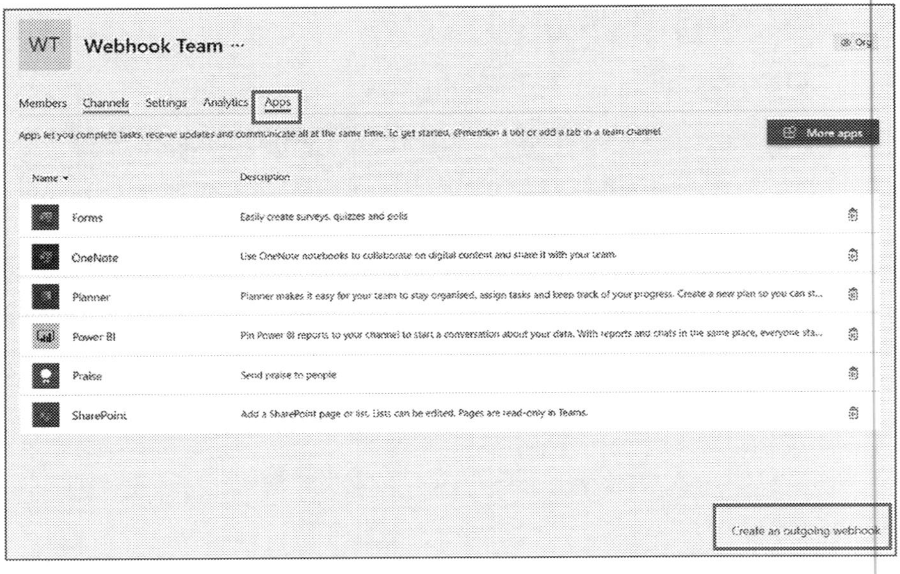

Figure 7-5. Create an outgoing webhook

- In the Create an outgoing webhook dialog, enter the following values and select Create (Figure 7-6):

  - **Name**: Planet Details

  - **Callback URL**: `https://{{REPLACE_NGROK_SUBDOMAIN}}.ngrok.io/api/webhook`

  - **Description**: Planet Details outgoing web hook

  - **Upload an image to identify**

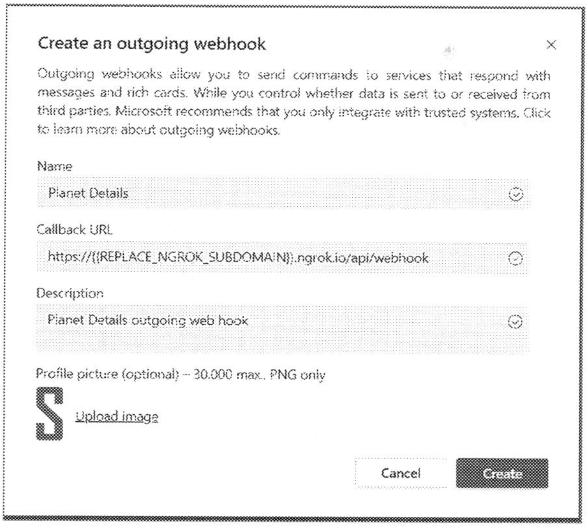

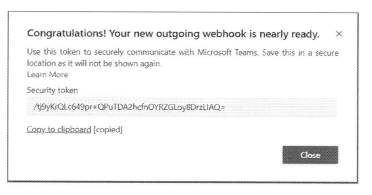

Figure 7-6. *Create an outgoing webhook form*

After creating the outgoing webhook, Microsoft Teams will display a security token (Figure 7-7).

Figure 7-7. *Outgoing webhook security token*

- Copy this value and set the **SECURITY_TOKEN** property in the ./.env file in the project.

- From the command line, navigate to the root folder for the project and execute the following command:

```
gulp ngrok-serve
```

In the console, locate the dynamic URL created by ngrok (Figure 7-8).

```
C:\Jenkins\JPower4\Book\MSTeamsBook\OutgoingWebhooks>gulp ngrok-serve
[18:31:12] Using gulpfile C:\Jenkins\JPower4\Book\MSTeamsBook\Outgoing
[18:31:12] Starting 'ngrok-serve'...
[18:31:12] Starting 'start-ngrok'...
[18:31:12] [NGROK] starting ngrok...
[18:31:13] [NGROK] Url: https://b73772b97945.ngrok.io
[18:31:13] [NGROK] You have been assigned a random ngrok URL that will
he Teams manifest next time you run this command.
[18:31:13] [NGROK] HOSTNAME: b73772b97945.ngrok.io
```

Figure 7-8. *Gulp ngrok serve execution*

- Go to Team ➤ Select Apps.
- Select the Planet Details web hook (Figure 7-9).

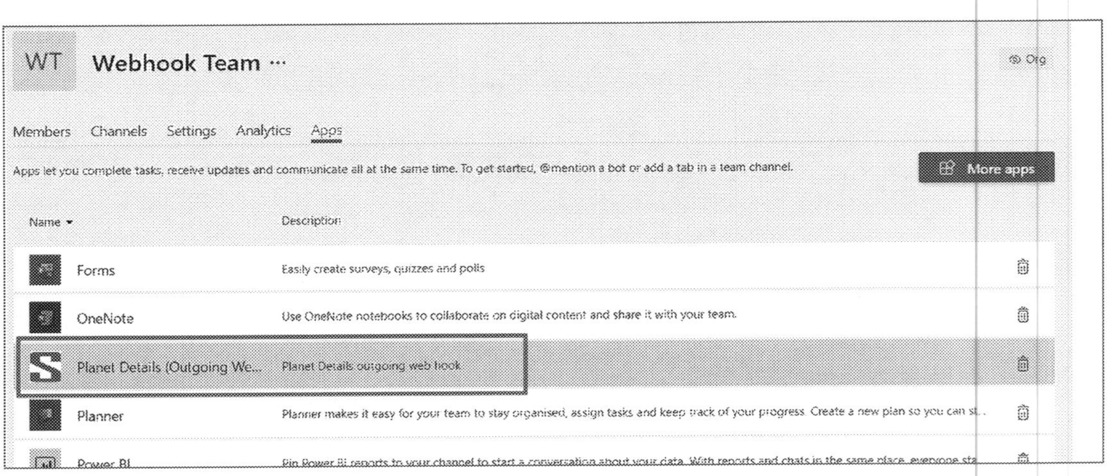

Figure 7-9. *Outgoing webhook apps*

- Click to open and update the ngrok dynamic URL and save it. See
  Figure 7-10.

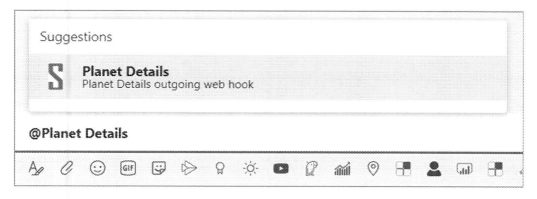

Figure 7-10. *Edit Outgoing webhook apps configuration*

- That is, replace the **{{REPLACE_NGROK_SUBDOMAIN}}** with the
  value of your dynamically created Ngrok URL (**b73772b97945**)

- Now you can test the webhook. Go to a channel Conversation tab
  within the team and enter the message **@Planet Details**. Notice that
  as you're typing the message, Microsoft Teams detects the name of
  the webhook (Figure 7-11).

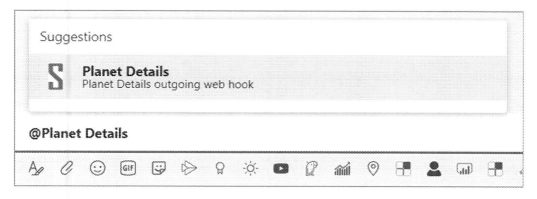

Figure 7-11. *Outgoing webhook apps Testing*

- Enter Mercury and click the send icon (Figure 7-12).

Planet Details Mercury

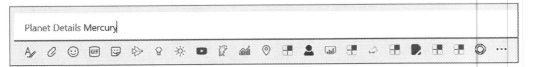

Figure 7-12. *Outgoing webhook apps add parameter*

- A few seconds after submitting the message, you will see a reply to your message that contains the customized Adaptive Card with details about the planet and sends the notification. Refer to Figure 7-13.

Custom bot replied to your conversation
Webhook Team / General

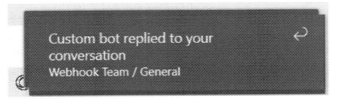

Figure 7-13. *Bot Notification*

Then Figure 7-14 show the outgoing webhook message output using a card.

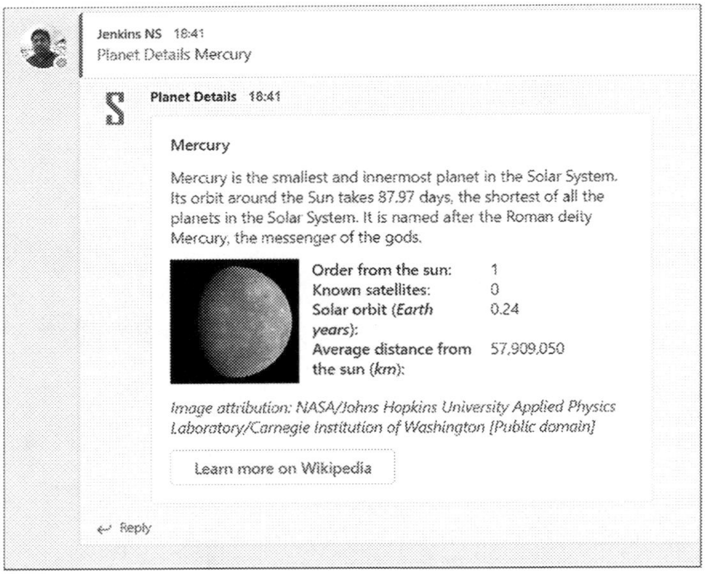

Jenkins NS 18:41
Planet Details Mercury
Planet Details 18:41
Mercury
Mercury is the smallest and innermost planet in the Solar System. Its orbit around the Sun takes 87.97 days, the shortest of all the planets in the Solar System. It is named after the Roman deity Mercury, the messenger of the gods.
Order from the sun: 1
Known satellites: 0
Solar orbit (Earth years): 0.24
Average distance from the sun (km): 57,909,050
Image attribution: NASA/Johns Hopkins University Applied Physics Laboratory/Carnegie Institution of Washington [Public domain]
Learn more on Wikipedia
Reply

Figure 7-14. *Outgoing webhook output*

You have successfully tested your outgoing webhook!

In this exercise, you have learned how to create an outgoing webhook and register it in Microsoft Teams. Without bot registration, you can get the custom bot reply to the conversation.

Exercise 2 - Create Incoming Webhooks

In this exercise, you will learn how to register an incoming webhook in a Microsoft Teams channel and post a message to it.

Register a New Incoming Webhook

Add the outgoing webhook to a team in Microsoft Teams. In the browser, navigate to `https://teams.microsoft.com` and sign in with the credentials of a Work and School account.

- Once you are signed in, select a team you want to add to the incoming webhook.

- Click and Select Manage team (Figure 7-15).

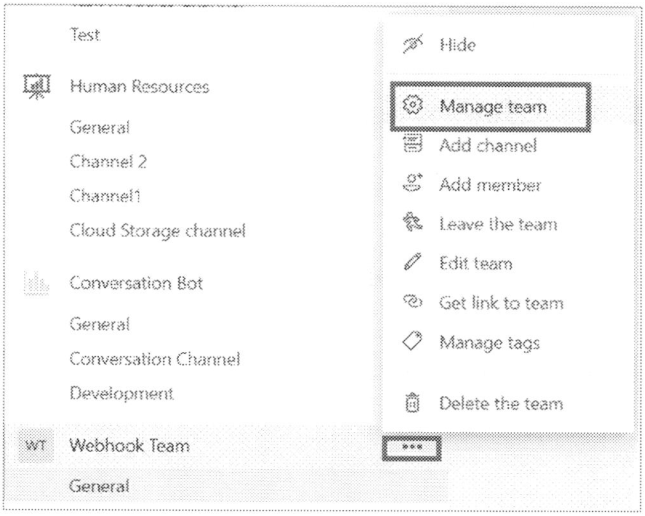

Figure 7-15. *Manage team*

- Select Apps and Click 'More Apps' in the right top (Figure 7-16).

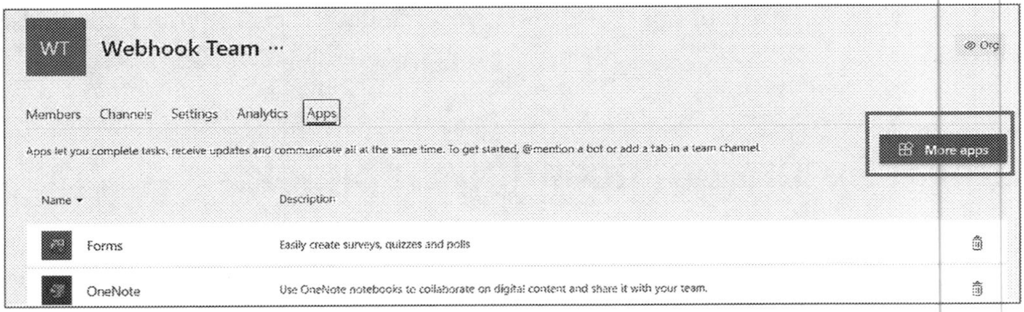

Figure 7-16. *More apps*

- On the Apps page, search for the incoming webhook app.
- Click the "Incoming Webhook" app and open it (Figure 7-17).

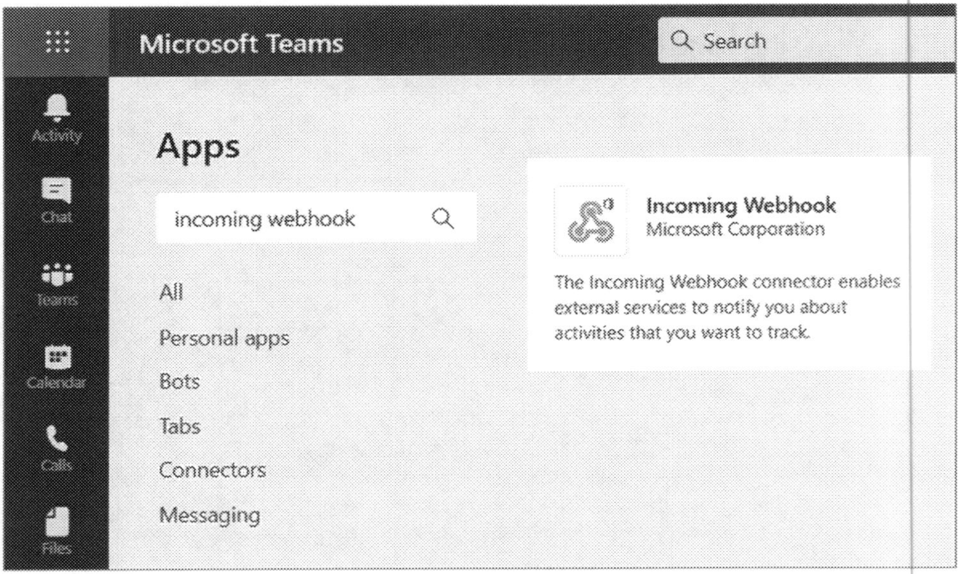

Figure 7-17. *MS Teams Apps list*

- Select the Add to a team button (Figure 7-18).

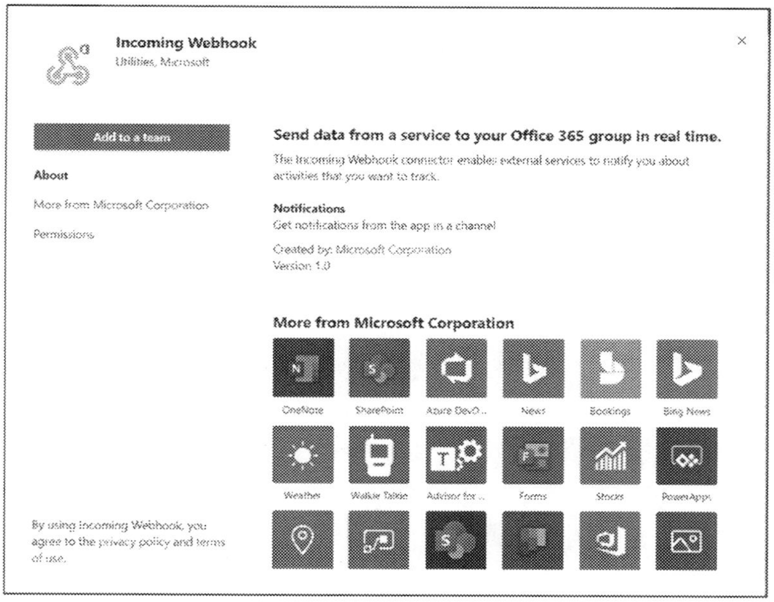

Figure 7-18. *Add to a team*

- Enter the name of a channel to add the webhook to and select the '**Set up a connector**' (Figure 7-19).

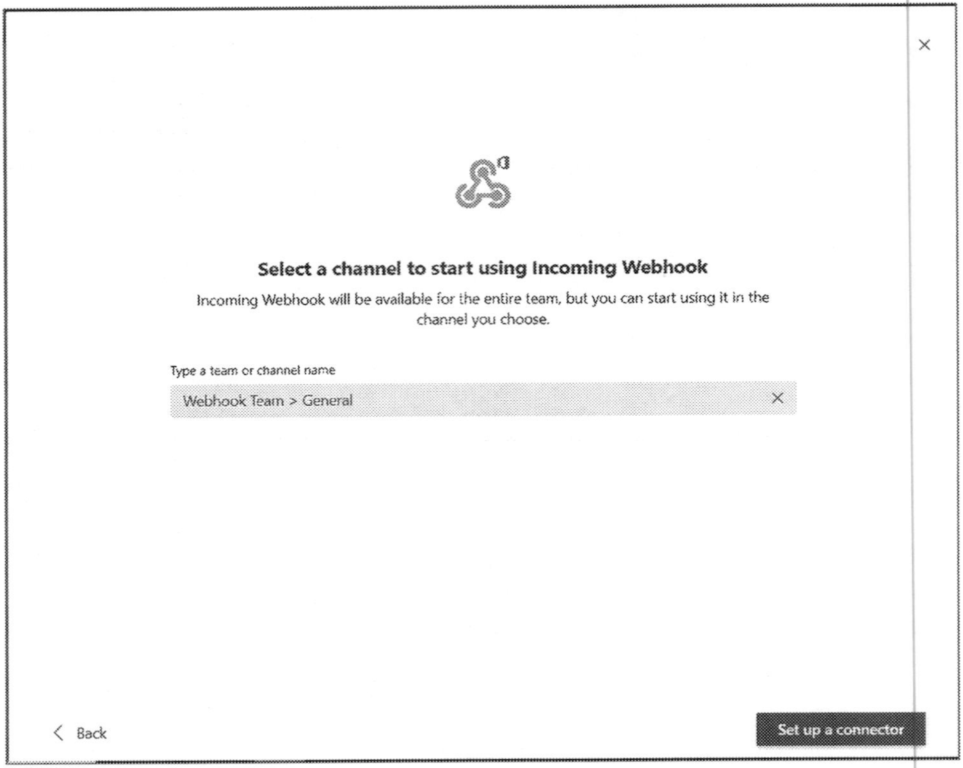

Figure 7-19. *Set up connector for incoming webhook*

On the Incoming Webhook configuration screen:

- Enter the name "JPOWER4 Services."

- Upload image.

- Select the Create button (you may need to scroll down in the dialog as the Create button isn't visible by default, as in the following screenshot of Figure 7-20).

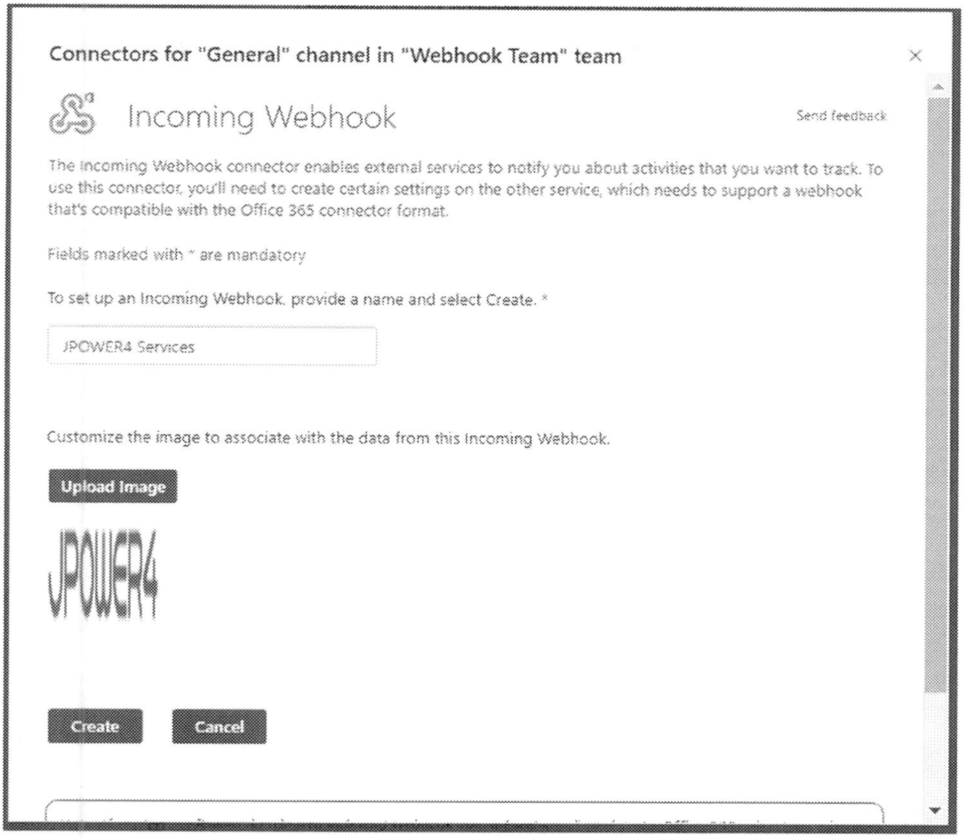

Figure 7-20. Configure incoming webhook

- After creating the incoming webhook, the dialog will add a new input box that contains the endpoint for you to post to. Copy this value (Figure 7-21).

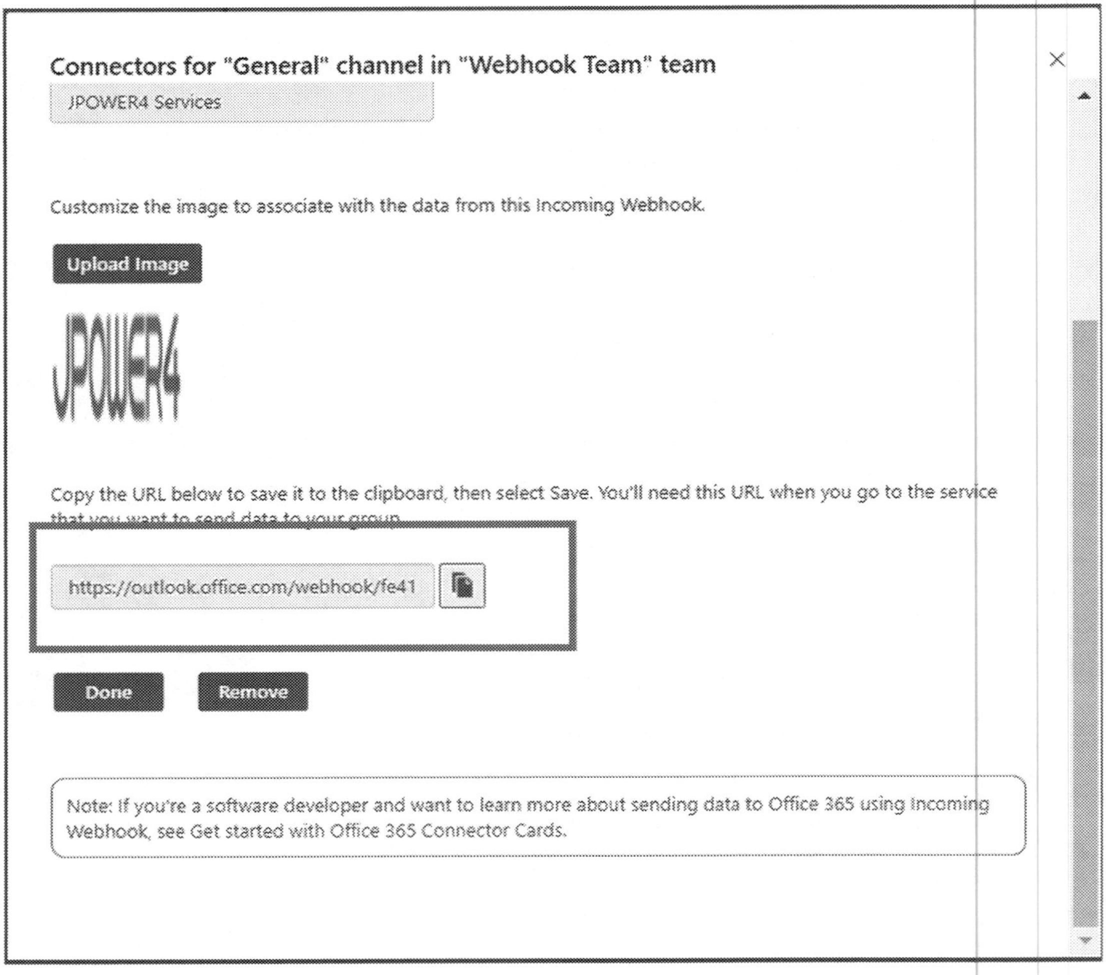

Connectors for "General" channel in "Webhook Team" team

JPOWER4 Services

Customize the image to associate with the data from this Incoming Webhook.

Upload Image

Copy the URL below to save it to the clipboard, then select Save. You'll need this URL when you go to the service that you want to send data to your group.

https://outlook.office.com/webhook/fe41

Done   Remove

Note: If you're a software developer and want to learn more about sending data to Office 365 using Incoming Webhook, see Get started with Office 365 Connector Cards.

Figure 7-21. *Copy incoming webhook URL*

- The copied URL looks like what is below:

  ```
  https://outlook.office.com/webhook/fe4183ab-49ea-4c1b-
  9297-2658ea56164c@f784fbed-7fc7-4c7a-aae9-d2f387b67c5d/
  IncomingWebhook/4d2b3a16003d47b080b7a083b5a5e533/74f315
  eb-1dde-4731-b6b5-2524b77f2acd
  ```

- It will add a conversation in the channel about an incoming webhook configuration to other channel members (Figure 7-22).

Figure 7-22. Incoming webhook added to the channel

Test the Incoming Webhook

Let's test it:

- After configuring the incoming webhook, the next step is to submit a post to it to display a message in the channel. Do this by submitting an HTTPS request to the webhook endpoint provided.

- Using the free tool **Postman** https://www.postman.com/ , create a new request to the point endpoint (Figure 7-23):

  - set the **request** to a **POST**

  - set the **endpoint** to the webhook endpoint you copied at the end of the previous section

  - set the **Content-Type** header to **application/json** on the Headers tab

Figure 7-23. Postman configuration

- Then add the following JSON to the **Body** tab and select the raw option.

- **Note**: This JSON contains Office 365 Connector Cards.

- Incoming webhook only supports Office 365 Connector Cards.

- Adaptive Cards aren't supported when sending messages to incoming webhooks. See Figure 7-24.

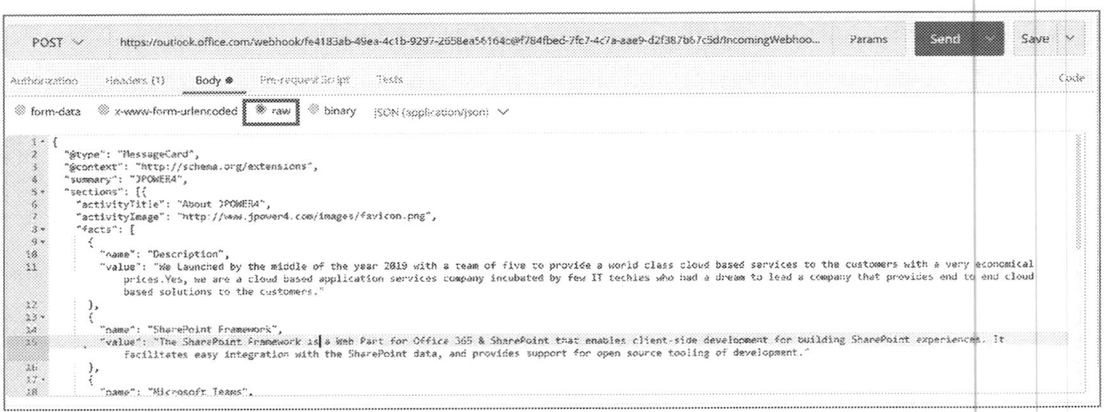

Figure 7-24. *Postman request body content*

```
{
    "@type": "MessageCard",
    "@context": "http://schema.org/extensions",
    "summary": "JPOWER4",
    "sections": [{
      "activityTitle": "About JPOWER4",
      "activityImage": "http://www.jpower4.com/images/favicon.png",
      "facts": [
        {
          "name": "Description",
          "value": "We Launched by the middle of the year 2019 with a team
          of five to provide a world class cloud based services to the
          customers with a very economical prices.Yes, we are a cloud based
          application services company incubated by few IT techies who had
          a dream to lead a company that provides end to end cloud based
          solutions to the customers."
        },
```

```
{
    "name": "SharePoint Framework",
    "value": "The SharePoint Framework is a Web Part for Office 365
    & SharePoint that enables client-side development for building
    SharePoint experiences. It facilitates easy integration with the
    SharePoint data, and provides support for open source tooling of
    development."
},
{
    "name": "Microsoft Teams",
    "value": "Microsoft Teams is a collaboration workspace in Office
    365 that integrates with apps and services people use to get work
    done together. We develop custom applications for Microsoft Teams
    and help the customer to upgrade from Skype for Business."
},
{
    "name": "Power Apps",
    "value": "Build apps in hours, not months, that easily connect
    to data, use excel like expressions to add logic, and run on the
    web, iOS, and Android devices"
},
{
    "name": "Power Automate",
    "value": "Include powerful workflow automation directly in your
    apps with a no-code approach that connects to hundreds of popular
    apps and services."
},
{
    "name": "Power BI",
    "value": "Make sense of your data through interactive, real-time
    dashboards and unlock the insights needed to drive your business
    forward."
}
]
}],
```

```
"potentialAction": [{
  "@context": "http://schema.org",
  "@type": "ViewAction",
  "name": "Know more about JPOWER4",
  "target": ["http://www.jpower4.com/"]
}]
}
```

- Click Send the card to Microsoft Teams by selecting the Send button.

- It will process the request and send a message card to the channel.

- Go to Microsoft Teams, and navigate back to the Conversations tab in the channel where you have installed the incoming webhook. You can see the message given below in your message card (Office 365 Connector card). Refer to Figure 7-25.

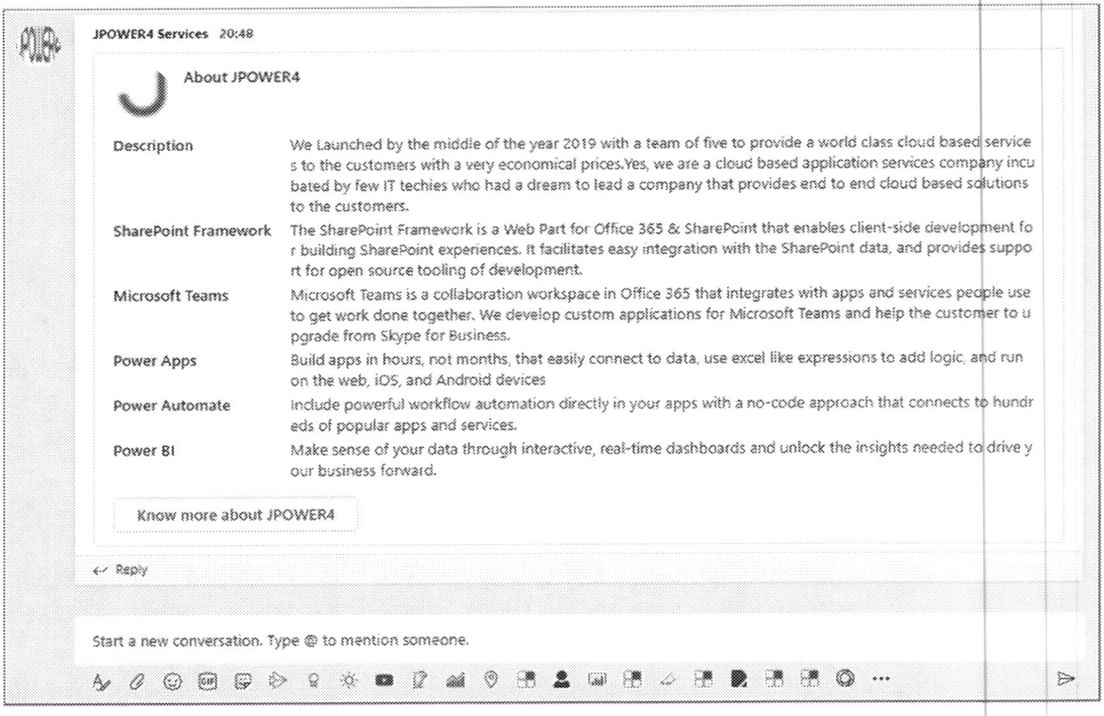

Figure 7-25. *Incoming webhook output*

In this exercise, you have learned how to register an incoming webhook in a Microsoft Teams channel and post a message with an Office 365 Connector card to it.

Conclusion

In this chapter, you have learned various features of webhooks. Outgoing webhooks allow your users to send text messages from a channel to your web services. Connectors and incoming webhooks allow users to subscribe to receive notifications and messages from your web services. We learned about Office 365 connectors cards that can be invoked by sending them from the postman extension, the same way that we are able to use it from our own application. Along with this, you will start learning different options and features of Microsoft Teams apps in our upcoming chapters.

CHAPTER 8

Extend Your Solution with Microsoft Graph

In this chapter, I will be covering the automation of Teams lifecycle management, messages, webhooks, and resource-specific permission consent. Microsoft Graph is a unified API endpoint for dealing with data so that there is a graph endpoint for SharePoint, Teams, exchanges, and planning a whole variety of different Microsoft products, all exposed under a common API endpoint. Teams allows you to build a variety of different apps like tabs, bots, connectors, etc.

Overview of Graph API

Microsoft Graph is the unified REST API for accessing all the data in Microsoft's applications, and Microsoft Teams is the hub for teamwork in Office 365 allowing you to communicate through chat messages, online meetings, and calls. It allows you to collaborate with all of those Office 365 applications.

The API enables you to access Microsoft Cloud service resources. After you register your app and get authentication tokens for a user or service, you can make requests to the Microsoft Graph API. It exposes REST APIs and client libraries to access data on the following Microsoft 365 services:

- Office 365 services: Delve, Excel, Microsoft Bookings, Microsoft Teams, OneDrive, OneNote, Outlook/Exchange, Planner, and SharePoint;

- Enterprise Mobility and Security services: Advanced Threat Analytics, Advanced Threat Protection, Azure Active Directory, Identity Manager, and Intune;

- Windows 10 services: activities, devices, notifications (Figure 8-1).

267

© Jenkins NS 2021
J. NS, *Building Solutions with Microsoft Teams*, https://doi.org/10.1007/978-1-4842-6476-8_8

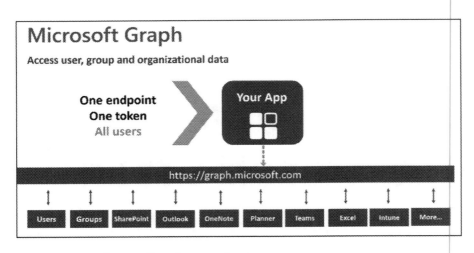

Figure 8-1. *Microsoft Graph – One endpoint*

Teams Graph APIs

Microsoft Graph provides APIs for accessing data and you can call graph APIs from tabs, bots, and websites and services that don't have user interfaces or even Graph APIs in your command-line tools.

A Microsoft Teams Graph API allows you to create new teams and add channels to those teams, add members to the teams, and add tabs into those channels that you have created. Once the team has run its life cycle, you then have a fully functioning team. You can then archive or delete the team using the Graph API for that functionality. Also, there are different things that people build with this first Graph API; for example, they bulk provision teams – maybe 100 teams for each department at the beginning of a year.

The second thing is that you can create temporary teams. For instance, if you are an airline and you want to fly a flight each day and have a team for each flight, you can do so at the stroke of midnight. The third thing is that people create a lot of admin tools; they just administer their teams so the PowerShell command that teams have are built on this. The modern portal for admin is also built on the Graph API so that the developer can get started with the teams Graph API to manager all teams admin activities.

You have a bunch of APIs today to do that (Table 8-1), and you have access to the team resources. You can read, write, add, remove, update, delete, as well as enumerate the teams that a member has. You have APIs for manipulating membership, adding and removing people to the membership list, adding and removing people to the owner list, and also enumerating who those owners and members are; and getting additional information about them such as what their full name is, their email address, their user picture, etc.

Table 8-1. *APIs Available Today for Microsoft Teams*

Resource	Methods
team	List your teams, list all teams, create, read, update, delete, clone, archive, unarchive
group	Add member, remove member, add owner, remove owner, get files, get notebook, get plans, get calendar
channel	List, create, read, update, delete
teamsTab	List, create, read, update, delete
teamsApp	List, publish, update, remove
teamsAppInstallation	List, install, upgrade, remove
chatMessage	Send
call	Answer, reject, redirect, mute, unmute, change screen sharing role, list participants, invite participants
schedule	Create or replace, get, share
schedulingGroup	Create, List, Get, Replace, Delete
shift	Create, List, Get, Replace, Delete
timeOff	Create, List, Get, Replace, Delete
timeOffReason	Create, List, Get, Replace, Delete

Team settings is another one of the things you can get access to - both reading and writing the settings of a team. With channels, we have the full ability to add, read, update, delete channels, as well as enumerate the channels in a team. And you can post channel messages to those channels.

Graph API for Lifecycle Management

One of the powerful things you can do with Graph APIs is to automate the life cycle of your team. So, you can create a team and then add members and owners to that team, add some channels to that team, configure the team settings, post a welcome message to the team, and then let your users party on that team and when they are done, when the business issue that you are trying to that team is resolved, you can then go ahead and delete the team (Figure 8-2).

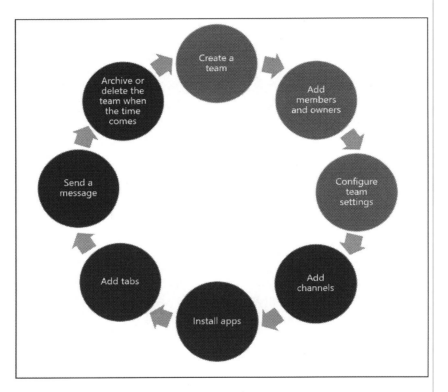

Figure 8-2. *Graph can automate team life cycle [REF – MSDN]*

Teams and Groups

Microsoft 365 groups address the various needs of group collaboration and having 19 Microsoft 365 applications endpoints including Microsoft Teams. All Microsoft group features are applicable to Microsoft Teams. Every Team associated with a group communicates in the context of a specific team. Group members communicate by group conversations, which are email conversations that occur in the context of a group in Outlook. To differentiate the group associated with the team, any group that has a team has a '**resourceProvisioningOptions'** property that contains "Team." Do not change "Team" from the '**resourceProvisioningOptions'** property or the result will be incorrect when you list all the teams.

The following are the differences at the API level between teams and groups:

- Persistent chat is available only to Microsoft Teams. This feature is hierarchically represented by the channel and 'chatMessage' resources.

- Group conversations are available only to Microsoft 365 groups. This feature is hierarchically represented by the conversation, 'conversationThread', and post resources.

- The List joined teams method applies only to Microsoft Teams.

- Calling and online meeting APIs apply only to Microsoft Teams.

You can create teams:

- From scratch, using your own team

- From an existing O365 group

- By cloning an existing team

- From a template

Here is the syntax:

```
POST https://graph.microsoft.com/v1.0/teams
Content-Type: application/json
{
  "template@odata.bind": "https://graph.microsoft.com/beta/
  teamsTemplates('standard')",
  "displayName": "My Sample Team",
  "description": "My Sample Team's Description",
  "owners@odata.bind": [
    "https://graph.microsoft.com/beta/users('userId')"
  ]
}
```

Team Templates

Spin up new teams quickly with preconfigured templates that include things like channels, owner settings, and preinstalled apps.

Out-of-the-box templates:

- Standard

- Education (class, staff, or PLC)

- Retail store (basic or manager collaboration)

- Health care (ward or hospital)

Set Up Your Team Using Graph API

You can configure your team when you create it or update it later.

Configure things like:

- Display name and description

- Guest and member permissions

- Visibility

- Messaging permissions

- Create channels

- Add members and roles

Here is the syntax:

```
PATCH https://graph.microsoft.com/v1.0/teams/{id}
Content-type: application/json
Content-length: 211
{
  "memberSettings": {
    "allowCreateUpdateChannels": true
  },
  "messagingSettings": {
    "allowUserEditMessages": true,
```

```
    "allowUserDeleteMessages": true
  },
  "funSettings": {
    "allowGiphy": true,
    "giphyContentRating": "strict"
  },
  "discoverySettings": {
    "showInTeamsSearchAndSuggestions": true
  }
}
```

Add Apps and Tabs Using Graph API

Preinstall apps, add tabs, and configure your tabs to install apps for your team:

- Your app must be in either your organizational app Catalog or the public app store.

- To add tabs for your team:

  - The app must be installed first.

  - You can preconfigure them, or leave them to be configured when a user first interacts with the tab.

  - Preconfiguring tabs can be challenging, make sure you use the documentation (https://docs.microsoft.com/en-us/graph/teams-configuring-builtin-tabs).

Here is the syntax:

```
POST https://graph.microsoft.com/v1.0/teams/{team-id}/channels/{channel-id}/tabs
{
    "displayName": "Document%20Library1",
    "teamsApp@odata.bind": "https://graph.microsoft.com/v1.0/appCatalogs/
    teamsApps/com.microsoft.teamspace.tab.files.sharepoint",
    "configuration": {
        "entityId": "",
```

```
        "contentUrl": "https://microsoft.sharepoint.com/teams/WWWtest/
        Shared%20Documents",
        "removeUrl": null,
        "websiteUrl": null
    }
}
POST https://graph.microsoft.com/v1.0/teams/{id}/installedApps
Content-type: application/json
{
"teamsApp@odata.bind":"https://graph.microsoft.com/v1.0/appCatalogs/
teamsApps/12345678-9abc-def0-123456789a"
}
```

Archive Your Team

When the time comes, use Graph to archive your team in an agile manner and if necessary, un-archive the team.

Common archive operations:

- Retrieve and archive messages in important channels (beta)

- Archive the team

- Set the SharePoint Online team site to read only (or delete the group)

- Archive or move stored files

Here is the syntax:

```
GET https://graph.microsoft.com/v1.0/teams/{id}/channels
GET https://graph.microsoft.com/beta/teams/{id}/channels/{id}/messages/
delta
GET https://graph.microsoft.com/beta/teams/{id}/channels/{id}/messages/
{id}/replies
POST https://graph.microsoft.com/v1.0/teams/{id}/archive
{
    "shouldSetSpoSiteReadOnlyForMembers": true
}
```

Graph and Bots: Better Together

A Teams app with a bot can proactively send messages to a chat or channel. It can only send messages to conversations. If it has the right information for a 1:1 chat, the bot needs to be installed in a group chat or channel the user is a part of or installed as a personal app for that user. The bot must store a reference to that user when they are made aware of them.

With Graph, you can install the app for any user, enabling proactive messaging regardless of where the app is previously installed. This is particularly useful in scenarios where you need to message a large portion of your organization reliably.

Bots can only read messages, and they are @mentioned:

- Use messaging APIs to get additional information for your bot

- Get the root message in a reply chain

- Retrieve all replies to a message

- Get previous messages from a chat thread

Microsoft Graph Toolkit

The Microsoft Graph Toolkit is a collection of reusables, framework-agnostic web components, and helpers for accessing and working with Microsoft Graph. The components are fully functional right of out of the box, with built-in providers that authenticate with and fetch data from Microsoft Graph. The Microsoft Graph Toolkit makes it easy to use Microsoft Graph in your application.

```
<mgt-login></mgt-login>
<mgt-agenda></mgt-agenda>
```

What's in the Microsoft Graph Toolkit?

Components

The Microsoft Graph Toolkit includes a collection of web components for the most commonly built experiences powered by Microsoft Graph APIs.

Component	Description
Login	A button and a flyout control to authenticate a user with the Microsoft Identity platform and display the user's profile information on sign in.
Person	Displays a person or contact by their photo, name, and/or email address.
People	Displays a group of people or contacts by their photos or initials.
Agenda	Displays events in a user or group's calendar.
Tasks	Displays and enables adding, removing, completing, or editing of tasks from Microsoft Planner or Microsoft To-Do.
People picker	Provides the ability to search for people and renders the list of results.
Person card	A flyout used on the person component to display more profile information about a user.
Get	**Make a GET query to any Microsoft Graph API directly in your HTML.**
Channel picker	Provides the ability to search for Microsoft Teams channels to select a channel from a rendered list of results.

Providers

The components work best when used with a provider. Providers enable authentication and provide the implementation for acquiring the access tokens for calling the Microsoft Graph APIs.

Providers	Description
MSAL	Uses MSAL.js to sign in users and acquire tokens to use with Microsoft Graph.
SharePoint	Authenticates and provides Microsoft Graph access to components inside of SharePoint web parts.
Teams	Authenticates and provides Microsoft Graph access to components inside of Microsoft Teams tabs.
Proxy	Allows the use of back-end authentication by routing all calls to Microsoft Graph through your back end.
Custom	Creates a custom provider to enable authentication and access to Microsoft Graph with your application's existing authentication code.

Why Use the Microsoft Graph Toolkit?

The Microsoft Graph Toolkit makes it quick and easy to integrate common experiences powered by Microsoft Graph into your own applications.

Cut Development Time

The work to connect to Microsoft Graph APIs and render the data in a UI that looks and feels like a Microsoft 365 experience is done for you, with no customization required.

Works Everywhere

All components are based on web standards and work seamlessly with any modern browser and web framework (React, Angular, Vue, etc.).

Beautiful but Flexible

The components are designed to look and feel like Microsoft 365 experiences but are also customizable using CSS custom properties and templating.

Styling Components in the Microsoft Graph Toolkit

Use CSS custom properties to modify component styles. Each component documents a set of CSS custom properties that you can use to change the look and feel of certain elements. For example:

```
mgt-person {
  --avatar-size: 34px;
}
```

You can't style internal elements of a component unless you provide a CSS custom property. The component child elements are hosted in a shadow dom https://developer.mozilla.org/en-US/docs/Web/Web_Components/Using_shadow_DOM.

Templates in the Microsoft Graph Toolkit

Use custom templates to modify the content of a component. All web components support templates based on the <template> element. For example, to override the template of a component, add a <template> element inside a component.

```
<mgt-agenda>
  <template data-type="event">
      <div>{{event.subject}}</div>
      <div data-for='attendee in event.attendees'>
          <mgt-person person-query="{{attendee.emailAddress.name}}">
           <template>
             <div data-if="person.image">
               <img src="{{person.image}}" />
              </div>
             <div data-else>
                 {{person.displayName}}
             </div>
           </template>
          </mgt-person>
        </div>
    </template>
</mgt-agenda>
```

Data Type

Each component can have multiple parts that can be templated.

For example, in the mgt-agenda component, you can template individual events, individual section headers, loading view, no data view, and more. To indicate the template, use the data-type attribute on a template.

```
<mgt-agenda>
  <template data-type="event"> </template>
</mgt-agenda>
```

If no data type is specified, the entire component will be replaced with the template. You can also use data type="default" for the same purpose.

Binding Data

Many templates allow binding of data that is passed to the template as data context. For example, the event template in the mgt-agenda component passes an {event} object that can be used directly in the template. To expand an expression, such as event, the subject uses the double curly brackets.

```
<template data-type="event">
  <div>{{event.subject}}</div>
</template>
```

This format can also be used inside attributes:

```
<template data-type="event">
  <a href="{{ event.onlineMeetingUrl }}" />
</template>
```

Change Binding Syntax

By default, to expand an expression, you use double curly brackets ({{expression}}). However, you can change this syntax for environments where the double curly bracket syntax is already used. For example, the following example uses double square brackets ([[expression]]).

```
import { TemplateHelper } from '@microsoft/mgt';
TemplateHelper.setBindingSyntax('[[', ']]');
```

Data Context Helper Properties

The following properties can also be used with the data context object in your templates.

Property	Description
$index	Numerical index of item being rendered while being looped with data-for.
$parent	If a template is rendered inside another template, this property allows you to access the parent data context.

The following example shows how to use the $index property in a data-for loop.

```
<mgt-person>
  <mgt-person-card>
    <template data-type="additional-details">
      <span data-for="language in languages">
        {{ language.displayName }}<span data-if="$index < languages.
        length - 1">, </span>
```

```
      </span>
    </template>
  </mgt-person-card>
</mgt-person>
```

Conditional Rendering

You might only want to render elements when a condition is true or false based on the data context. The data-if and data-else attributes can evaluate an expression and render only if they are true or false.

```
<mgt-person person-query="john doe">
  <template>
    <div data-if="person.image">
      <img src="{{ person.image }}" />
    </div>
    <div data-else>
      {{ person.displayName }}
    </div>
  </template>
</mgt-person>
```

Looping

There will be cases where the data context object contains a loop and you will need to loop over the data. For this scenario, use the data-for attribute.

```
<template data-type="event">
  <ul>
    <li data-for='attendee in event.attendees'>
    {{ attendee.displayName }}
    </li>
  </ul>
</template>
```

Template Context

In scenarios where you need to convert data in your bindings, bind to events, or just use external data in your template's bindings, the templates support binding to external data context. You can add additional template context in two ways.

Directly on the Component

Each component defines the *templateContext* property, which you can use to pass additional data to any template in the component.

```
document.querySelector('mgt-agenda').templateContext = {

  someObject: {},
   formatDate: (date: Date) => { /* format date and return */ },
  someEventHandler: (e) => { /* handleEvent */  }

}
```

The properties in the *templateContext* object will now be available to be used in the binding expressions in the template.

Globally for All Components

The TemplateHelper class exposes the globalContext object to add data or functions that should be globally available for all components.

```
import { TemplateHelper } from '@microsoft/mgt';
TemplateHelper.globalContext.someObject = {};
TemplateHelper.globalContext.formatDate = (date: Date) => { /* format
date and return */ };
TemplateHelper.globalContext.someEventHandler = (e) =>
{ /* handleEvent */  }
```

Converters

In many cases, you might want to transform the data before presenting it in the template. For example, you might want to properly format a date before it is rendered. In these cases, you might want to use a template converter.

To use a template converter, you first need to define a function that will do the conversion. For example, you might define a function to convert an event object to a formatted time range.

```
document.querySelector('mgt-agenda').templateContext = {

  getTimeRange: (event) => {
    // TODO: format a string from the event object as you wish
    // timeRange = ...

      return timeRange;
  }
}
```

To use the converter in your template, use it as if you would use a function in the code behind.

```
<template data-type="event">
  <div>{{ getTimeRange(event) }}</div>
</template>
```

Event or Property Binding

The data-props attribute allows you to add an event listener or set a property value directly in your templates.

```
<template>
    <button data-props="{{@click: myEvent, myProp: value}}"></button>
</template>
```

The data-props accepts a comma delimited string for each property or event handler you might want to set. To add an event handler, prefix the name of the event with @. The event handler will need to be available in the *templateContext* of the element.

```
document.querySelector('mgt-agenda').templateContext = {

    someEventHandler: (e, context, root) => { /* handleEvent */ }
}
<template>
    <button data-props="{{@click: someEventHandler}}"></button>
  </template>
```

The event args, data context, and root element of the template are passed to the event handler as parameters.

Template Rendered Event

In certain cases, you might want to get a reference to the rendered element. This can be useful if you want to handle the rendering of the content yourself, or you want to modify the rendered element.

In this scenario, you can use the *templateRendered* event, which fires after the template has been rendered.

```
let agenda = document.querySelector('mgt-agenda');
agenda.addEventListener('templateRendered', (e) => { });
```

The event details will contain a reference to the element that is being rendered, data context object, and type of template.

```
agenda.addEventListener('templateRendered', (e) => {
  let templateType = e.detail.templateType;
  let dataContext = e.detail.context;
  let element = e.detail.element;

  if (templateType === 'event') {
    element.querySelector('.some-button').addEventListener('click',
    () => {});
  }
});
```

Microsoft Graph Toolkit Playground

To find a tool used for interacting with the Microsoft Graph Toolkit, try out the components in this playground: https://mgt.dev. See Figure 8-3.

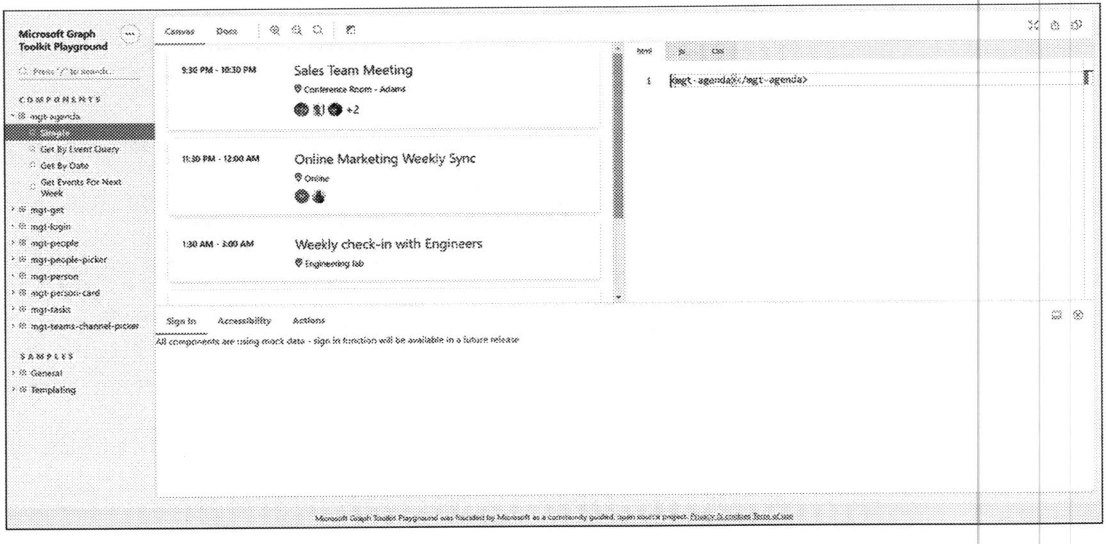

Figure 8-3. *Graph Toolkit playground*

Microsoft Graph Explorer

Microsoft Graph Explorer is a tool to explore graph APIs, and you can see the image in Figure 8-4 of the screenshot of the Microsoft Graph Explorer that I have captured. As you can see, this console gives you the option to type in the API or address of a specific entity type or object for which you are looking for some information, and then you also need to sign in with a specific account that has the privilege to query this particular API, Next it will also show you some of the sample queries that you can use to understand the explorer. You can access Graph Explorer at: `https://developer.microsoft.com/graph/graph-explorer`

The following example shows a request that returns information about *joinedteams* in my tenant.

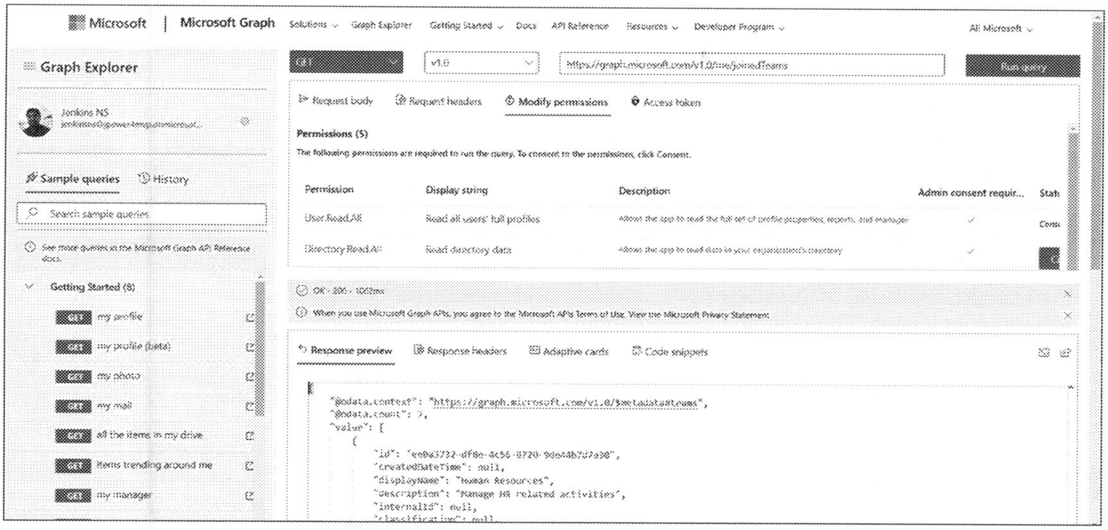

Figure 8-4. *Graph API Explorer*

A status code and message are displayed after a request is sent and the response is shown in the Response Preview tab.

Postman

Postman is a collaboration platform for API development that you can use to build and test Microsoft Graph API requests. You can download Postman from `https://www.getpostman.com`. To interact with Microsoft Graph in Postman, you use the Microsoft Graph collection. To learn more about postman, refer here: `https://learning.postman.com/`

Microsoft Teams Toolkit for Visual Studio Code

The Microsoft Teams Toolkit extension enables you to create, debug, and deploy Teams apps directly from Visual Studio Code.

Prerequisites:

- Visual Studio Code v1.44 or newer

- NodeJS 6 or newer

To access the Microsoft Teams Toolkit: - `https://marketplace.visualstudio.com/items?itemName=TeamsDevApp.ms-teams-vscode-extension`. See Figure 8-5.

Figure 8-5. *Microsoft Teams Toolkit*

Exercise – Microsoft Teams Tabs Using Microsoft Graph Toolkit

In this exercise, you will learn the basics of Microsoft Graph in Microsoft Teams and how to use Microsoft Graph API Toolkit, Microsoft Graph Explorer, and AAD Permission Implementation. This exercise develops using Microsoft Teams Toolkit for Visual Studio Code.

Before starting the exercise, verify your environment. In this exercise, I am using the tools mentioned below, which are installed in my environment:

1. Visual Studio Code

2. Microsoft Teams Toolkit

3. Ngrok account

Steps to build a Teams tab using Microsoft Graph API Toolkit:

1. Install Microsoft Teams Toolkit extension for Visual Studio Code

2. Build Microsoft Teams tab

   - Implement Microsoft Graph Toolkit

     - Login component: login button to authenticate a user with the Microsoft Identity platform

     - Teams provider: Microsoft Teams tab to facilitate authentication

     - Person component: displays user

3. Set up ngrok for tunneling

4. Register your app in Azure Active Directory

5. Execute the app

6. Test your App in Microsoft Teams

Enable Microsoft Teams Toolkit Extension for Visual Studio Code

Install Microsoft Teams Toolkit from the Extensions tab on the left sidebar in Visual Studio Code. See Figure 8-6.

Figure 8-6. *Microsoft Teams Toolkit Installation*

Build Microsoft Teams Tab

Here are the steps (Figure 8-7):

1. Open Visual Studio Code

2. Select Microsoft Teams icon on the left sidebar in Visual Studio Code and **Sign in**

3. Log in with your tenant account

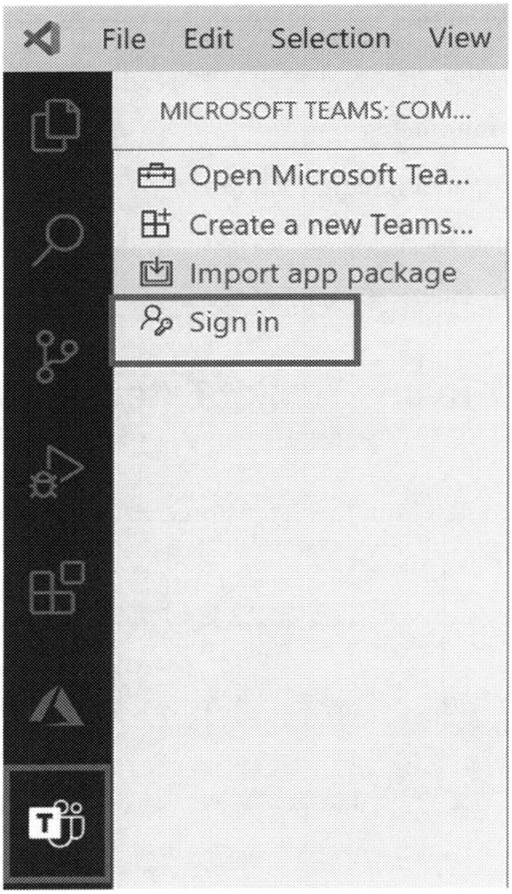

Figure 8-7. *Microsoft Teams Toolkit Sign In*

4. Navigate to "Create a New Teams app" and Click to enter new app name (Figure 8-8)

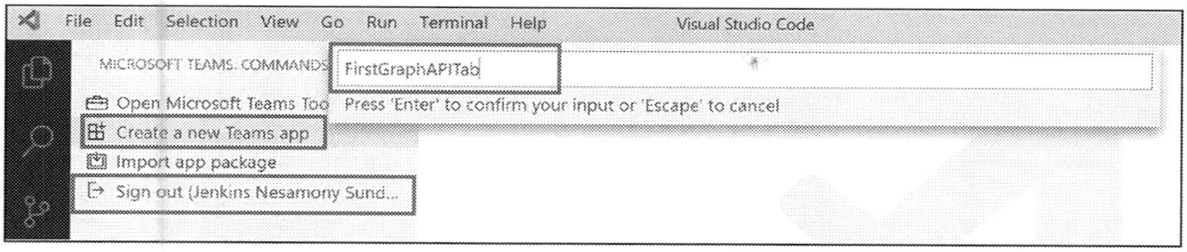

Figure 8-8. *Create new App*

5.   Press 'Enter' to select the app path

6.   Choose **Tab** to create Microsoft Teams Tab (Figure 8-9)

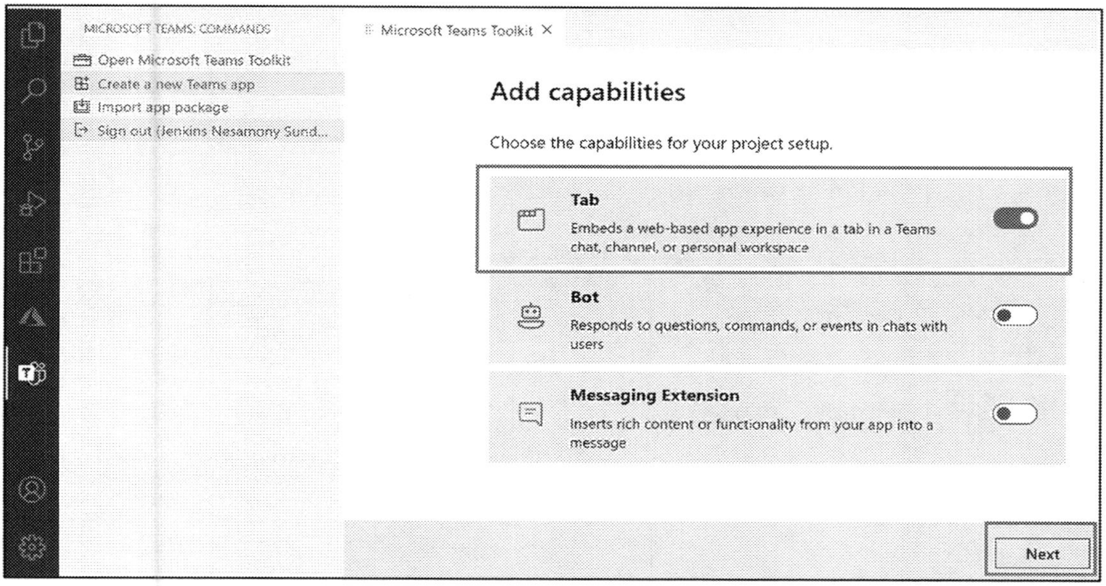

Figure 8-9. *Select new tab App*

7.   Click Next button

8.   Select Personal tab (Figure 8-10)

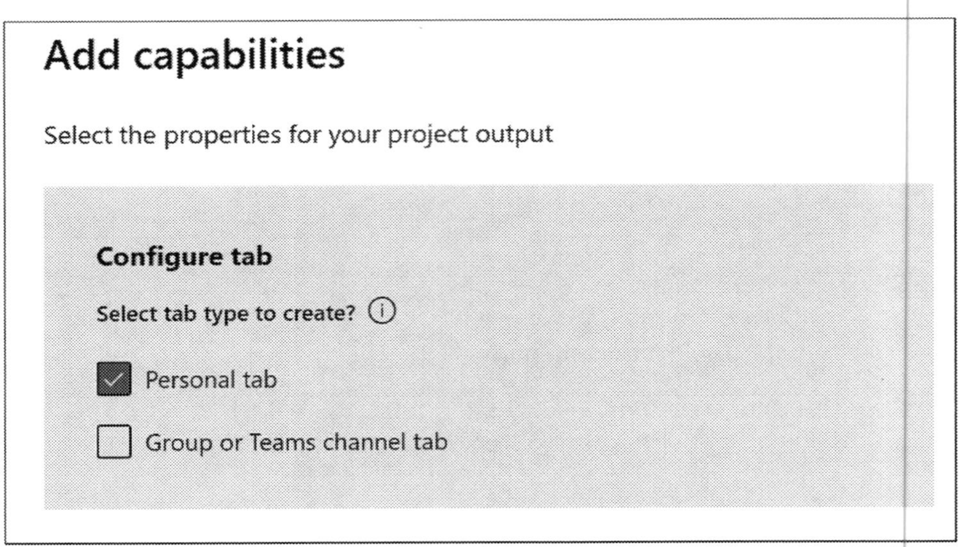

Figure 8-10. *Select Personal App*

9. Click the Finish button to create the Teams app (Figure 8-11)

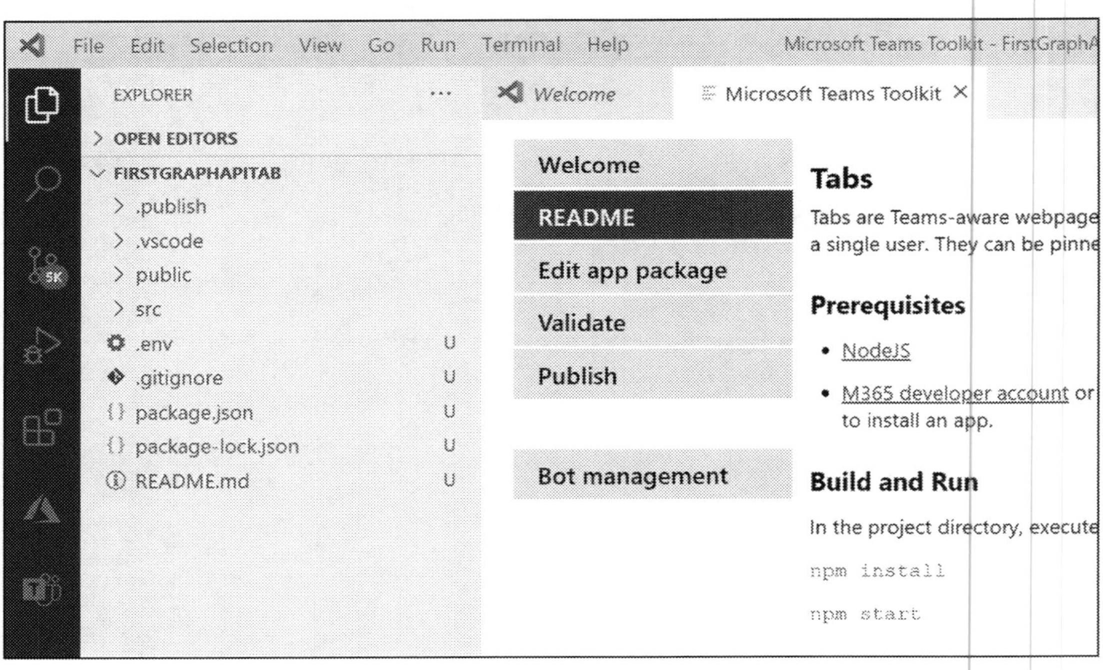

Figure 8-11. *Microsoft Teams Tab App Created*

Implement Microsoft Graph Toolkit

Let's implement it:

- Add a new file under **src** folder and name it as **auth.js**

- Then add the code below in it:

```
import React from 'react';
import ReactDOM from 'react-dom';
import './index.css';
import App from './components/App';
import { Provider, themes } from '@fluentui/react-northstar'

ReactDOM.render(
    <Provider theme={themes.teams}>
        <App />
    </Provider>, document.getElementById('auth')
);
```

- Add a new file under public folder and name as **auth.html**

- Then add below code

```
<!DOCTYPE html>
<html>
<head>
    <meta charset='utf-8'>
    <meta http-equiv='X-UA-Compatible' content='IE=edge'>
    <title>Auth Tab</title>
    <meta name='viewport' content='width=device-width, initial-scale=1'>
    <link rel='stylesheet' type='text/css' media='screen'
    href='main.css'>
    <script src='main.js'></script>
</head>
```

```
<body>
    <div id="auth"></div>
    <script src="https://unpkg.com/@microsoft/teams-js/dist/
    MicrosoftTeams.min.js" crossorigin="anonymous"></script>
    <script src="https://unpkg.com/@microsoft/mgt/dist/bundle/mgt-
    loader.js"></script>
    <script>
        mgt.TeamsProvider.handleAuth();
    </script>
</body>

</html>
```

- Add the code below in **index.html,** inside <body> tag:

```
<div id="root"></div>
    <script src="https://unpkg.com/@microsoft/teams-js/dist/
    MicrosoftTeams.min.js" crossorigin="anonymous"></script>
    <script src="https://unpkg.com/@microsoft/mgt/dist/bundle/mgt-
    loader.js"></script>
    <mgt-teams-provider client-id=" YOUR-CLIENT-ID" auth-popup-
    url="YOUR-NGROK-URL/auth.html"></mgt-teams-provider>
    <mgt-login></mgt-login>
    <mgt-person id="with-presence" person-query="me" person-
    card="hover" view="twoLines" show-presence></mgt-person>
```

Set Up Ngrok for Tunneling

Follow these steps:

- Go to the ngrok(https://ngrok.com/) website and log in with your tenant id

- Download ngrok.exe and Complete the setup and installation guide

- Copy the Authtoken from the ngrok site

- Save Authtoken in the default configuration file **C:\Users\[user name]\.ngrok>** (Figure 8-12)

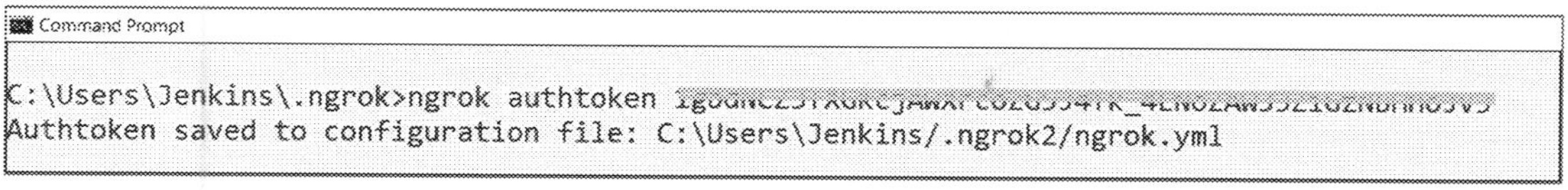

```
Command Prompt

C:\Users\Jenkins\.ngrok>ngrok authtoken 1guuNCZJ1AuKtjANAftOzuJJ4rK_4LNuzANJJz1uzNunnuJVJ
Authtoken saved to configuration file: C:\Users\Jenkins/.ngrok2/ngrok.yml
```

Figure 8-12. *configUre ngrok auth token*

- Run the script below (Figure 8-13) to create an ngrok tunnel for
  https://localhost:3000

  ngrok http -host-header="localhost:3000" 3000

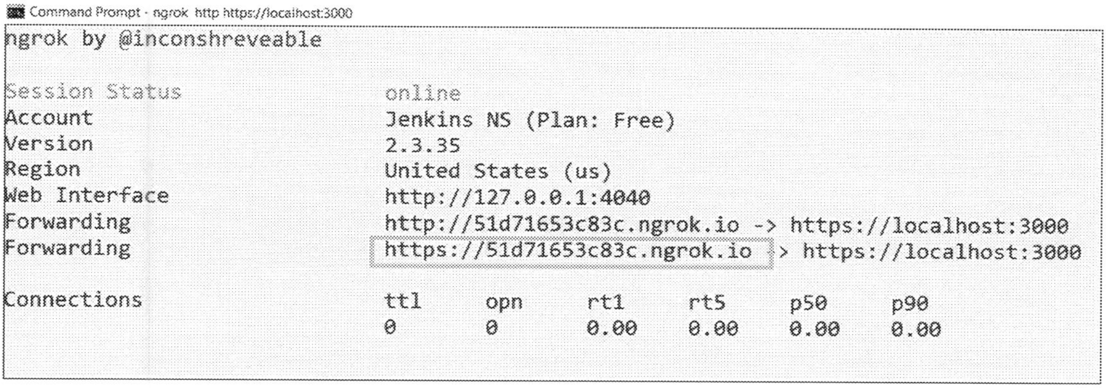

```
Command Prompt - ngrok http https://localhost:3000

ngrok by @inconshreveable

Session Status                online
Account                       Jenkins NS (Plan: Free)
Version                       2.3.35
Region                        United States (us)
Web Interface                 http://127.0.0.1:4040
Forwarding                    http://51d71653c83c.ngrok.io -> https://localhost:3000
Forwarding                    https://51d71653c83c.ngrok.io > https://localhost:3000

Connections                   ttl      opn      rt1      rt5      p50      p90
                              0        0        0.00     0.00     0.00     0.00
```

Figure 8-13. *Ngrok created the tunnel*

- Go to your project **.publish** > **Development.env**, and replace baseUrl0
  with ngrok URL (Figure 8-14), https://51d71653c83c.ngrok.io

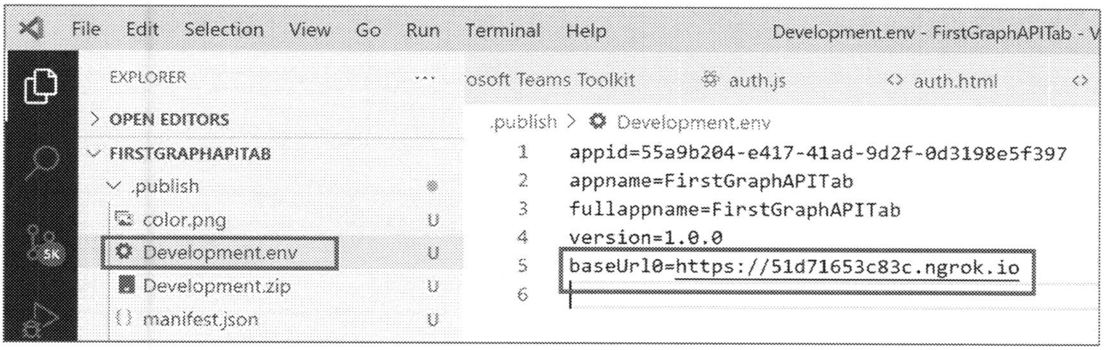

Figure 8-14. *Update URL in .env file*

- Go to your project **public > index.html**, replace YOUR-NGROK-URL with ngrok URL `https://51d71653c83c.ngrok.io` in **mgt-teams-provider > auth-popup-url** (Figure 8-15).

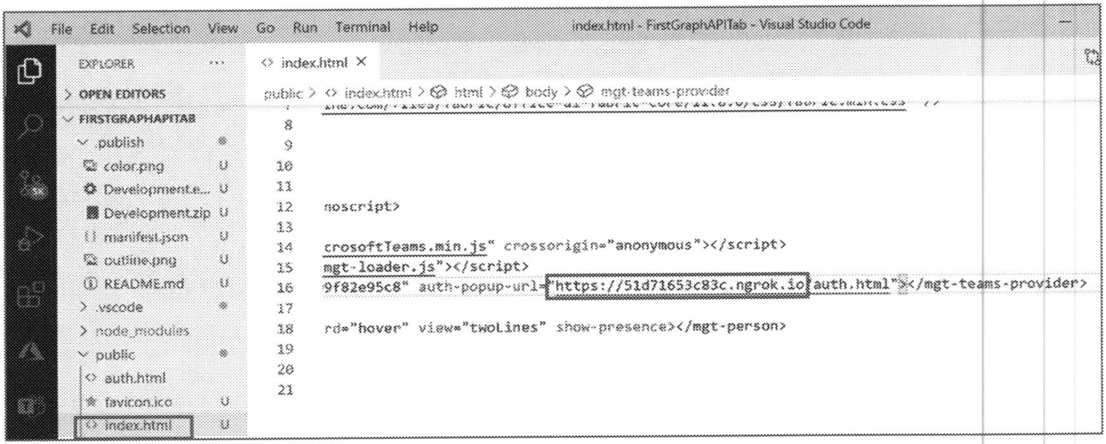

Figure 8-15. *Update URL in index file*

- Navigate Terminal ➤ New Terminal

- Run the solution (Figure 8-16). Default Teams tab will be running `https://localhost:3000`

```
npm install
npm start
```

```
PS C:\Jenkins\JPower4\Book\MSTeamsBook\FirstGraphAPITab> npm start
Compiled successfully!

You can now view microsoft-teams-ext in the browser.

  Local:            http://localhost:3000
  On Your Network:  http://10.0.1.1:3000

Note that the development build is not optimized.
To create a production build, use npm run build.
```

Figure 8-16. *Compiled the app*

Register Your App in Azure Active Directory

Now we register the app:

1. Go to the Azure Portal, then Azure Active Directory ➤ App Registration and select New Registration

2. Azure Active Portal URL - `https://aad.portal.azure.com/`

3. Login

4. Click Azure Active Directory

5. Select App registrations

6. Then Click New Registration (Figure 8-17)

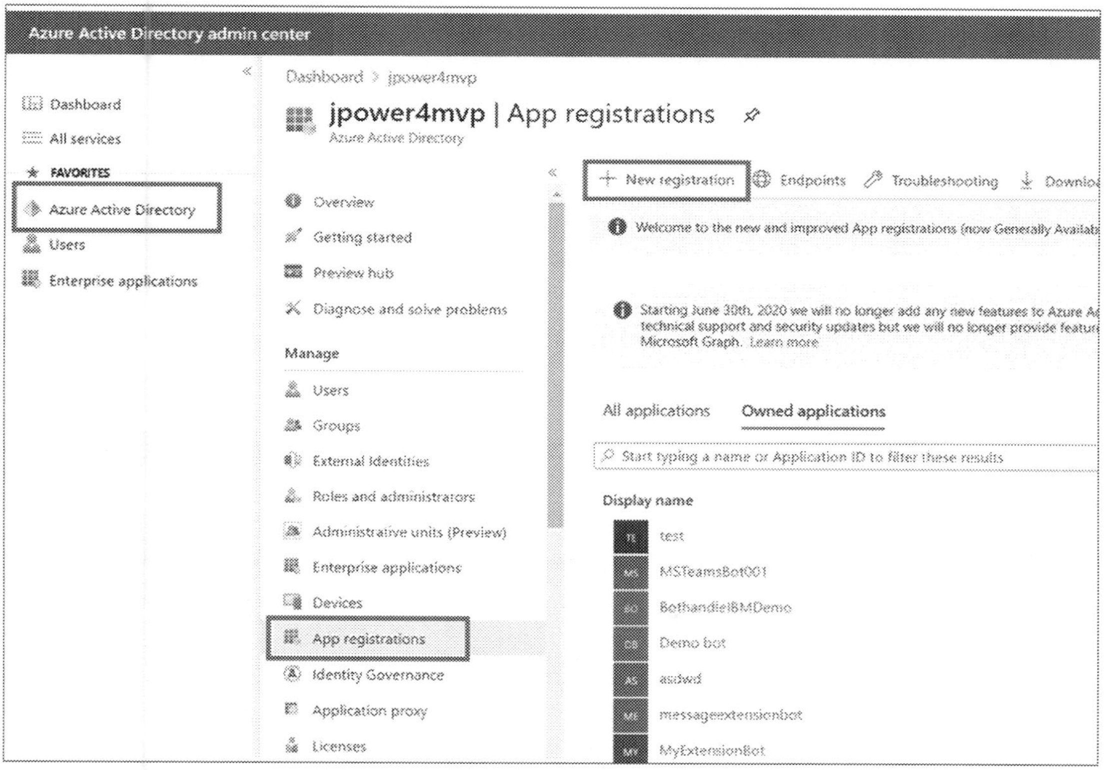

Figure 8-17. *App registrations*

7. Fill in the Details for registering an app:

- Name: TeamsTabApp

- Supported Account type : Accounts in any organizational directory (Any Azure AD directory - Multitenant) and personal Microsoft accounts (e.g., Skype, Xbox)

- Redirect URL for web: *https://REPLACE_NGROKDOMAIN.ngrok. io/auth.html*

- Click 'Register' button to register an application (Figure 8-18)

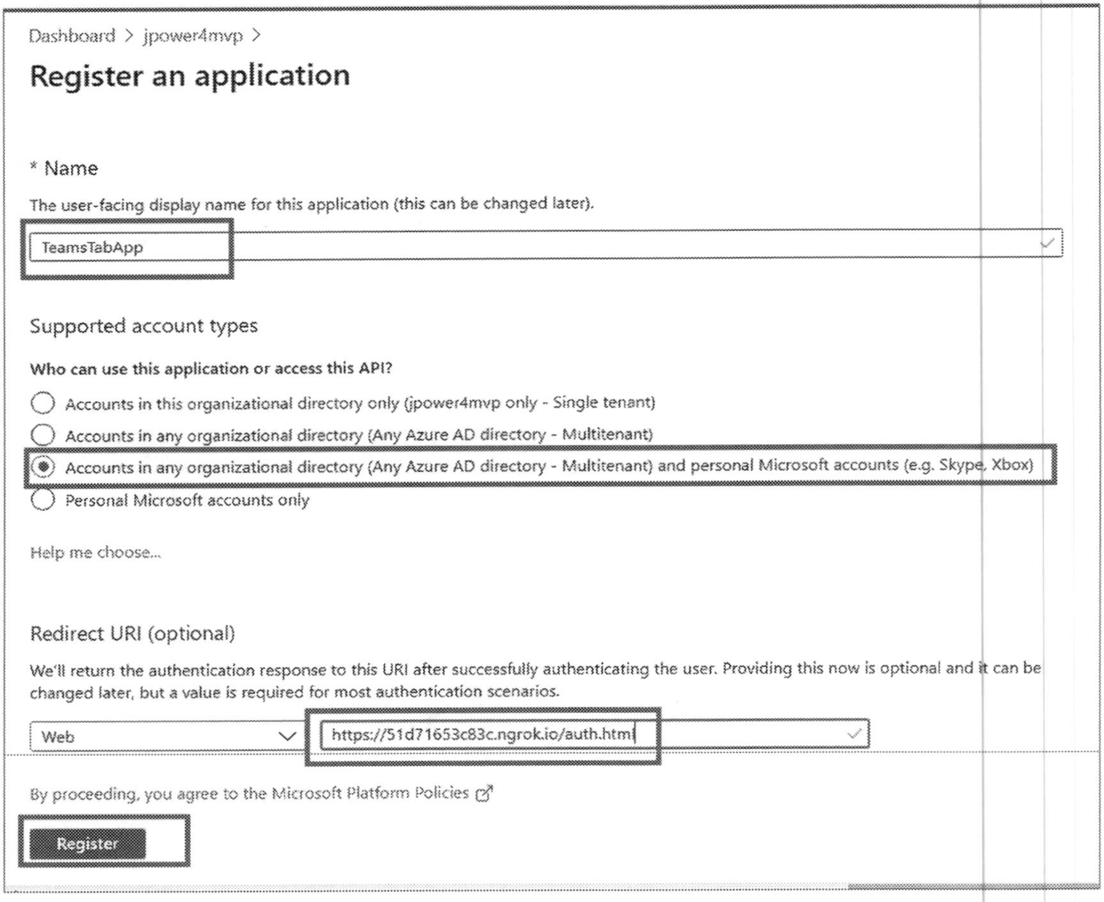

Figure 8-18. *Register an application*

8. Go to the Authentication tab *and* Enable Implicit grant by selecting *Access tokens and ID tokens* (Figure 8-19)

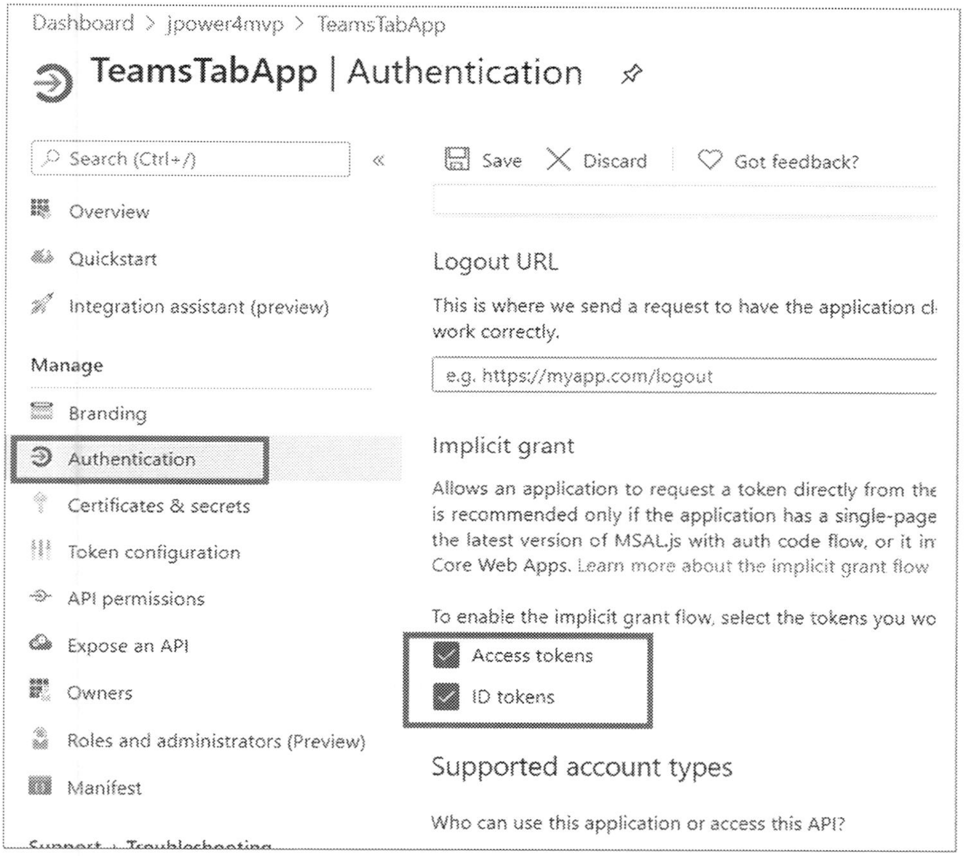

Figure 8-19. *Authentication*

9. Click Save

10. Go to API permissions tab (Figure 8-20), select **Add a permission ➤ Microsoft Graph ➤ Delegated permissions and add permission**

    a. *Calendar.Read*

    b. *Calendar.ReadWrite*

    c. *Directory.AccessAsUser.All*

    d. *Directory.Read.All*

    e. *Directory.ReadWrite.All*

    f. *User.Read*

    g. *User.Read.All*

    h. *User.ReadWrite.All*

    i. *Mail.Read*

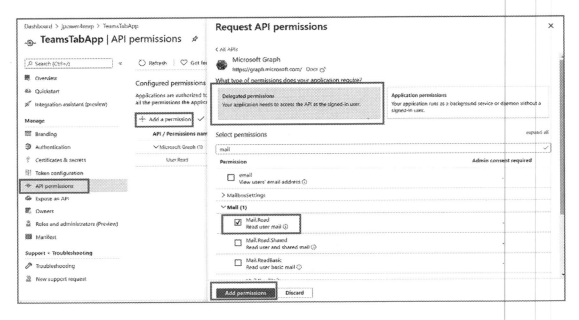

Figure 8-20. *Request API permission*

11. Then, select Grant admin consent (Figure 8-21)

Configured permissions

Applications are authorized to call APIs when they are granted permissions by users/admins as part of the all the permissions the application needs. Learn more about permissions and consent

─ Add a permission   ✓ Grant admin consent for jpower4mvp

API / Permissions name	Type	Description
∨ Microsoft Graph (8)		
Calendars.Read	Delegated	Read user calendars
Calendars.ReadWrite	Delegated	Have full access to user calendars
Directory.Read.All	Delegated	Read directory data
Directory.ReadWrite.All	Delegated	Read and write directory data
Mail.Read	Delegated	Read user mail
User.Read	Delegated	Sign in and read user profile
User.Read.All	Delegated	Read all users' full profiles
User.ReadWrite.All	Delegated	Read and write all users' full profiles

Figure 8-21. *Grant Admin consent*

12.   Go to Overview tab and copy ***Application (client) ID*** (Figure 8-22)

Dashboard > jpower4mvp > TeamsTabApp

🔢 TeamsTabApp 📌

🔍 Search (Ctrl+/) «	🗑 Delete ⊕ Endpoints
🔢 Overview	⋀ Essentials
📖 Quickstart	Display name : TeamsTabApp
🖋 Integration assistant (preview)	Application (client) ID : 3229da43-347e-4fd5-8300-695f6ce1d2a3
Manage	Directory (tenant) ID : f784fbed-7fc7-4c7a-aae9-d2f387b67c5d
🗒 Branding	Object ID : 4eab3b29-5047-4375-a3f6-791770a5da3a
🕙 Authentication	ℹ Starting June 30th, 2020 we will no longer add any new features to Az technical support and security updates but we will no longer provide f

Figure 8-22. *Application client ID*

13. Then go to your project public > index.html, and replace YOUR-
CLIENT-ID with Application (client) ID in mgt-teams-provider >
auth-popup-url (Figure 8-23).

```
EXPLORER                          <> index.html ●
> OPEN EDITORS   1 UNSAVED        public > <> index.html > ⊘ html > ⊘ body > ⊘ mgt-teams-provider
∨ FIRSTGRAPHAPITAB                      lnk rel="stylesheet" href="https://static2.sharepointonline.com/files/fabric/offilce-ui-fab
  > .vscode                    8       itle>Microsoft Teams Tab</title>
  > node_modules               9       >
  ∨ public                    10
    <> auth.html              11
    ★ favicon.ico      U      12       oscript>You need to enable JavaScript to run this app.</noscript>
    <> index.html      U      13       iv id="root"></div>
  ∨ src                       14       cript src="https://unpkg.com/@microsoft/teams-js/dist/MicrosoftTeams.min.js" crossorigin="a
    > components       ●       15       cript src="https://unpkg.com/@microsoft/mgt/dist/bundle/mgt-loader.js"></script>
    JS auth.js                 16       gt-teams-provider client-id="3229da43-347e-4fd5-8300-695f6ce1d2a3" auth-popup-url="https://
    # index.css        U       17       gt-login></mgt-login>
    JS index.js        U       18       gt-person id="with-presence" person-query="me" person-card="hover" view="twoLines" show-pres
                              19       >
                              20
                              21       >
```

Figure 8-23. *update client ID in index file*

Test Your App in Microsoft Teams

It is time to test it:

1. Go to **Microsoft Teams** (`https://teams.microsoft.com`)

2. Go to ... ➤ open **App Studio** (Figure 8-24)

Figure 8-24. *Open App Studio*

3. Select Manifest Editor and select Import an existing app (Figure 8-25)

Figure 8-25. *Import an existing app*

4. Select Development.zip under your project folder ➤ .publish
    (Figure 8-26)

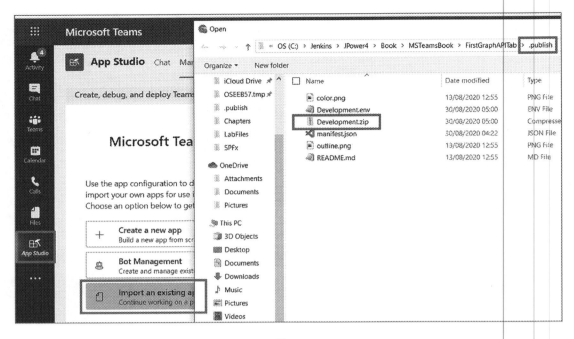

Figure 8-26. *Import Development.zip file*

5. Scroll down and select **Test and distribute**, then click **Install** (Figure 8-27)

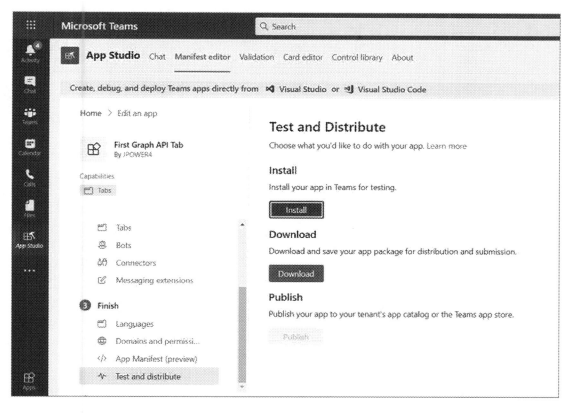

Figure 8-27. *Install the app for testing*

6.   Click the Add button to install the app (Figure 8-28)

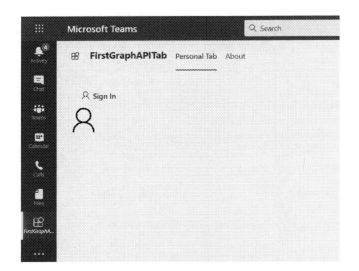

Figure 8-28. *Add the app for testing*

7. Click Sign in for the authentication using an AAD registered app
    (Figure 8-29)

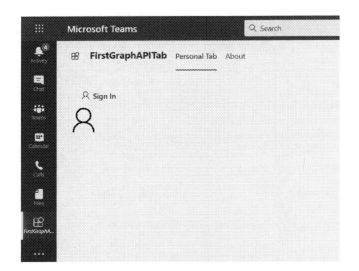

Figure 8-29. *Sign in the app*

8.   Give consent to the AAD registered app you created (Figure 8-30)

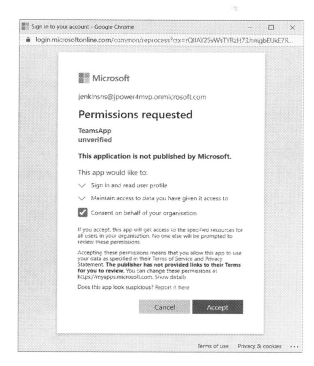

Figure 8-30.   *Give consent to AAD*

Figure 8-31.   *Get User info using Graph API toolkit*

9. Your profile information email and name should appear in your
    tab after the successful authentication (Figure 8-31)

In this exercise, you have learned how to use Microsoft Teams Toolkit for Visual
Studio code with Microsoft Graph API toolkit within Microsoft Teams for a tab app.

Conclusion

In this chapter, you have learned various features of Microsoft Teams Toolkit, Microsoft
Graph API Toolkit, and Graph API with examples that we can be able to use from our
own custom application. Along with this you will start learning different options and
features of Microsoft Teams apps in our upcoming chapters.

CHAPTER 9

Building Teams Apps Using Solution Accelerators

This chapter covers Building Teams Apps using Solution Accelerators, building Teams apps using power apps, power automate integration with teams, App templates, and team mobile platform extensibility. Today, using a low-code approach to building applications instead of writing code in an IDE like Visual Studio, you can actually draw your app like a picture and we take care of generating the code that you need on the back end to make your application actually work. The best part is built apps without writing code and easily adding them as tabs or integrating apps in Teams.

Overview of Solution Accelerators

Every customer is looking for application development and deployment to run more quickly and to upgrade at their own pace while also maintaining full control of solution designs and to tailor already deployed services to meet their needs. Microsoft Teams is the hub for teamwork in Microsoft 365 to enable people to work together and integrate all applications together without redevelopment. That is why solution accelerators are the best solution to reuse the existing application. Today the ways that customers work are changed; all are working remotely and need to quickly access information in minutes.

© Jenkins NS 2021
J. NS, *Building Solutions with Microsoft Teams*, https://doi.org/10.1007/978-1-4842-6476-8_9

Power Platform Overview

Microsoft's Power Platform provides users with the tools needed to create solutions that accelerate business. Microsoft Power Platform is a family of products that delivers innovative business solutions across one seamlessly integrated platform. Power Platform provides a graphical user interface that employs drag-and-drop components and model-driven logic (as opposed to traditional computer programming) that enables everyday users to quickly create apps with little to no coding required (also known as a low-code interface). At the same time, it also provides professional developers with a robust set of tools for creating advanced custom apps.

The business applications and process automations enabled by Power Platform can quickly become part of an organization's application ecosystem. For this reason, it is important that enterprise administrators understand what Power Platform is and how its citizen developers are leveraging its capabilities to connect to the services and data that are part of the managed enterprise environment.

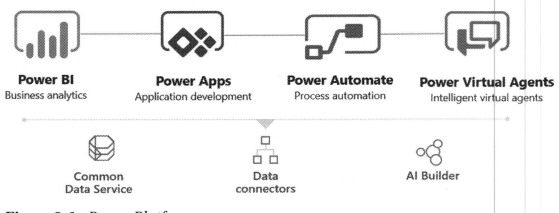

Figure 9-1. *Power Platform*

Power Platform family contains four key products (refer to Figure 9-1):

1. Power BI

2. Power Apps

3. Power Automate

4. Power Virtual Agents

Power Apps

Microsoft PowerApps is a powerful new way to turn business expertise into custom applications. With PowerApps you can quickly and easily create apps without writing a single line of code. PowerApps has an intuitive design interface to guide you the whole way as you create apps for your team or business, and your app can integrate with data you already have or instead use our line of business application. Power Apps is a cloud-based suite of apps, services, connectors, and a data platform that provides organizations with a rapid application development environment to build custom apps that address their business needs. By employing Power Apps, users can quickly build custom business apps that connect to business data stored in the underlying, built-in data platform (known as the Common Data Service) or in various online and on-premises data sources (such as SharePoint, Excel, Office 365, Dynamics 365, SQL Server, and so on).

Power Automate

Power Automate is a service that helps users create automated workflows for their application and services and then can be integrated with Microsoft Teams working together.

Power BI (Business Intelligence)

Power BI is a visualization tool to help you create stunning reports and dashboards to help you gain insights into your business and make better business decisions. Also, you integrate Power BI reports as tabs or apps in Microsoft Teams to enable working together and making good decisions.

Power Virtual Agents

Power Virtual Agents enable us to create a chatbot easily: that is, easily build powerful conversion bots through a simple and easy graphical interface and integrate the conversation bots to your Microsoft Teams channel.

PowerApps Integration

Every PowerApps Is a Teams App

We have three options to make your PowerApps a Teams App:

- Option 1: Add as a channel tab

- Option 2: Embed an app in Teams

- Option 3: Upload to the tenant app Catalog, and provision as a personal app using setup policies

Benefits

PowerApps are available in Teams where critical work and collaboration already happen, so IT admins can distribute PowerApps in a scalable manner by publishing them to the tenant app Catalog in Teams and the frontline workers can access PowerApps in Teams mobile.

While we have a way to go, there are great examples of how customers are running their businesses with PowerApps loaded in Teams – let's just share a few here.

Education: Tacoma Public Schools

An assistant principal at the Tacoma School District – with ZERO technical experience! – has built power apps for teachers to track student reading comprehension and provide much more helpful recommendations. Figure 9-2 references this customer experience.

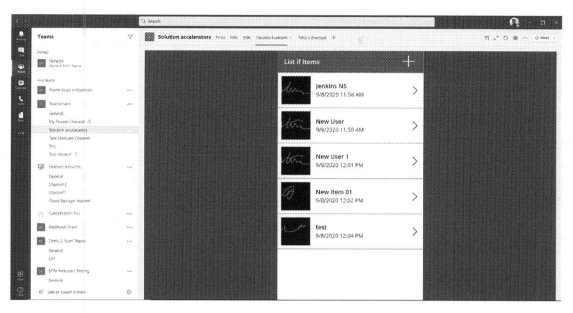

Figure 9-2. *Tacoma public schools*

Telecommunications: Telstra

Telstra, the Australian telecom provider, has built tools to empower their field technicians to work more effectively, like accessing knowledge documents, submitting issues to leadership, and better documenting damage claims. Figure 9-3 references this for implementation

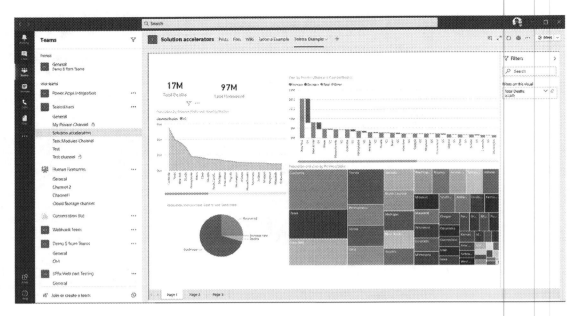

Figure 9-3. *Telstra Communication*

Not for Profit: American Red Cross

The American Red Cross has digitized their supply chain, allowing for better management and tracking of vital resources. Figure 9-4 references this for implementation.

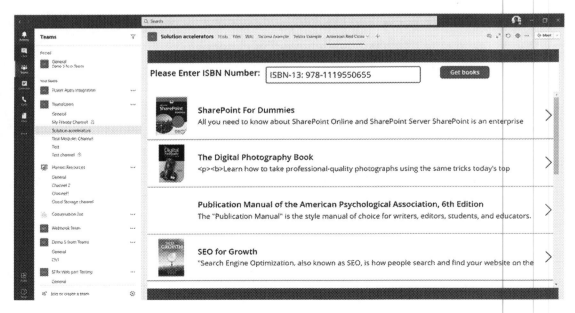

Figure 9-4. *American Red Cross*

Exercise 1 –Add a PowerApps App as a Channel App

These are the steps involved to add PowerApps app as a channel tab:

1. Create a data source using SharePoint

    a. Create SharePoint list 'UserInfo' with Name, Photo, description (Figure 9-5)

    b. Then add a few records

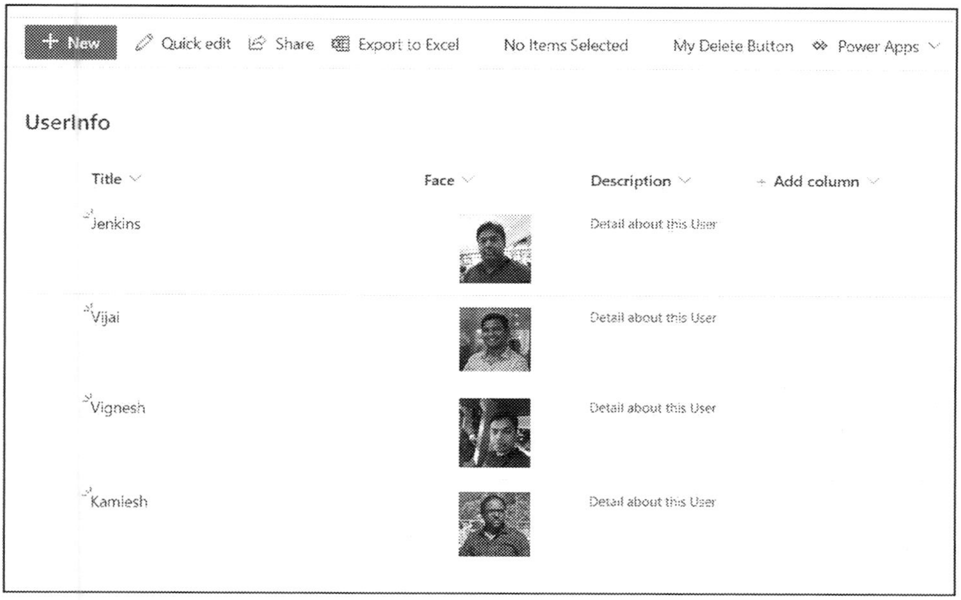

Figure 9-5. *SharePoint List*

2. Create a Canvas app in Power Apps (`https://powerapps. microsoft.com`) (Figure 9-6):

    - Go to `https://powerapps.microsoft.com`

    - Sign in

    - Click Create ➤ Select Canvas app from blank

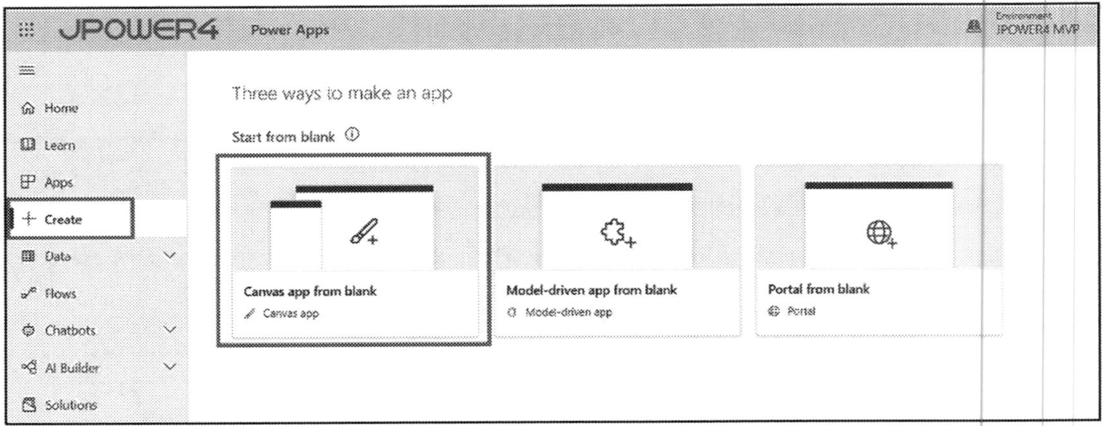

Figure 9-6. *Create Power Apps*

- Enter App Name

- Select Tablet Format

- Click Create button to create an App (Figure 9-7)

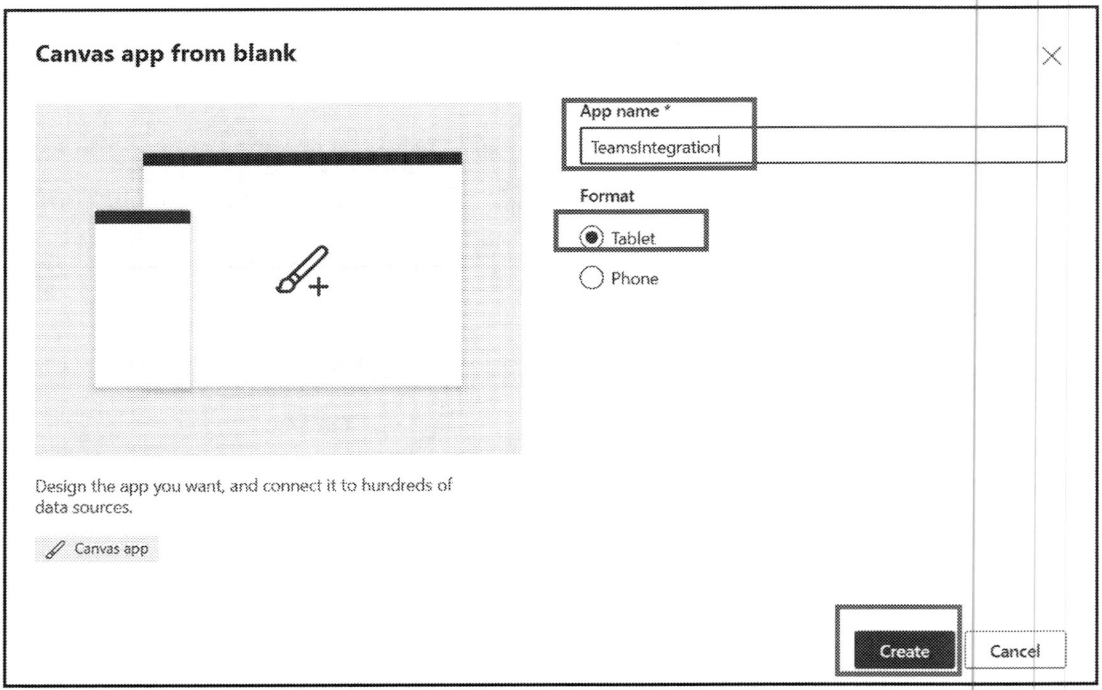

Figure 9-7. *Canvas App from blank*

- Add a Header

- Add a Vertical Gallery and select data source as SharePoint list 'UserInfo'

- Then add Display Form and select data source as SharePoint list 'UserInfo'

- Add Gallery1.Selected in Display form Item property (Figure 9-8)

Figure 9-8. *Design Canvas App*

- Save and Publish the app

3. Add the Power Apps to Teams as tab (Figure 9-9)

- Go to Teams (`https://teams.microsoft.com`)

- Select Teams and go to your teams and select the channel

- Click + in the channel

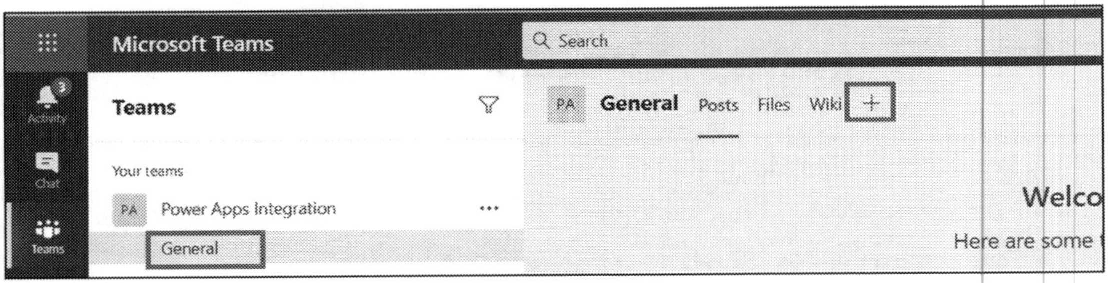

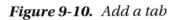

Figure 9-9. *Add tab in Channel*

- Search Power and Select PowerApps (Figure 9-10)

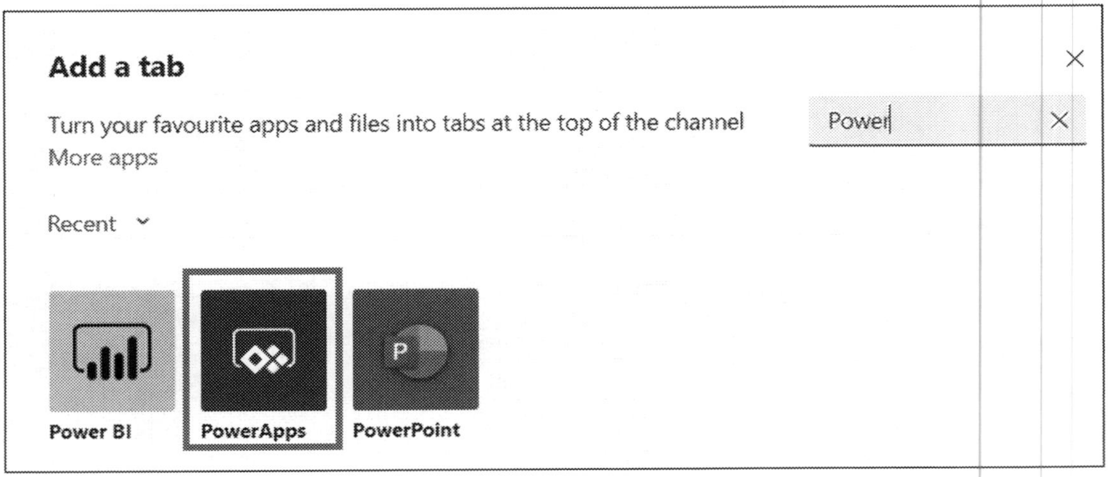

Add a tab   ✕

Turn your favourite apps and files into tabs at the top of the channel   Power   ✕
More apps

Recent ∨

Power BI   PowerApps   PowerPoint

Figure 9-10. *Add a tab*

- Click Add button to add Power Apps to your channel
- Select the 'TeamsIntegration' App (Figure 9-11)

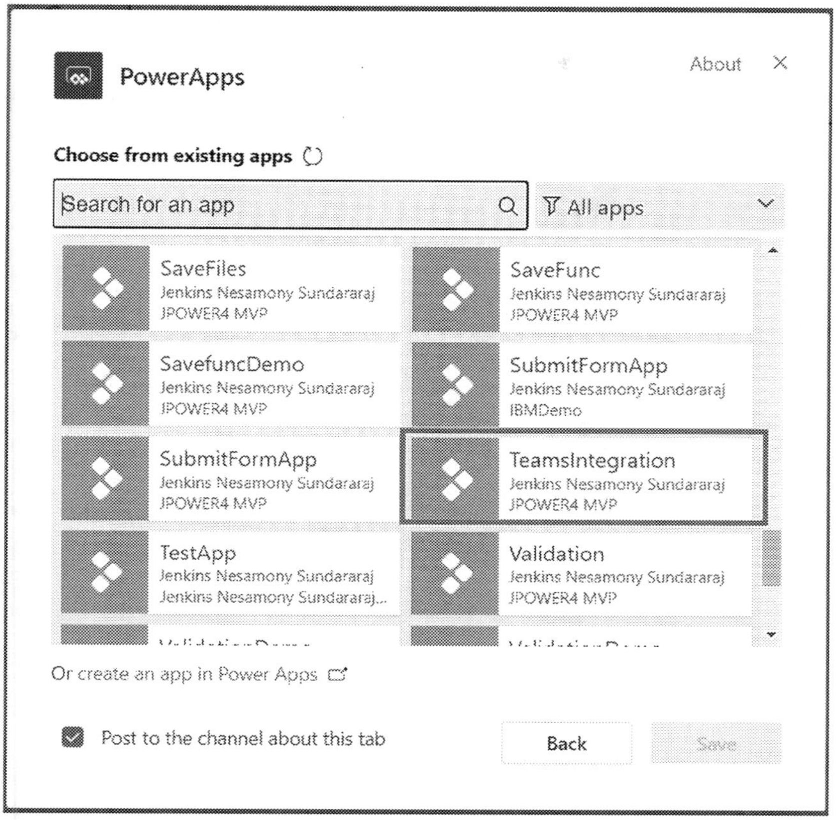

Figure 9-11. *Choose from existing app*

- Click Save to add the Power Apps as a tab (Figure 9-12)

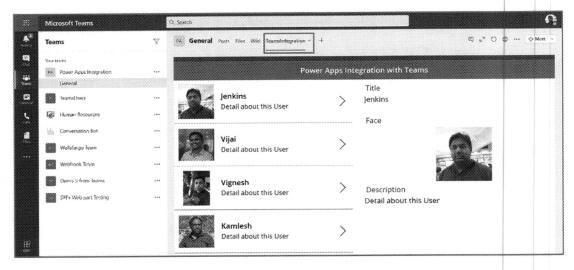

Figure 9-12. *Added the PowerApps in Teams tab*

In this exercise, you have learned how to use Integrate Power Apps as Teams within Microsoft Teams for a tab app.

Exercise 2 –PowerApps App Embed an App in Teams

You can share an app you have created by embedding it directly into Microsoft Teams. When completed, users can select + to add your app to any of your team channels or conversations in the team you are in. The app appears as a tile under Tabs for your team. Also, an admin can upload the app so it shows up for all teams in your tenant under the All tabs section.

Download the App

Let's get started.

- Sign in to https://powerapps.microsoft.com, and then select Apps in the menu (Figure 9-13).

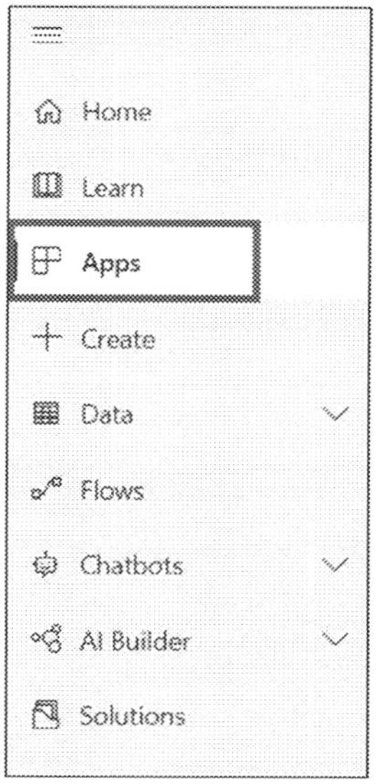

Figure 9-13. *PowerApps Apps list*

- Select More actions (...) for the app you want to share in Teams, and then select Add to Teams (Figure 9-14).

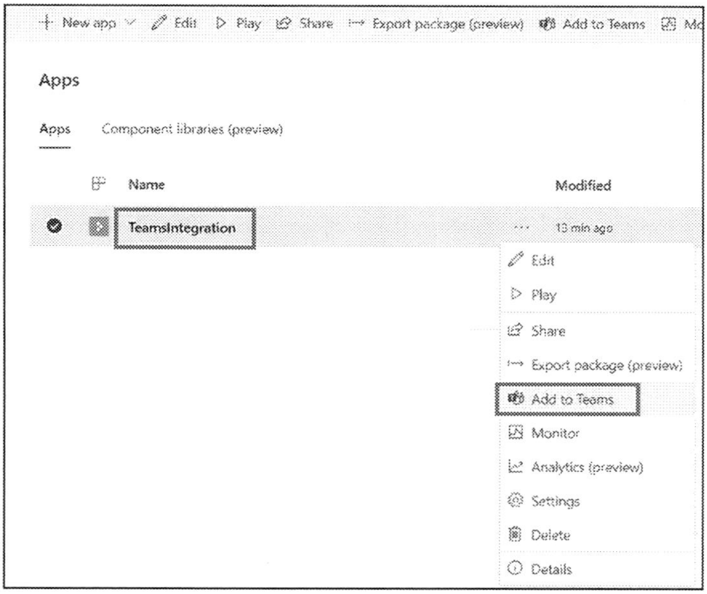

Figure 9-14. *Select the PowerApps Apps*

- In the Add to Teams panel, select **Download**. Power Apps will then generate your Teams manifest file using the app description and logo you've already set in your app (Figure 9-15).

Figure 9-15. *Download the app*

Add the App as a Personal App

Now we need to add it.

- To add the app as a personal app or as a tab to any channel or conversation, select **Apps** in the left navigation and then select **Upload a custom app** (Figure 9-16).

Figure 9-16. *Upload a custom app*

- Upload the downloaded zip file

- Select Add to add the app as a **personal app or select Add to team to add** the app as a tab within an existing channel or conversation.

In this exercise, you have learned how to use Power Apps App as a Teams App (i.e., embed the app in Teams) within Microsoft Teams for a tab app.

Power Automate Integration

Power Automate is a service that helps users create automated workflows between their favorite apps and services for the purpose of synchronizing files, ending notifications, collecting data, and more. Workflows, which are referred to simply as flows in Power Automate, consist of triggering events, conditions, and actions.

A flow is started when a triggering event occurs. A trigger can include things like a record being created, a scheduled activity occurring, or even button clicks from the Power Automate mobile application. Once a flow is triggered, the workflow logic checks the conditions defined in the flow, and for any condition that is true, the actions that are associated with the condition are executed.

This creates flows that automate repetitive work tasks with Power Automate - and trigger right from your Microsoft Teams data.

Exercise 3 – Power Automate Integration with Teams

Follow these steps to install the Power Automate app in Microsoft Teams.

- Sign into Microsoft Teams.

- Tap the **Apps** icon at the lower left of the Teams navigation bar (Figure 9-17).

Figure 9-17. *Select Teams Apps*

- Search **flow** (Figure 9-18).

- Select the **Flow** app.

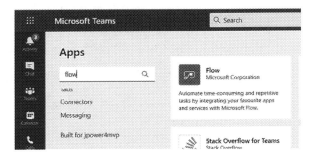

Figure 9-18. *Search flow*

- Select and Click **Add ➤ Add to team** button to Install (Figure 9-19).

- Power Automate is now installed.

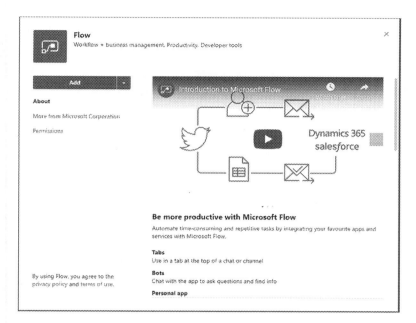

Figure 9-19. *Add flow app*

- Select the Team and Channel (Figure 9-20).

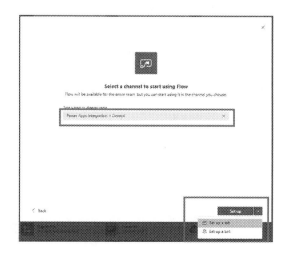

Figure 9-20. *Set up flow app*

- Click Set up a tab or Set up a bot (Figure 9-21).

- I have selected Set up a tab.

- Now you can create a flow from Teams.

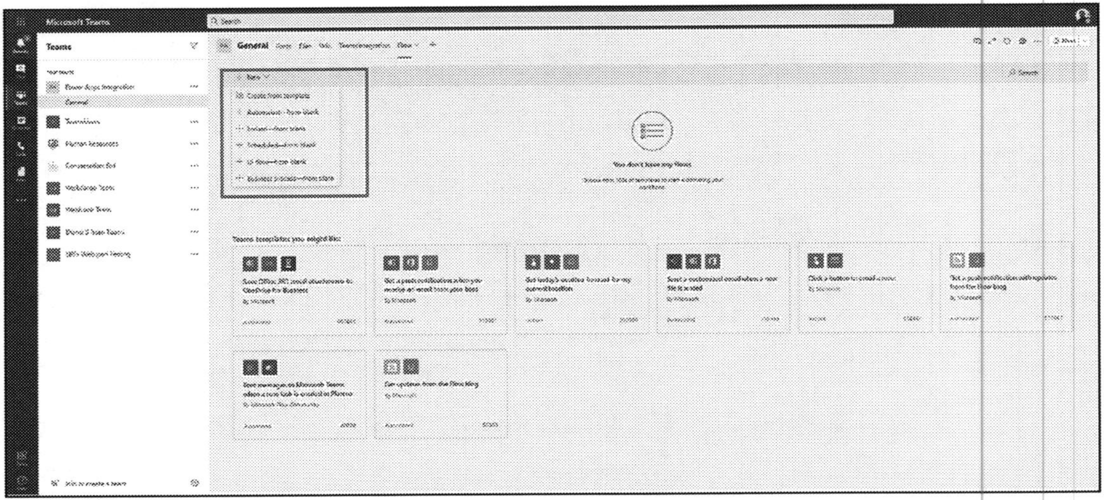

Figure 9-21. *Set up flow app as tab*

Also, you can set up as bot and access from the conversation.

- Go to (…) in the Teams Menu (Figure 9-22)

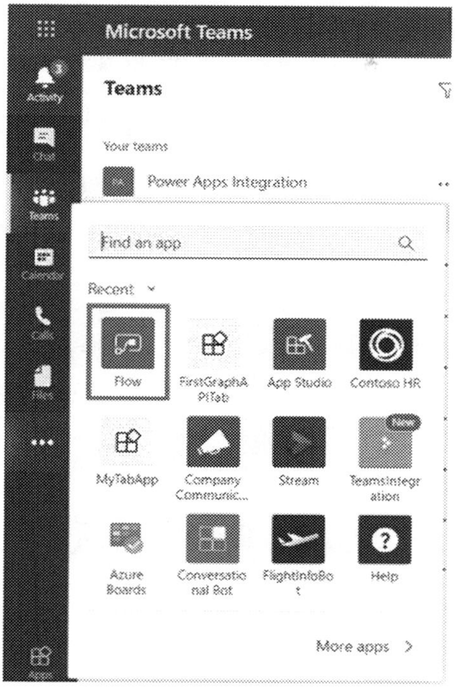

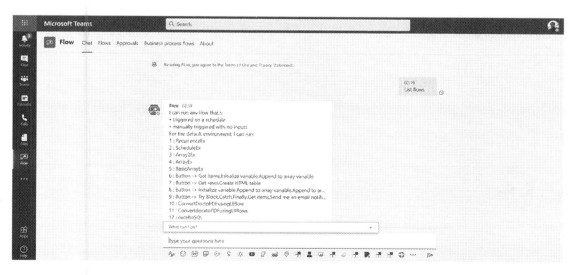

Figure 9-22. *Add flow as bot*

- Select list flows

- It displays all my flows (Figure 9-23)

Figure 9-23. *Set up flow app as bot*

App Templates for Teams Apps

App templates are production-ready apps for Microsoft Teams that are developed by community members and published by Microsoft. This App's templates are open source and available in GitHub. All app templates contain detailed deployment instructions with screenshots. Also, Microsoft tested these apps and published them, so you can deploy them directly to your organization tenant or alter the source code based on your line of business. These app templates are very useful for most of your daily activities for your team. You are a developer or IT pro no matter what-you can deploy and use this app without any help from Microsoft or Community members.

What Are App Templates?

Today we have 30+ app templates available provided by Microsoft, that are production-ready apps to deploy in your tenant. All these apps solve most of the real-world generic problems. No need to spend extra money for your apps. They come with functionality documentation, deployment documentation, and complete source code. Any time you want to, you can alter the source code based your LOB (Figure 9-24).

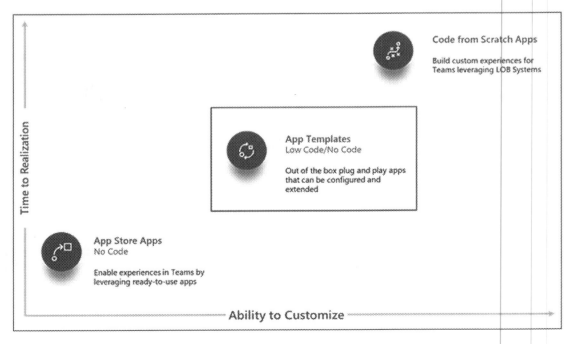

Figure 9-24. App template ability to customize

Key Benefits

Plug and play experience

The app templates come with deployment scripts with detailed documentation, but it does not require the developer use it to deploy the apps.

Production-ready code

All app templates follow best practices, security, compliance, and standard governance. Also, Microsoft tested the app template submitted by the community before published.

Customizable and extensible

They provide the entire code to you, that is, open source. Both code and deployment scripts are customizable and extend based on your line of busines.

Detailed documentation and support

The app templates are included with end-to-end documentation with screenshots and solution architecture, deployment scripts, and configuration steps. If you find any issues, you can raise an issue on GitHub. Microsoft and community members can help.

The APPS Templates

As of September 2020, we have 30+ App Templates available, and they are increasing daily based on community submissions. Also the community adds new features in the same app template, so you can easily upgrade it if those features fit with your organization.

Production-ready app templates Go to `https://aka.ms/teamsapptemplates`. It contains an overview of all available app templates, along with links to GitHub repos (Figure 9-25).

Associate Insights
Attendance
Book-a-room
Celebrations
Company Communicator
Contact Group Lookup ☆
CrowdSourcer
Custom Stickers
E-Prescriptions ☆
Expert Finder
FAQ Plus
Goal Tracker ☆
Great Ideas ☆
Group Activities
Grow Your Skills ☆
HR Support
Icebreaker
Incentives
Incident Reporter ☆
Open Badges
Quick Responses
Remote Support ☆
Request-a-team ☆
Scrums for Channels ☆
Scrums for Group Chat ☆
Share Now ☆
SharePoint List Search
Staff Check-ins ☆
Visitor Management ☆
Workplace Awards ☆

Figure 9-25. *List of App templates*

How to Deploy App Templates?

Deploying App templates are very easy and not required by any developers. You just need to follow the documentation. First set up the prerequisites and configuration, and then one-click deployment is available. To know more about apps deployment, read the documented instructions and architecture diagram (Figure 9-26).

Documentation | Deployment guide | Architecture

Figure 9-26. *Deploy App Templates*

FAQs?

1. Are these apps secure?

    The app templates conform to recommended best practices around security and infrastructure, and all community-submitted changes to them are reviewed to ensure continued conformance.

2. What would it take to take these apps and deploy them in my tenant?

    All App Templates come with detailed deployment instructions and take minutes to set up. You don't require a developer to deploy and use these app templates out of the box.

3. Can everyone deploy these app templates?

    Typically, organizations have their own review processes to upload an app to their internal catalog. Anyone with these permissions can deploy these apps.

4. Do these apps cost anything?

    These app templates are free to use as they are open sourced. They may incur Azure consumption charges but there are free trials available.

License

This app template is provided under the MIT License terms. In addition to these terms, by using this app template you agree to the following:

- You are responsible for internal or external privacy and security regulations.

- You are responsible for all data-related incidents.

- Microsoft does not grant you rights to use any Microsoft names, logos, or trademarks.

- Use of this template does not guarantee acceptance of your app to the Teams app store.

Teams Mobile Platform Extensibility

The Teams platform was designed from the beginning to allow the features of external services to appear as if they were native features of Teams, including Microsoft services and those from third parties. In the year 2019 Microsoft released the ability for organizations to have their own private app catalogs for publishing LOB apps. As you will hear more about later, we have a rich selection of industry vertical solutions that are built on the Teams platform (Figure 9-27).

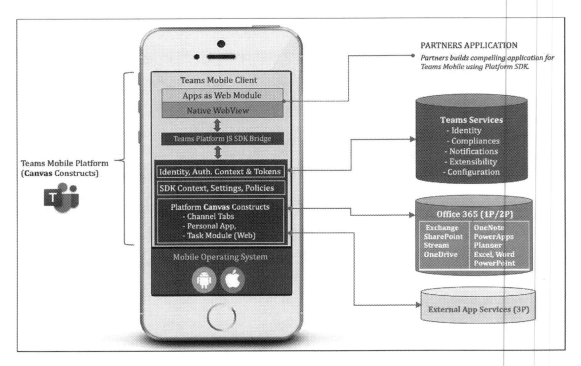

Figure 9-27. *Mobile Platform [REF – MSDN]*

The Teams platform is composed of a set of distinct capabilities classified into a 2 x 2 grid based on how the user interacts: either in a personal or group context, or in a conversation surface or a dedicated canvas owned by the external service.

Connectors are just a way to post a card to a conversation when something happens in an external system.

Icebreaker Bot

An Icebreaker bot allows users in a group to connect and network with other members. It is available in Teams app templates: `https://docs.microsoft.com/en-us/microsoftteams/platform/samples/app-templates#icebreaker`. It also makes use of other functionality like 'Deep link to meeting schedule' or 'Deep link to chats'. See Figure 9-28.

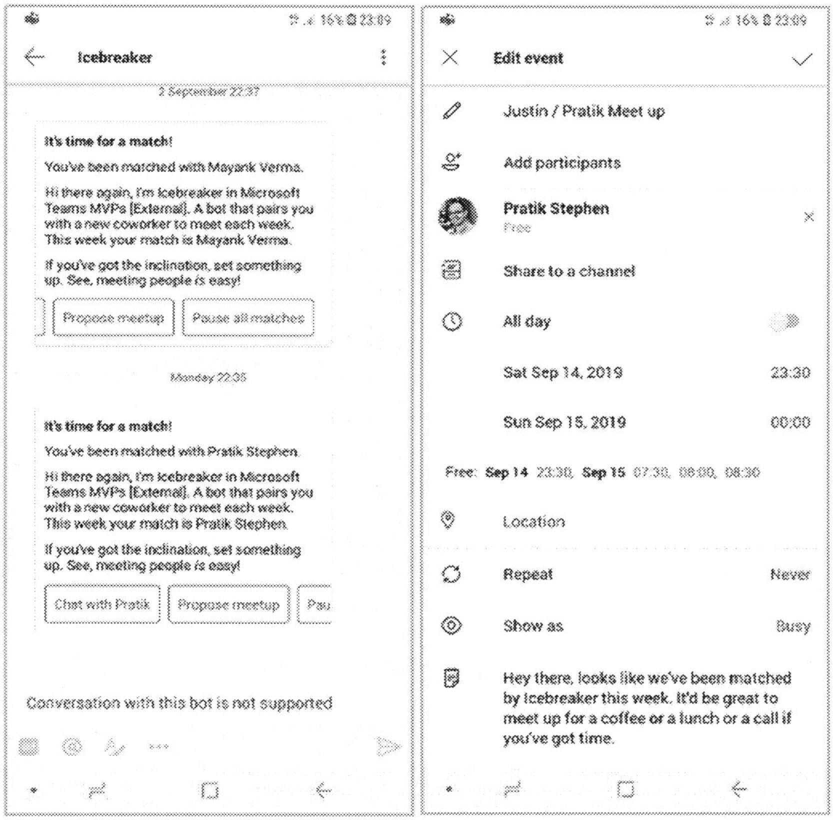

Figure 9-28. *IceBreaker App Mobile view [REF – MSDN]*

Praise Messaging Extension

The Praise Messaging Extension app is for for sending praise to people and it is available in a mobile platform. You can make people happier and more productive by giving them recognition for their efforts. This app is fully supported in the Teams Mobile Platform (Figure 9-29).

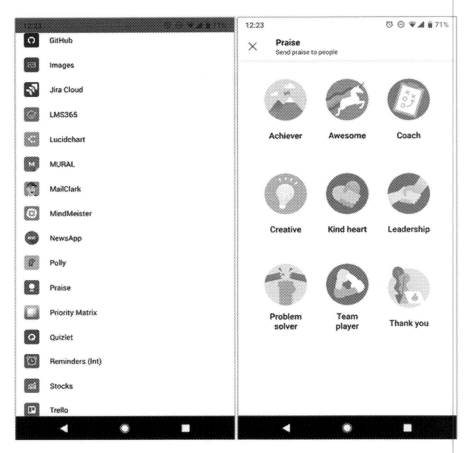

Figure 9-29. *Praise Messaging Extension [REF – MSDN]*

Conclusion

In this chapter, you have learned various features of Microsoft Teams Integration with App templates, Mobile Apps, and Power Platform with examples, and now we can use them for our own applications. Along with this you will start learning about different options and features of Microsoft Teams apps in our upcoming chapters.

CHAPTER 10

SharePoint and Teams: Better Together

In this chapter we are going to look at how we can build Microsoft Teams customizations using the SharePoint Framework. We will understand Microsoft Teams' development and the benefits of using the SharePoint Framework to extend Microsoft Teams. Next we will learn how to surface SharePoint Framework customizations in Microsoft Teams. Microsoft teams provides many different extensibility options for creating a team's app, which could consist of a custom tab. As you learned from previous chapters, it could also leverage bots' messaging extensions and connectors, or you can also build a custom bot that would reply and receive messages from a user to have a nice little interaction experience with your users.

What Is SharePoint Framework?

The SharePoint Framework (SPFx) is a fully supported client-side SharePoint client web part or extension or library. With SharePoint Framework, we can use SharePoint lists and libraries and extend the SPFx web part to Microsoft Teams, Microsoft Outlook web apps, and other Microsoft 365 apps. You can use modern toolchain web technologies and tools based on your preferred JavaScript libraries. Also, all SharePoint Framework web parts are responsive and mobile ready.

Surfacing SharePoint Framework to Teams

Extend SharePoint Framework web parts to Microsoft Teams without any code change. You can leverage the existing knowledge and reuse the same line of business. If already developed for SharePoint and you want to use the same functionality into Teams, then you can add an SPFx web part as a tab in Microsoft Teams.

© Jenkins NS 2021
J. NS, *Building Solutions with Microsoft Teams*, https://doi.org/10.1007/978-1-4842-6476-8_10

Bring SPFx Solutions into Teams Tab

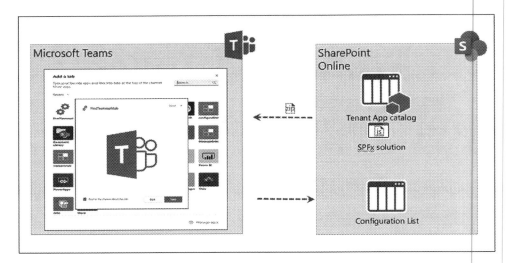

Figure 10-1. *Bring SPFx Solutions into Teams Tab*

Figure 10-1 represents the SPFx solutions to Teams tab, and here are the details:

- First SPFx Teams solutions are deployed to Office 365 tenants using tenant app catalog.

- You have two options: one is to Sync the web part to Teams or create a custom manifest file and deploy in Teams as Apps.

- Then user selects the SPFx application like any other tab in MS Teams "Add a tab" experience.

- Configuration panel is displayed and, once saved, information is stored in the SharePoint Online site connected to the group.

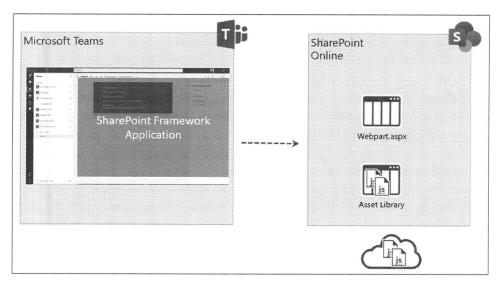

Figure 10-2. *Bring SPFx Solutions into Teams Tab*

Figure 10-2 represents the SPFx web part loads in theTeams tab, and here are the details:

- While loading, SPFx components render in a dedicated _layout page which is iFramed in Teams.

- Teams and SharePoint site context are available to the developer, and you can validate where the webpart loading is and whether it is SharePoint or Teams.

- Code is loaded from the SharePoint asset library where it was deployed at the time the package was uploaded.

- Also, code can run in different CDN locations like Azure, SharePoint Library, etc., based on where you deployed the code.

Common Needs

Why would you need a SharePoint Framework web part to extend to Teams? Here we will discuss the based end user or IT Admin or developer perfective.

End User

The information the team cares about should be available regardless of the tool/workload and make it possible to bridge team collaboration and external communication.

IT Administrator

It can reduce the number of places and ways to manage and deploy solutions to end users.

Developers

They can reach multiple workloads with a single solution and reduce the number of developer concepts and experiences.

Solution

Figure 10-3. *Surface SPFx and Teams Solution*

For this, Microsoft enables users to collaborate around the same content in SharePoint and Teams and centralized Admin experience and tools, including LOB app distribution and common developer frameworks for building solutions targeting both SharePoint and Teams experiences. See Figure 10-3.

SharePoint Framework Targeting Teams Tabs

- SPFX is the standard way for Enterprise Devs and SIs to Develop "O365-hosted" solutions across SharePoint and Teams.

- Developers will be able to "target" the environments in the 'manifest.json'.

- Single point of governance in the App Catalog.

- Standard "features" of SPFx

  - Toolchain

  - Authentication

  - SP, Graph, and Web API Access

  - CDN hosting

  - Config experience

  - Solution hosting

- Component can get the right application context.

Catalog Synchronization

Build your app using familiar technology and deploy and host it in the app Catalog and sync to teams by one-click synchronization:

- Development happens in a familiar environment for SPFx developers:

  - Yeoman

  - NPM

  - Visual Studio Code

- Once the package is created, Admins deploy it in the SharePoint Tenant App Catalog.

- "Sync to Teams" option available to sync SPFx components are marked to work in Teams in the Teams LOB Catalog.

  - Teams Manifest is created on the fly at that point with all the tenant-specific information.

Why Build for Microsoft Teams Using SharePoint Framework?

There are two main benefits for using the SharePoint Framework to build for Microsoft Teams:

- Single platform for hosted experience
- Automatic solution hosting

Single Platform for Hosted Experiences

Build your solution to run across Teams, SharePoint, Outlook and all of Office's applications. See Figure 10-4.

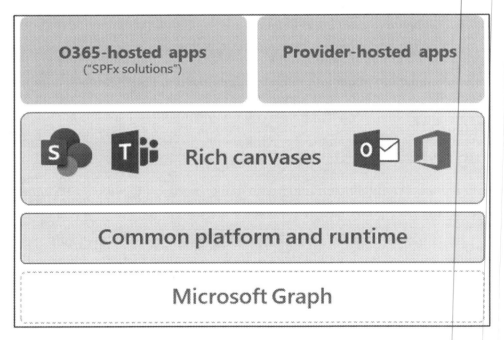

Figure 10-4. *Single platform for hosted experiences*

Automatic Solution Hosting

When you build apps for Microsoft Teams, you need to host the app in Azure or the app store. We need extra infrastructure and require extra money budgeted for this. If you have already developed a same functionality SPFX web part using your favorite technologies, then we are not required to develop and deploy for Microsoft Teams. Additionally, if you have Office 365 CDN enabled, assets for your Teams tabs and personal apps will be served from the CDN offering your users a significantly better experience without any extra cost or configuration. It will also not require any extra cost for development.

Authentication

Microsoft Teams solutions require you to connect any APIs and authenticate them before using them. When you build your Microsoft Teams application yourself, you need to ensure all APIs are securely connected. But in the SharePoint Framework, it has already integrated with managing API permission access in the SharePoint Admin center. It contains ready-to-use libraries for communicating with the Microsoft Graph and other APIs. Using these classes, you can access the APIs without worrying about authentication. Here's how it will happen:

- Silent authentication between Teams rich client and SharePoint

  - Teams provides the token client side to SharePoint.

  - It converts it to a cookie server side.

  - The _layout system page that hosts the SPFx solution renders this: no additional auth required.

  - Full access to SharePoint REST APIs.

- If the component requires you to access Graph/Web APIs:

  - You get the auth token from the client: no permissions there, we use it as a bootstrap token.

  - SPFx client libraries understand that the call is coming from a Teams rich client environment.

  - Bootstrap token is sent to AAD using the "on behalf of" flow to obtain an access token for the requested resource in exchange for the bootstrap token.

  - AAD returns the access token to SPO. The component can now execute the Web API call.

Building Microsoft Teams Tabs Using SharePoint Framework

From SharePoint Framework v1.8, you can build tabs for Microsoft Teams with the SharePoint Framework tooling and use SharePoint as a host for your solutions. But you need to deploy manifest.json file manually. As part of the SharePoint Framework v1.10, you can also publish your solution as a Microsoft Teams personal app and sync automatically.

The benefits of using the SharePoint Framework as the platform for your Microsoft Teams tabs include the following:

- Development platform is like SharePoint Framework web parts and does not require a separate development environment.

- All SharePoint Framework web parts can be synced and added as a tab or personal app in Microsoft Teams.

- Also controls Teams/SPFx context and scope to expose a custom tab as a web part and tab in your tenant using this.context.sdks. microsoftTeams to get Teams context.

- Your Teams tab will be executed in the context of the underlying SharePoint site behind the specific team. This means that you can take advantage of any SharePoint-specific APIs or functionalities in your web part, that is, from your tab.

Development Process

From SharePoint Framework 1.8 or later versions, you can start developing Microsoft Teams tabs. The high-level steps to get started are as follows:

- Create a SharePoint Framework solution with a client-side web part.

- Add "**TeamsTab**" to the **supportedHosts** property of the webpart manifest file to use it as a tab in a channel:

```
"supportedHosts": ["SharePointWebPart", "TeamsTab"],
```

- Add "TeamsPersonalApp" to the supportedHosts property of the webpart manifest to use it as a personal app:

```
"supportedHosts": ["SharePointWebPart", "TeamsPersonalApp"],
```

- Deploy the web part using tenant-scoped deployment option to your SharePoint app catalog. Then it is available for all Teams.

- Activate the SharePoint Framework solution, which you deployed, and select **Sync to Teams** button in the App Catalog.

Enable Upload Custom Apps

As part of the Developer of SharePoint Framework Teams Tabs, you will need to explicitly deploy the Microsoft Teams app to a team in Microsoft Team. Your tenant will also need to support side loading of custom apps for the Microsoft Teams, so that you can deploy the app to a specific team and use it.

- Go to `https://admin.teams.microsoft.com`

- Select Teams apps

- Then select Setup policy

- Add new Setup policies

- Enable 'Upload custom apps'

- Manage users (Figure 10-5)

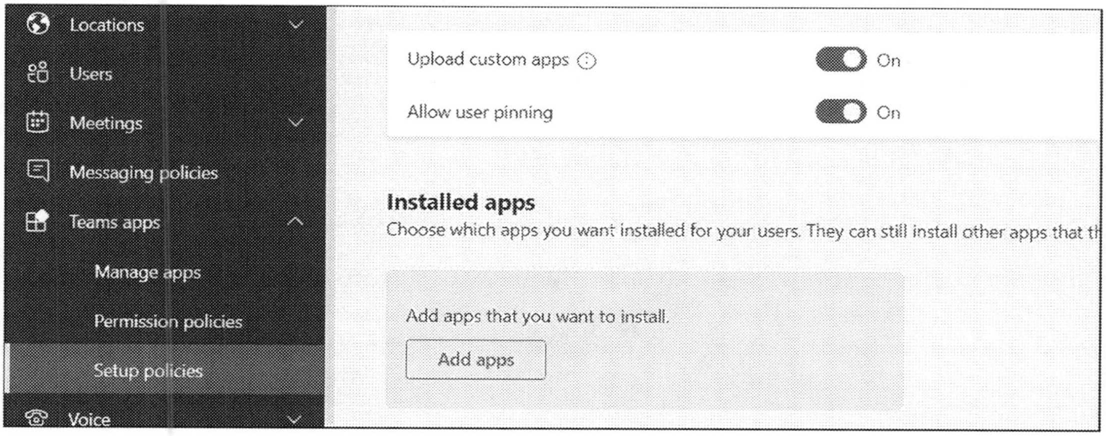

Figure 10-5. *Enable upload custom apps*

Deployment Options

There are two options to deploy the Microsoft Teams tab or as a personal app from the SharePoint Framework to Microsoft Team. As both SharePoint and Microsoft Teams have their own app catalogs, deployment requires operations on both services. Visibility of the new functionality can be controlled by the deployment steps taken.

- Sync with Teams from Tenant
- Manual Deployment

Tenant Deployment

You can use the **Sync with Teams** button in the App Catalog ribbon that will automatically create the Microsoft Teams app manifest and app package and install it in the Microsoft Teams store. This will make your solution available for all users in your tenant and Microsoft Teams 'teams'. Then you can add the web part as a tab from the channel.

Manual Deployment

There is a manual way to deploy your solution, which will, for instance, allow you to make a solution available only to one specific team in your tenant. See the Create Microsoft Teams manifest manually for a web part and deploy it to Microsoft Teams for details on how to create the manifest: `https://docs.microsoft.com/en-us/sharepoint/dev/spfx/web-parts/guidance/creating-team-manifest-manually-for-webpart`

- Build your SharePoint Framework solution the standard way:

  ```
  gulp bundle --ship
  gulp package-solution --ship
  ```

- You will be able to see two image files in the './teams' folder.

- Create a custom manifest file for Teams, and refer to the url below:

  - `https://docs.microsoft.com/en-us/sharepoint/dev/spfx/web-parts/guidance/creating-team-manifest-manually-for-webpart`

- Create Microsoft Teams manifest manually for a web part and deploy it from Microsoft Teams to this folder. This file should be named '*manifest.json', and you can add a webpart component ID to refer to from the teams tab.

- After you added the manifest to the './teams' folder, zip the two image files and manifest.json together to into a zip file. This means that the zip file should only contain the manifest.json and the two images.

- You can deploy this directly to Microsoft Teams as an app.

- Also deploy the code in Microsoft 365 CDN or your preferred CDN.

Detecting if Web Part Is in Teams Context

The context in a web part contains a reference to the Teams JavaScript SDK object so that you can easily get access on the Teams context when your web part is rendered as a tab.

```
this.context.sdks.microsoftTeams
```

- The property **this.context.microsoftTeams** has been deprecated in the SharePoint Framework v1.10 release and Microsoft introduced this.context.sdks.microsoftTeams from SPFx v1.10

- You should use **this.context.sdks.microsoftTeams** for all solutions created with the **SharePoint Framework v1.10 and later**.

Exercise – Create an SPFx Web Part and Distribute to Teams

Before starting the exercise, verify your environment for SharePoint Framework Development.

Set Up Your SharePoint Framework Development Environment

You can use Visual Studio or your own custom development environment to build SharePoint Framework solutions. You can use a Mac, PC, or Linux environment as well.

Install Node.js

Install the latest version of **Node.js LTS 10.x**.

If you installed as per the setup for app development in Chapter 2, please verify the version. Node.js v9.x, v11.x, and v12.x are not currently supported with the SharePoint Framework development.

Install Gulp

Gulp is a JavaScript-based task runner used to automate repetitive tasks. The SharePoint Framework build toolchain uses Gulp tasks to build projects, create JavaScript bundles, and the resulting packages used to deploy solutions.

If you already installed as per instructions in Chapter 2, then you are not required to install it again.

Enter the following command to install Gulp:

```
npm install gulp –global
```

Install Yeoman

Yeoman helps you kick-start new projects and prescribes best practices and tools to help you stay productive. SharePoint client-side development tools include a Yeoman generator for creating new web parts. The generator provides common build tools, common boilerplate code, and a common playground website to host web parts for testing.

Enter the following command to install Yeoman:

```
npm install yo –global
```

Install Yeoman SharePoint Generator

You use the Yeoman SharePoint webpart generator to create a SharePoint client-side solution project.

To install the SharePoint Framework Yeoman generator globally, enter the following command:

```
npm install @microsoft/generator-sharepoint –global
```

Trusting the Self-Signed Developer Certificate

While running a SharePoint Framework web part locally using gulp serve, it executes using HTTPs by default and implementing by using a development self-signed SSL certificate. By default, self-signed certificates are not trusted in your development environment.

To trust the development environment, execute the command below in the project folder:

```
gulp trust-dev-cert
```

Create the Project

In this exercise, you will learn how to create a SharePoint Framework web part and deploy/Sync to Microsoft Teams without any extra code.

- Open your command prompt and navigate to a directory where you want to save your work

- Create a new project directory

  ```
  md teamsspfx-tab
  ```

- Navigate to teamsspfx-tab folder

  ```
  cd teamsspfx-tab
  ```

- Create a new solution by running the Yeoman SharePoint Framework Generator:

  ```
  yo @microsoft/sharepoint
  ```

- When prompted, enter the following values:

  - What is your solution name? **teamsspfx-tab**

  - Which baseline packages do you want to target for your component(s)? **SharePoint Online only (latest)**

  - Where do you want to place the files? **Use the current folder**

  - Do you want to allow the tenant admin the choice of being able to deploy the solution to all sites immediately without running any feature deployment or adding apps in sites? **Yes**

345

- Will the components in the solution require permissions to access web APIs that are unique and not shared with other components in the tenant? **No**

- Which type of client-side component to create? **WebPart**

- Add new Web part to solution? **teamsspfx-tab**

- What is your Web part name? **FirstTeamsspfxtab**

- What is your Web part description? **First Teams SPFx Tab**

- Which framework would you like to use? **No JavaScript framework**

At this point, Yeoman installs the required dependencies and scaffolds the solution files. Creation of the solution might take a few minutes. Yeoman scaffolds the project to include your **FirstTeamsspfxtab** web part as well. See Figure 10-6.

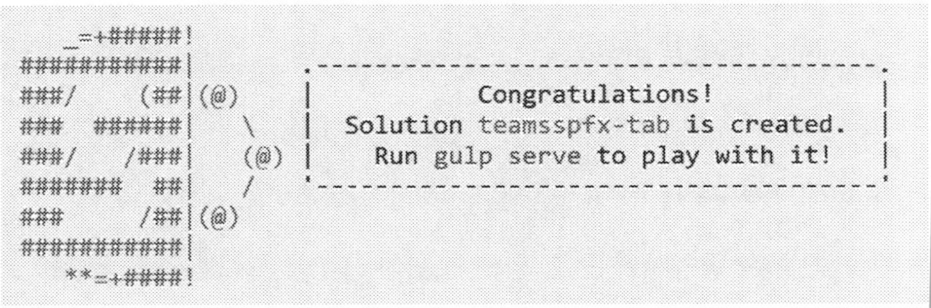

```
    _=+#####!
###########|
###/     (##|(@)        .------------------------------------------.
### ######|   \    |            Congratulations!               |
###/  /###|   (@) |    Solution teamsspfx-tab is created.   |
####### ##|   /    |     Run gulp serve to play with it!      |
###     /##|(@)        '------------------------------------------'
###########|
  **=+####!
```

Figure 10-6. *teamsspfx-tab web part created*

- Enter **code .** and the following to open the webpart project in Visual Studio Code:

code

- SharePoint Framework v1.8 and later projects will include the ./ teams folder in the solution structure (Figure 10-7)

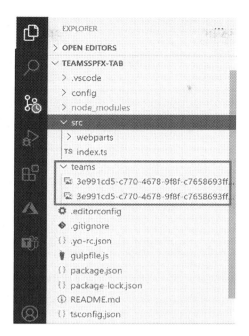

Figure 10-7. *Solution Structure*

- Teams folder contains the following two files:

  - [componentId]_color.png: Default small picture for a tab

  - [componentId]_outline.png: Default large picture for a tab#

These images will be used as icons in Microsoft Teams. You can replace them with custom images, but you will need to use the same name for ensuring they get packaged properly with the solution deployment.

For tenant deployment, go to **./config/package-solution.json,** add attribute "skipFeatureDeployment": **true** like below.

```
{
  "$schema": "https://developer.microsoft.com/json-schemas/spfx-build/
  package-solution.schema.json",
  "solution": {
    "name": "teamsspfx-tab-client-side-solution",
    "id": "f9892e3b-9a82-4fc6-83fb-bae21492b82e",
    "version": "1.0.0.0",
    "includeClientSideAssets": true,
```

```
    "skipFeatureDeployment": true,
    "isDomainIsolated": false
  },
  "paths": {
    "zippedPackage": "solution/teamsspfx-tab.sppkg"
  }
}
```

If you enter false in "skipFeatureDeployment": false, then you will have to individually add this solution on the MS Team site collection. Also consider the points below:

- Make sure Teams – Team and SharePoint site are the same.

- Deploy the web part in the SharePoint site before deploying it in Teams.

In this exercise I have selected **skipFeatureDeployment:true**.

Update the Webpart Manifest to Make It Available for Microsoft Teams

Locate the **./src/webparts/firstTeamsspfxtab/ FirstTeamsspfxtabWebPart.manifest. json** file for the web part you want to make available to Teams and modify the supportedHosts properties to include the "**TeamsTab**." Refer to Figure 10-8.

```
"supportedHosts": ["SharePointWebPart","TeamsTab"]
```

```
  "requiresCustomScript": false,
  "supportedHosts": ["SharePointWebPart",""],

                                      "SharePointFullPage"
  "preconfiguredEntries": [{         "SharePointWebPart"
    "groupId": "5c03119e-3074-46f   "TeamsPersonalApp"
    "group": { "default": "Other"   "TeamsTab"
```

Figure 10-8. *Supported Hosts*

Starting in SharePoint Framework v1.10, you are able to use SharePoint Framework web parts as personal Microsoft Teams apps. This can be controlled by including **"TeamsPersonalApp"** in the supportedHosts value. Personal App SPFx web parts don't have the configuration option.

Update Code to Be Aware of the Microsoft Teams Context

- Open **./src/webparts/helloWorld/FirstTeamsspfxtabWebPart**. It's for the needed edits to make the solution aware of the Microsoft Teams context if it is used as a tab.

- Update the render() method as follows.

- How are we rendering different content is dependent on if the code is rendered as a tab in Microsoft Team or as a web part in SharePoint. We can detect if the solution is hosted by Microsoft Teams by checking the **this.context.sdks.microsoftTeams** property.

- Then replace the render() method with the code below:

```
public render(): void {
    let teamsMessage: string = `<p class="${styles.
    description}">Welcome to SharePoint!</p>`;

    if (this.context.sdks.microsoftTeams) {
    teamsMessage = `
    <p class="${styles.description}">Welcome to Teams!</p>
    <p class="${ styles.description}">Team Name - ${escape(this.
    context.sdks.microsoftTeams.context.teamName)}</p>
<p class="${ styles.description}">Channel Name - ${escape(this.
context.sdks.microsoftTeams.context.channelName)}</p>
<p class="${ styles.description}">Group Id - ${escape(this.
context.sdks.microsoftTeams.context.groupId)}</p>
<p class="${ styles.description}">Team Site Url - ${escape(this.
context.sdks.microsoftTeams.context.teamSiteUrl)}</p>`;
    }
```

```
this.domElement.innerHTML = `
  <div class="${ styles.firstTeamsspfxtab }">
    <div class="${ styles.container }">
      <div class="${ styles.row }">
        <div class="${ styles.column }">
          <p class="${ styles.description }">${teamsMessage}</p>
        </div>
      </div>
    </div>
  </div>`;
}
```

- The code above displays Team Name, Channel Name, Group ID, and Team Site URL when you added the spfx web part as a tab.

- The same will display 'Welcome to SharePoint' when you add the spfx web part in SharePoint.

Package and Deploy Your Web Part to SharePoint

1. Go back to the command prompt.

2. Execute the following commands to build and bundle your solution. This will create a release build and map with a dynamic label as the host URL for your assets.

   - gulp build

   - gulp bundle –ship

3. Execute the following task to package your solution. This creates a **teamsspfx-tab.sppkg** package on the **sharepoint/solution** folder.

   - gulp package-solution --ship

4. Then deploy the package that was generated to the tenant App Catalog.

5. Go to your tenant's SharePoint App Catalog.

6. Upload or drag and drop the **teamsspfx-tab.sppkg** to the App Catalog (Figure 10-9).

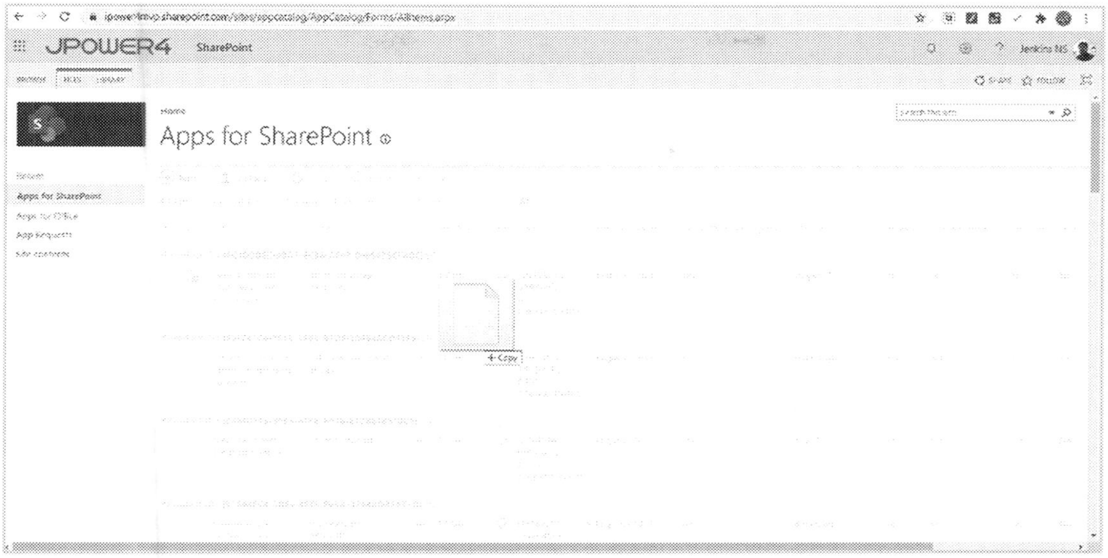

Figure 10-9. *Deploy Spfx Web Part*

This deploys the client-side solution package. Because this is a full trust client-side solution, SharePoint displays a dialog and asks you to trust the client-side solution to deploy. See Figure 10-10.

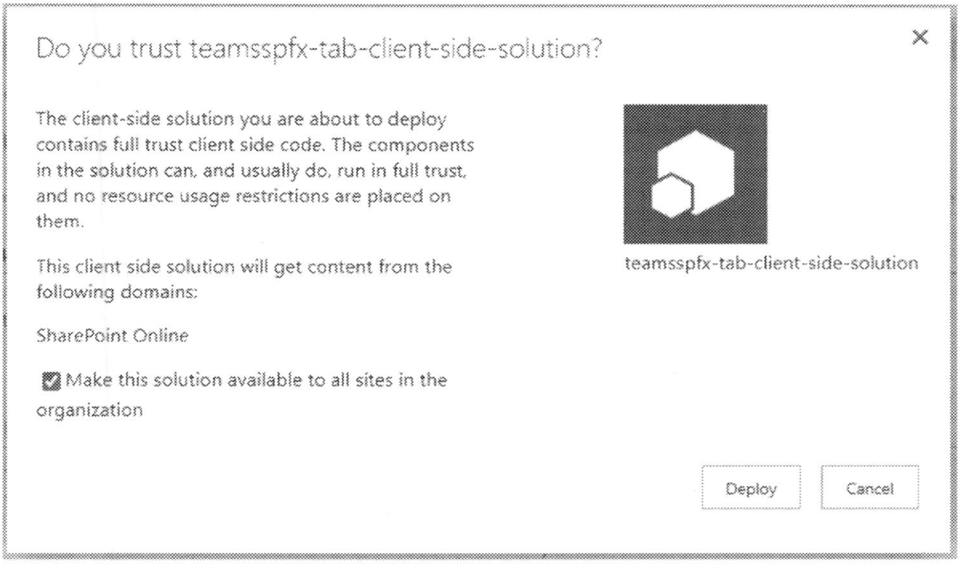

Figure 10-10. *Trust SPFx Web Part*

- Trust the solution, and ensure that the Make this solution available to all sites in the organization option is selected, so that the web part can be used from the Microsoft Teams side.

- Then Click the Deploy button to deploy the web part (Figure 10-11).

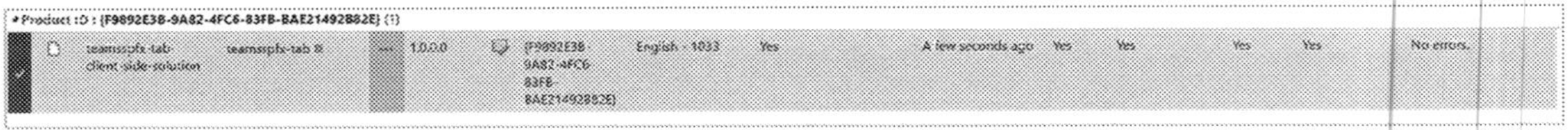

Figure 10-11. *Deployed Spfx Web Part*

Sync and Make the Web Part Available in Microsoft Teams

Select the **teamsspfx-tab-client-side-solution** package in the SharePoint tenant App Catalog webpart solution list and select the **Sync to Teams** button in the ribbon in the Files tab. Refer to Figure 10-12.

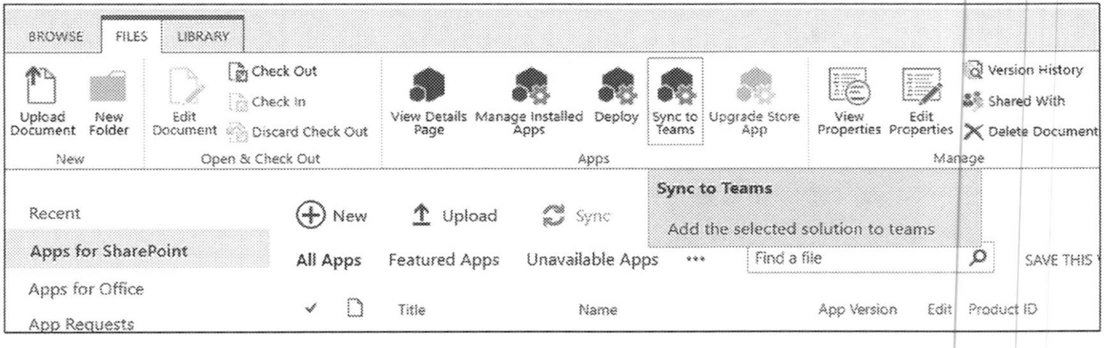

Figure 10-12. *Sync to Teams*

- Confirmation status message can be seen on the top-right corner.

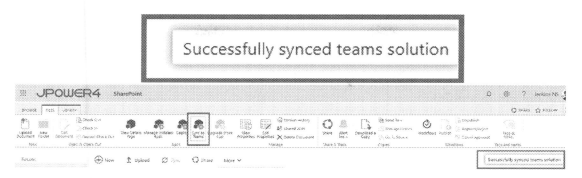

Figure 10-13. *Successfully synced to teams*

Your SharePoint Framework web part deployed and synced to Teams Successfully (Figure 10-13).

Failed to Sync Solution to Teams

If you received a notification of **Failed to sync solution to teams**, which might appear on the top right of your page, follow the steps below to delete your app from Microsoft Teams, and then try to sync it again:

Open Microsoft Teams.

- When viewing your team channel, click + to Add a tab.

- Select the More apps link at the top.

- Find your app in the list and click on the ... menu.

- Select Delete to remove the app from Microsoft Teams.

- You can now sync your new version to Microsoft Teams.

Add SPFx Web Part as Tab in Microsoft Teams

- Wait a few minutes – sync to Teams can take a few minutes due to caching.

- Then open to the Microsoft Teams client and check the App Catalog status by selecting **Apps** from the left navigation (Figure 10-14).

Figure 10-14. *Teams check available Apps*

- Click Apps and select Built for jpower4mvp (tenant name). See Figure 10-15.

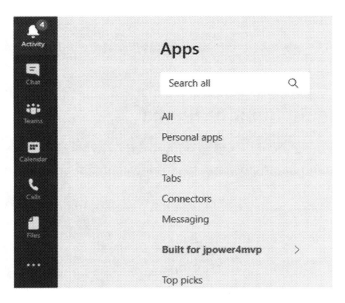

Figure 10-15. *Build for your organization*

- You can see your **FirstTeamsspfxTab** web part in the team's app catalog (Figure 10-16).

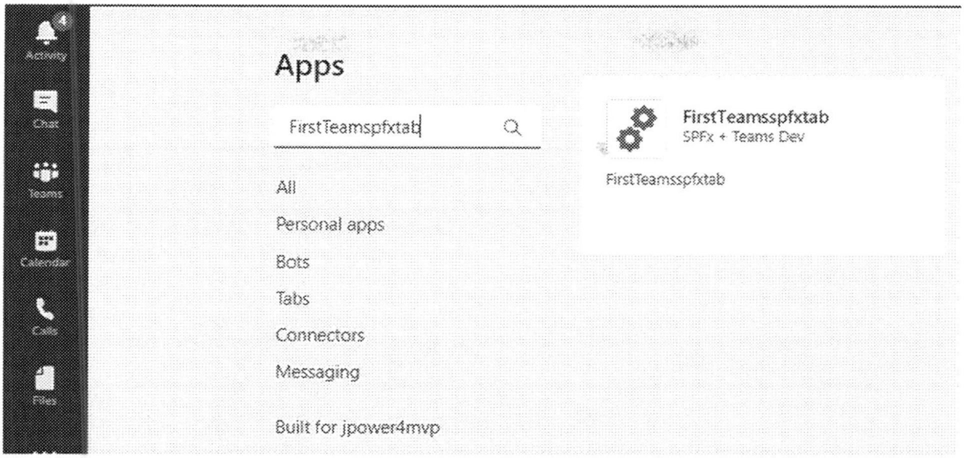

Figure 10-16. *Find the web part from teams*

- Select the **FirstTeamsspfxtab** app

- Click **Add to team** button (Figure 10-17)

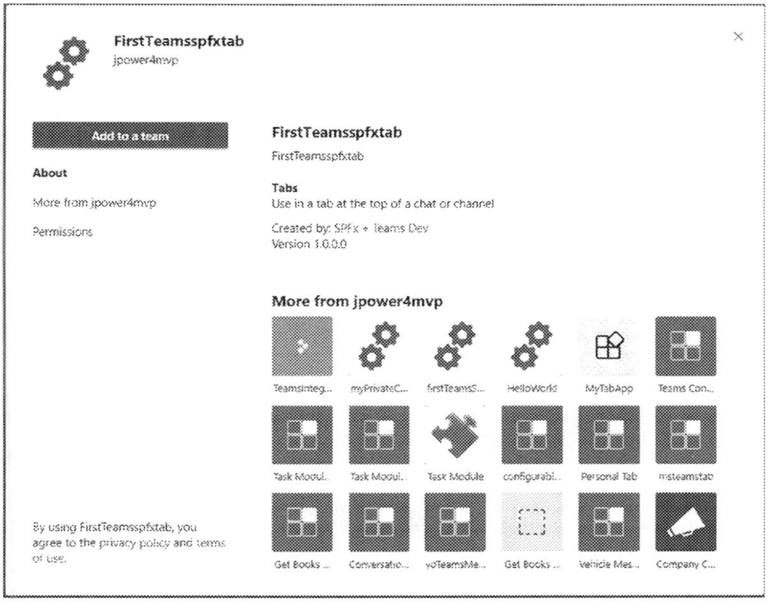

Figure 10-17. *Add to a team*

- Select the Team and channel where you want to test the solution.

- Then click the **Setup to tab** button to confirm the tab to be selected (Figure 10-18).

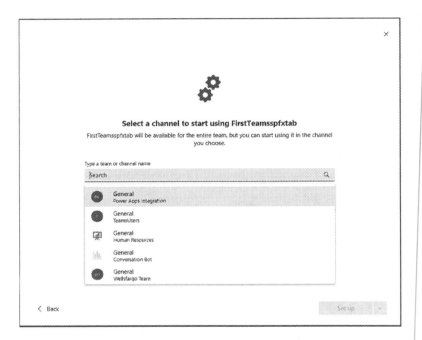

Figure 10-18. *Select Team and channel to setup*

- Click the **Save** button to confirm the tab to be installed on the channel (Figure 10-19)

Figure 10-19. *Save the app into channel*

- Your custom tab has been added on the Microsoft Teams channel and you can see how the code is reacting now that it's in the Microsoft Teams context. The theme of the web part is by default and coming from the underlying SharePoint site (Figure 10-20).

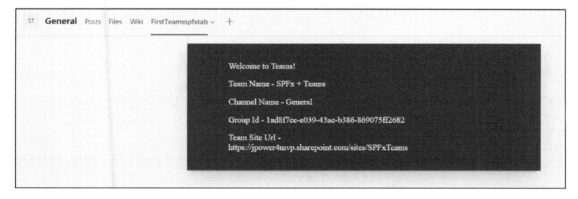

Figure 10-20. *Custom app add in Teams*

You have successfully deployed an SPFx web part to the Microsoft Teams tabs.

Conclusion

In this chapter, you have learned about Surfacing a SharePoint Framework Web Part to Microsoft Teams as a tab; now we can use this with our own application. Along with this, you will start learning about deployment options of Microsoft Teams apps in our next chapter.

CHAPTER 11

Teams Lifecycle Management and Design Guideline for Apps

In this chapter we are going to look at how we can deploy the custom Teams apps for your organization. You'll decide what to build, build your web services, create an app package, and distribute that package to your target end users.

Overview to Deploy the Apps

There are multiple different hosting options for your Microsoft Teams Apps assets. In this chapter, I am going to show how to deploy Teams Apps assets to Azure using Git.

The built and tested apps in previous exercises are ready to deploy to Azure and include a variety of features such as modifying the Microsoft Teams schema, support for Azure Application Insights, and a pluggable framework to add additional features.

Run and Debug Your Microsoft Teams App

Microsoft Teams apps can be run or hosted with multiple options based on your favorite technology and customer preferred CDN. For debugging we have the following options to run your app in Microsoft Teams.

- Purely local
- Locally hosted in Teams
- Cloud-hosted in Teams

© Jenkins NS 2021
J. NS, *Building Solutions with Microsoft Teams*, https://doi.org/10.1007/978-1-4842-6476-8_11

Purely Local

In purely local for tabs, you can run locally with your browser and access content through `http://localhost`. You run and test your application from your own laptop. This allows you to compile and run within your IDE and take full advantage of such techniques as breakpoints and step debugging. I always recommend development, Testing, UAT, and Production environment for all of your development in real-life app development.

With purely local for bots you can use a Bot Emulator, and remember a run from a local Bot Emulator does not give full teams specific functions like roster calls and other channel-specific functionality. And some Bot Emulator functionality is not supported in Teams.

Your local bot can be run within the Bot Emulator. This allows you to test some of the core logic of the bot to perform simple tests and debugging, see a rough layout of messages, and perform simple tests. Here are the steps:

- Run the code locally

- Launch the Bot Emulator and set the URL:

  - Node.js: `http://localhost:3978/api/messages`

  - .NET/C#: `http://localhost:3979/api/messages`

- Leave the Microsoft app ID and Microsoft app password blank, to match the default environment variables

Locally Hosted in Teams

Locally hosted in Teams runs using ngrok or any tunneling software and creates an app package and uploads in a Microsoft Teams client. This allows you to run and debug your app within the Teams client. Same as the purely local option, you can run it from your laptop. The best part is that you can run within your IDE and debug using breakpoints. Here, also, I always recommend development, Testing, UAT, and Production environment for all of your development in real-life app development.

Why you need to use tunneling software like ngrok is because Microsoft Teams is a cloud-based product and supports only publicly enabled https endpoints, and http endpoints are not supported. Therefore, to enable your app to work within Teams, you need to either publish the code to the cloud of your choice or make your local running instance externally accessible. You can use any tunneling software, but Microsoft recommends ngrok: ngrok creates an externally addressable URL for a port you open locally on your laptop.

The ngrok-serve task builds your project and starts a local web server (`http://localhost:3007`). It then starts ngrok with a random subdomain that creates a secure URL to your local webserver.

In development, testing can be done using the tool ngrok that creates a secure rotatable URL to your local HTTP webserver. Ngrok is included as a dependency within the project so there is nothing to set up or configure. Ngrok has created the temporary URL, for example:841c87a33afc.ngrok.io that will map to our locally running web server. Then go to the Azure portal and open the Bot Channel registration App. Update the Messaging endpoint using the temporary URL 841c87a33afc.ngrok.io, for example: `https://841c87a33afc.ngrok.io/api/messages`. You can validate that ngrok is working by testing the bot response in the Bot Framework portal's Test chat window. Also you can update the endpoint anytime it is required.

Cloud-Hosted, in Teams

Cloud-hosted means you are going to deploy a production-ready app in your Cloud CDN. In this chapter, I am going to show you how to deploy an app in cloud and publish it in Microsoft Teams. Microsoft recommends Azure and GitHub and you can create a manifest package to upload into a Teams client. Also, you can create multiple manifests and packages to allow you to manage Development, Testing, UAT, and Production Apps. Microsoft also recommends that you use multiple manifests and packages to separate your Development, Testing, UAT, and Production Apps.

Microsoft recommends Azure, but you can use any hosting cloud environment with their HTTPS endpoints. Always remember that for Bot and Messaging environments, your app should be compiled with Bot Framework. To ensure a secure environment, be explicit about the exact domain and subdomains you reference, and those domains must be in your control and listed in the valid domain object in the manifest file.

Note   *.azurewebsites.net would not be recommended

Packaging Your App

Deploying your Microsoft Teams app in production is a two-step process; the first one we already discussed in hosting your code in cloud. The second one is packaging your app configuration and uploading and installing it in Microsoft Teams. You define your app configuration in a manifest JSON file with two icons and bundled in an app package. You will need an app package to upload and install your app in Teams and to publish into different channels. The app package is a .zip file with three files (manifest.json, outline. png, and color.png).

- A manifest file named "**manifest.json**," which specifies attributes of your app and points to required resources for your experience, such as the location of its tab configuration page or the Microsoft app ID for its bot and domain URLs and scope.

- A transparent "outline" icon and a full "color" icon.

Creating a Manifest

Yeoman generator creates the manifest automatically; if you want to create one, then use App Studio in Microsoft Teams. Your manifest file must be named "manifest.json" and add the general info; app version; app ID; and capabilities like tab, bot, messaging extension, and connectors.

Always use the current manifest schema:

```
"$schema": "https://developer.microsoft.com/json-schemas/teams/v1.7/
MicrosoftTeams.schema.json",
```

Icons

App Package requires two icons for your app experience to identify while adding the app and accessing the app. As discussed in a previous section, icons must be included in the package and referenced via relative paths in the manifest. The maximum length of each path is 2048 bytes, and the format of the icon is *.png.

Accent Color

The color icons are used in Microsoft Teams in app and tab galleries, bots, flyouts, etc. This icon should be 192 x 192 pixels; refer to Figure 11-1. Your icon can be any color, but the background should be an accent color.

For example, say your company is JPOWER4. You would submit two icons:

1. App gallery (192 x 192)

2. Transparent (32 x 32)

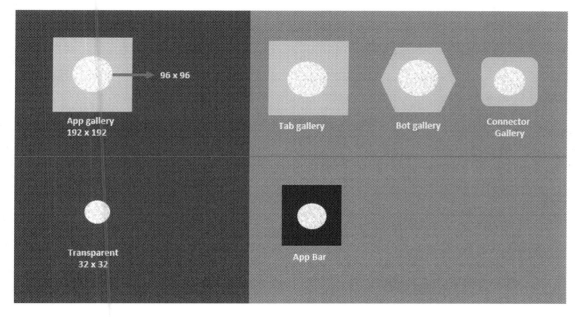

Figure 11-1. *Icons for App Gallery*

Deploy and Publish Your App

Once you have created your app, there are three options for distributing it:

- Upload your app directly.

- Publish your app to your organization's app Catalog.

- Publish your app through AppSource.

Upload an App Package to Microsoft Teams

To test your app, you need to upload it to Teams. Uploading adds the app to the team you select, and the team can interact with it like end users.

Publish Your App to Your Organization's App Catalog

Use the Manage apps page to publish apps that are built specifically for your organization. After you publish a custom app, it is available to users in your organization's app store. There are two ways to publish a custom app to your organization's app store. The way that you use depends on how you get the app.

- **Approve a custom app**: Use this method if the developer submits the app directly to the Manage apps page using the Teams App Submission API. You can then review and publish (or reject) the app directly from the app details page.

- **Upload an app package**: Use this method if the developer sends you the app package in .zip format. You publish the app by uploading the app package.

Publish your app through AppSource

Publishing your app to AppSource makes it available in the Teams app catalog on the Web.

Best Practices

Tabs

- **Always include a default state**: If your tab is configurable or static, always include a default state; it will help you to set up the tab easily.

- **Deep linking**: By always deep linking your cards and bots in a tab, then you can show richer data in a hosted tab.

- **Naming**: Always use a meaningful full name and map it with your line of business.

Bots

- **Bots are not assistants**: Bot act as specialists, so always include cognitive services.

- **Discourage chit chat**: Use your bot for conversational; otherwise, redirect it toward task completion.

- **Introduce some personality**: Example: Now that voice is very popular, introduce your bot to some speaking capabilities.

- **Maintain tone**: Always include friendly and light conversation.

- **Encourage easy task flow**: Always ask questions with multi-turn interactions with task flow; it will help users get a proper answer from the bot.

Messaging Extensions

- **Keep it simple**: A message extension should be lightweight and fast or it will lose its utility. If your search requirements are very complex or multiple parameters are necessary, even in the simplest cases, it is OK to include them.

- **Optimize your search results**: A snappy message extension will return an easily digestible list of search results. We recommend including an image and no more than two lines of text.

- **Optimize your cards**: Each message extension is produced in a card. Since it is the last thing your user will see, make sure your cards are useful, good-looking, and easy to share.

Cards

- **Keep the noise down**: For example: Microsoft Teams Apps support sends multiple cards together, but they become less useful, because users unable to see the response in a single view are required to scroll down.

- **Test on mobile**: While creating cards always consider mobile. Try to avoid big images, large data sets, and large text lengths. Also consider the title, width, and that text lengths truncate on mobile. Test in mobile before publishing to Production.

- **Check your graphics**: Always test images and videos in all platforms like mobile, desktop, and browser.

Avoid including text in a graphic: Load the test messages in a text field, but do not load it in images or videos. Since images and videos are dynamically scaled, any text in your image loads in the wrong place.

Task Modules

- **In a channel**: Use task modules to have a 1:1 interaction with a user. Task modules keep you from cluttering the channel with unnecessary bot responses and avoid redirecting the user to a 1:1 chat and losing context.

- **Test on mobile**: While Adaptive Cards hosted in a task module render well on mobile, if you choose to create custom HTML, it will need to use our CSS to handle theme changes and be responsive to handle the differences between desktop and mobile screen real estate.

- **Short interactions**: You can easily create multistep wizards but holding a user in a task module can be problematic as incoming messages encourage users to exit. Pop out to a web page instead of a task module if your task is really involved or time consuming.

- **Errors**: Keep errors inline. Do not pop a dialog on top of a dialog.

Message Actions

- **Simple action names**: Keep the name short: a couple of words at most.

- **Use a task module**: Allow some control over the action by exposing it in a task module or just open it to confirm that the action was completed.

- **Try using Natural Language Processing**: NLP can help your service listen for keywords or synonyms for your entities.

- **Try using graph queries too**: Once you are manipulating text sent by users, you can take advantage of MS Graph to get more context. There are additional permissions required to do so, and you'll need to inform the user.

Activity Feed

- **Keep it short**: Make sure to keep things brief because longer messages get truncated.

- **Bundle your notifications**: If your service regularly sends a lot of simultaneous notifications, try grouping them into a single notification. For example: "10 tasks were assigned to you."

Exercise – Publish Your App to Your Organization

In the previous chapters we developed Teams App and tested locally. Ngrok allows us to quickly test the apps. However, in real-life scenarios, we will have to deploy these Teams Apps to some hosting environments from where they can be served to Microsoft Teams.

In this exercise, we will have a look at how to deploy and publish your app to your organization production environment; that is, Create a new Teams app and deploy its assets to Azure Content Delivery Network as the hosting solution.

Before starting the exercise, verify your environment. In this exercise, I am using the tools mentioned below, which are installed in my environment:

- Microsoft Azure Subscription

- GitHub Account

- Node.js - v10.16.0

- NPM - 6.9.0

- Gulp

  - CLI version: 2.3.0

  - Local version: 4.0.2

- Yeomen Generator of MS Teams - 2.14.0
- Visual Studio Code

Steps Involved

If you want to deploy the Teams Apps for Production, follow these steps.

    A.   Create a Web App in Azure

    B.   Create a repository in GitHub

    C.   Create an App using 'yo teams'

    D.   Deploy to Azure using Git

    E.   Deploy the package to Teams to test the app

Create a Web App in Azure

In this section you are creating a web app to publish your application to the public domain to access from anywhere. Open a browser and navigate to the Azure portal `https://portal.azure.com/`. Sign in using your **username@tenantname.onmicrosoft.com** that was used from the Azure subscription.

    `- https://portal.azure.com/`

- Create a new Resource Group or use an existing one.
- In this exercise, I am using my existing Resource Group "Teams."
- Click 'Create a resource' (Figure 11-2).

Figure 11-2. *Create a resource*

- Select 'Web App' (Figure 11-3).

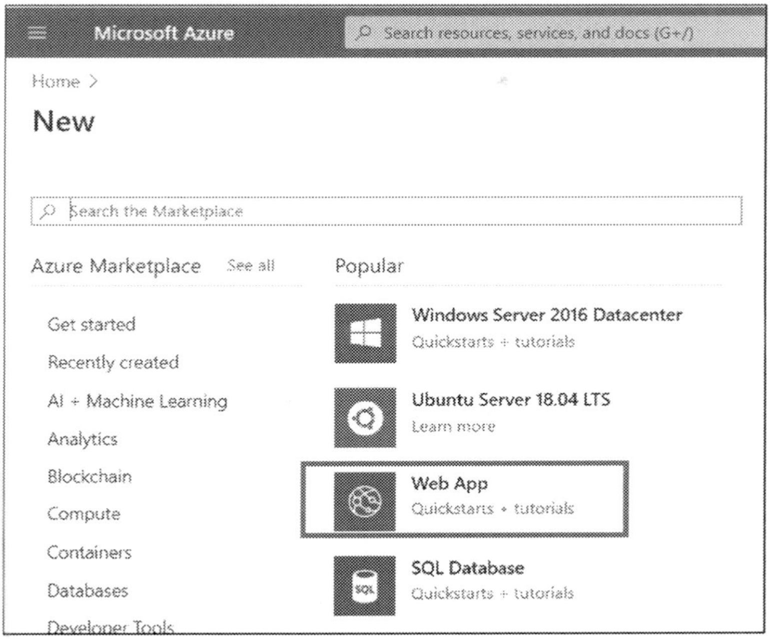

Figure 11-3. *Create a Web App*

- Create a Web App with a Windows App Service Plan and give it the name of your tab, the same one you used when asked for a URL in the Yeoman generator. In this example: `https://deployfirstteamsapp.azurewebsites.net` (Figure 11-4).

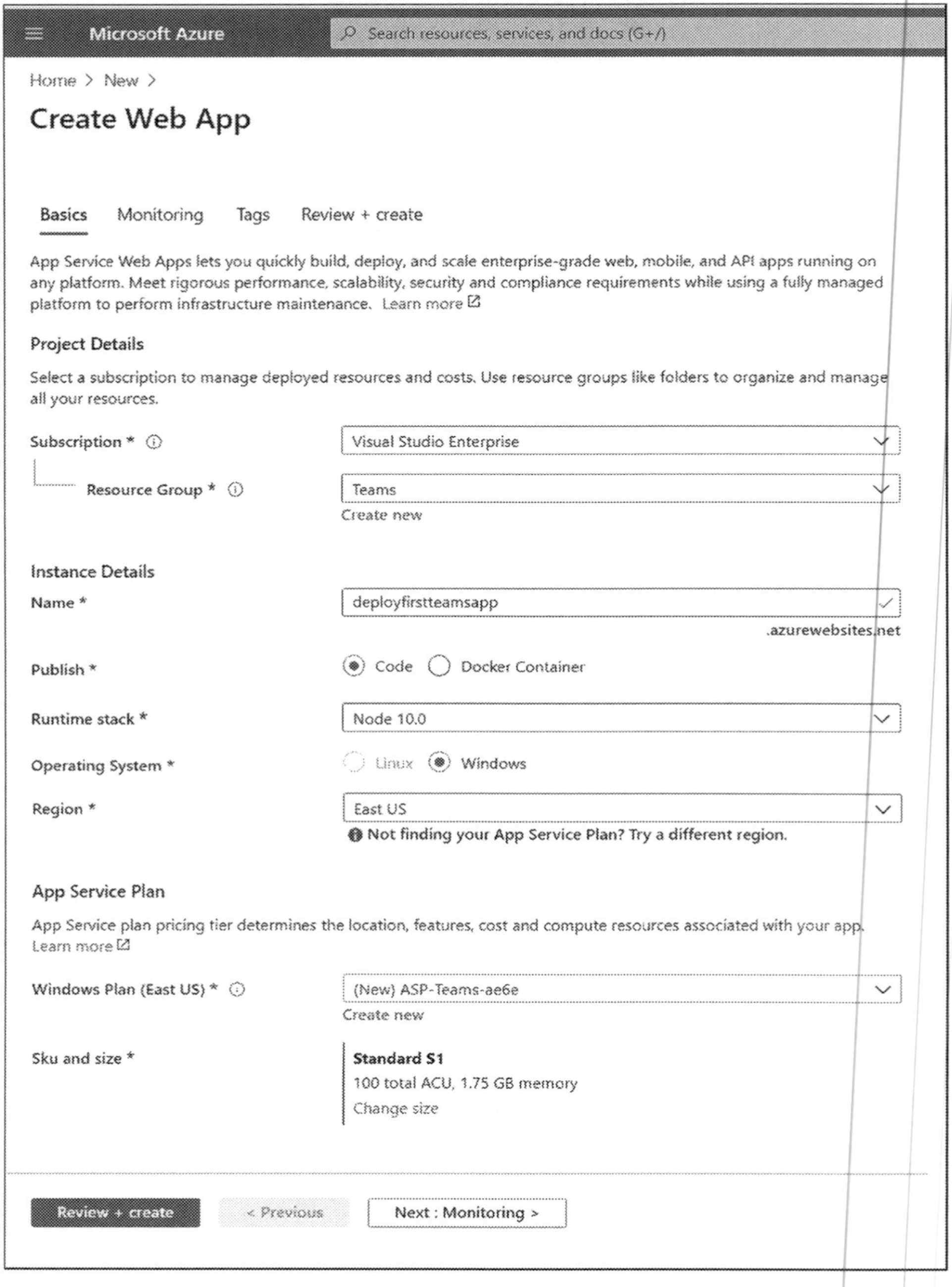

Figure 11-4. *Create and review Web App*

- Click the Review and Create buttons to Create a Web App (Figure 11-5).

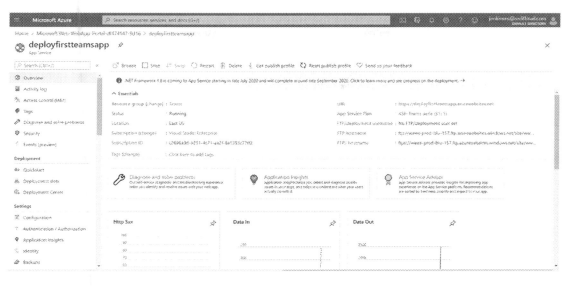

Figure 11-5. *Web App Created*

- Go to Configuration under Settings

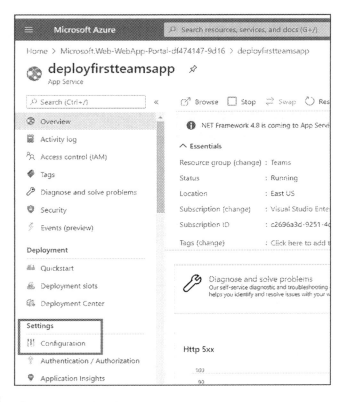

Figure 11-6. *Configuration Settings*

- Add the following keys in the Configuration ➤ **Application Settings** (Figure 11-6)

- New Application setting (Figure 11-7).

  Name = WEBSITE_NODE_DEFAULT_VERSION, Value = 8.10.0 and
  Name = SCM_COMMAND_IDLE_TIMEOUT, Value = 1800

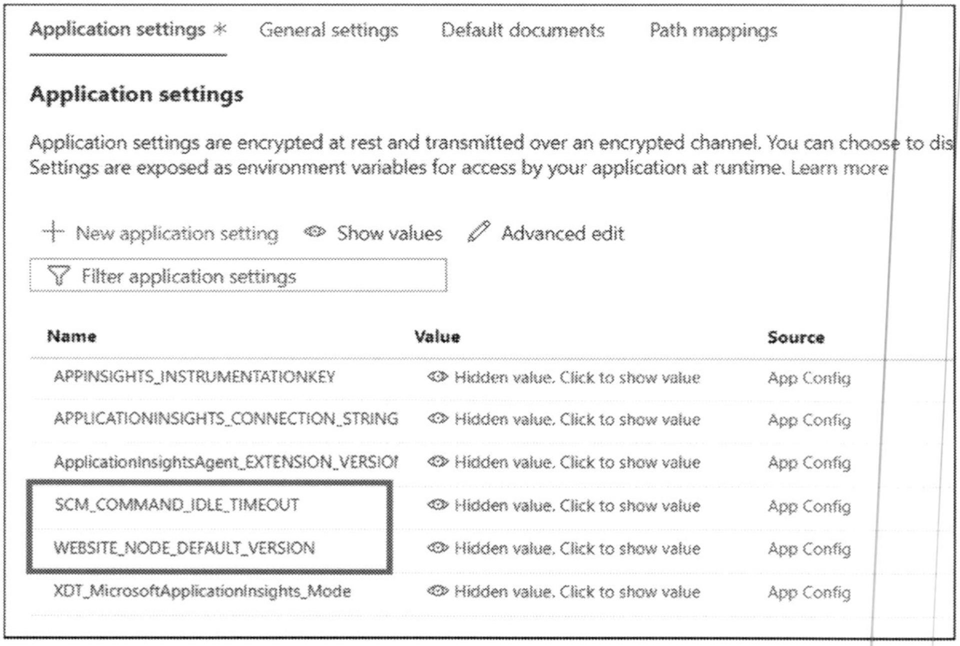

Figure 11-7. *Application Settings*

- Click Save.

Create a Repository in GitHub

In this section you create a new repository and map with your local project folder. Open a browser and log in into GitHub Example: https://github.com/jenkinsns (my repository), and if you don't have a GitHub repository account, then create one.

- Go to repositories

- Click New button and Create a new repository

- Repository Name: deployfirstteamsapp

- Click 'Create repository' button to Create new repository in your GitHub (Figure 11-8)

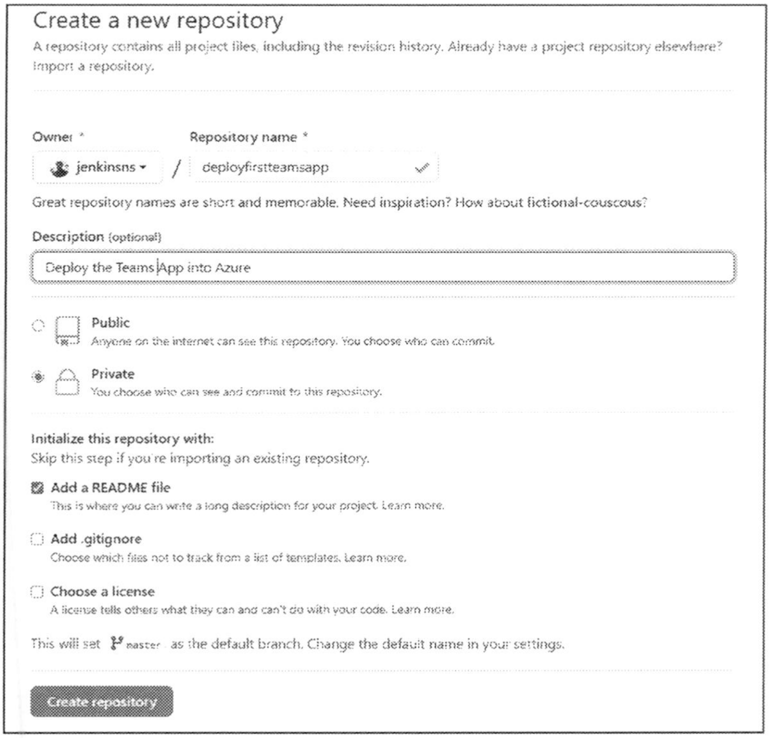

Figure 11-8. *Create a new repository*

- If you don't have GitHub Desktop in your Laptop or Desktop, install it.

- Click Code button ➤ Select Open with GitHub Desktop (Figure 11-9).

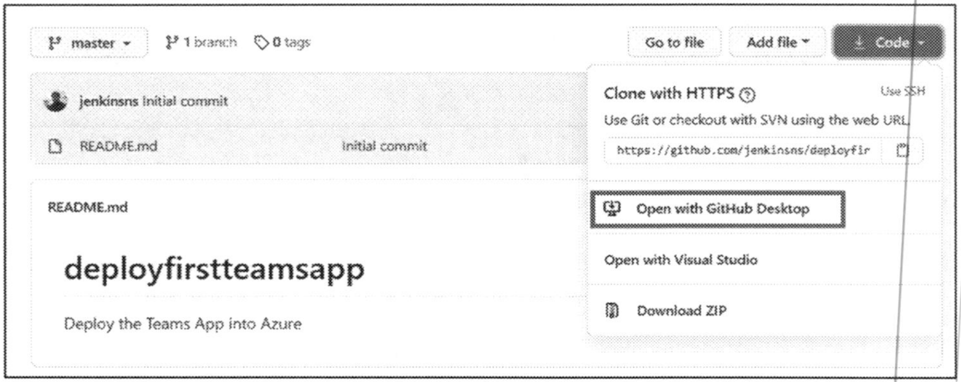

Figure 11-9. *Open with GitHub Desktop*

- Then map/clone your project folder for the new App (Figure 11-10).

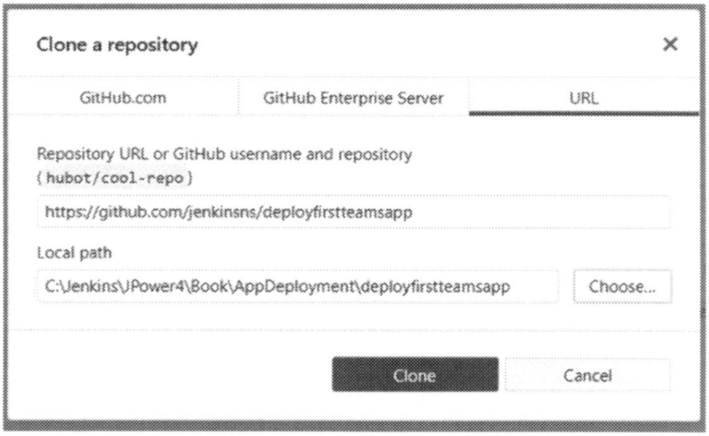

Figure 11-10. *Clone a repository*

Create an App Using 'yo teams'

In this section, you will create a new tab Teams app using Yeoman generator (yo teams):

- Open Command Prompt

- Navigate to Project folder mapped/clone from github

- **Example**: C:\Jenkins\JPower4\Book\AppDeployment\
  deployfirstteamsapp

- Run the Yeoman generator for Microsoft Teams by running the following command: **yo teams** (Figure 11-11).

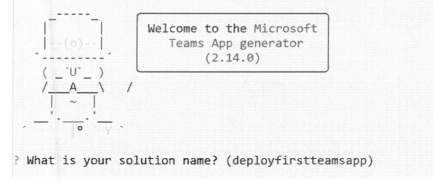

```
C:\Jenkins\JPower4\Book\AppDeployment\deployfirstteamsapp>yo teams

     ------
    |_    _|            +-----------------------------+
    |--(o)--|           | Welcome to the Microsoft    |
    `---------'         |    Teams App generator      |
                        |         (2.14.0)            |
    ( _`U`_ )           +-----------------------------+
   /___A___\   /
    |  ~  |
  __'.___.'__
`--    `  `--`

? What is your solution name? (deployfirstteamsapp)
```

Figure 11-11. *yo teams generator*

Yeoman will launch and ask you a series of questions. Answer the questions with the following values (Figure 11-12):

- What is your solution name? **deployfirstteamsapp**

- Where do you want to place the files? Use the current folder

- Title of your Microsoft Teams App project? **deployfirstteamsapp**

- Your (company) name? (max 32 characters) JPOWER4

- Which manifest version would you like to use? v1.6

- Enter your Microsoft Partner ID, if you have one? (Leave blank to skip)

- What features do you want to add to your project? A Tab

- The URL where you will host this solution? **https:// deployfirstteamsapp.azurewebsites.net (Enter the Web App URL created in Azure Portal)**

- Would you like show a loading indicator when your app/tab loads? No

- Would you like to include Test framework and initial tests? No

- Would you like to use Azure Applications Insights for telemetry? No

- Default Tab name? (max 16 characters) My Tab

- What kind of Tab would you like to create? Personal (static)

- Do you require Azure AD Single-Sign-On support for the tab? No

```
? What is your solution name? deployfirstteamsapp
? Where do you want to place the files? Use the current folder
? Title of your Microsoft Teams App project? deployfirstteamsapp
? Your (company) name? (max 32 characters) JPOWER4
? Which manifest version would you like to use? v1.6
? Enter your Microsoft Partner ID, if you have one? (Leave blank to skip)
? What features do you want to add to your project? A Tab
? The URL where you will host this solution? https://deployfirstteamsapp.azurewebsites.net
? Would you like show a loading indicator when your app/tab loads? No
? Would you like to include Test framework and initial tests? No
? Would you like to use Azure Applications Insights for telemetry? No
? Default Tab name? (max 16 characters) My Tab
? What kind of Tab would you like to create? Personal (static)
? Do you require Azure AD Single-Sign-On support for the tab? No
```

Figure 11-12. *answer Yeoman questionnaire*

Note   Most of the answers to these questions can be changed after creating the project. For example, the URL where the project will be hosted is not important at the time of creating or testing the project

---

- Open Visual Studio Code using **code.** in the command prompt (Figure 11-13).

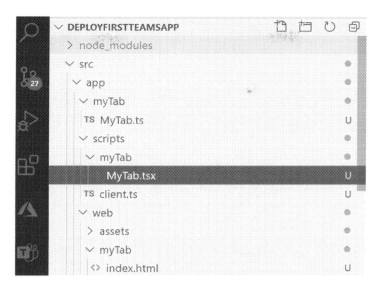

Figure 11-13. *Visual Studio Code*

- Add your functionality for the Teams Tab App

- Save it

Deploying to Azure Using Git

In this section you will set up the web app deployment center created in an earlier step and configure the deployment build service with the GitHub repository.

1. Log into the Azure Portal - `https://portal.azure.com/`

2. Open the WebApp **deployfirstteamsapp** created (Figure 11-14)

3. Go to the Deployment Center under Deployment (Figure 11-15)

4. Choose Local Git as source

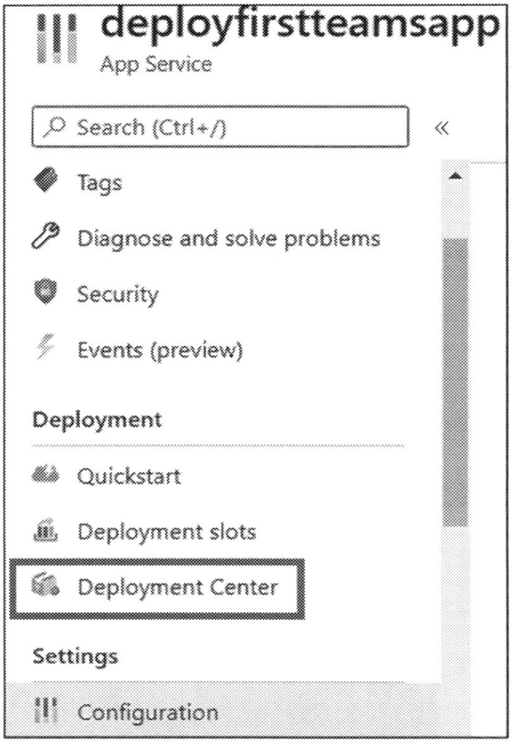

Figure 11-14. *Web App Deployment Center*

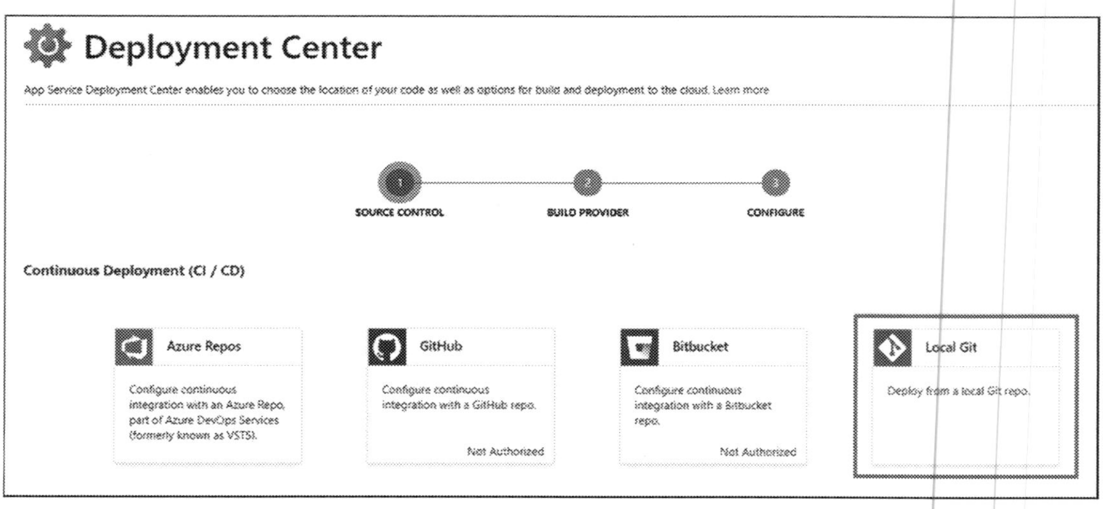

Figure 11-15. *Local Git in Deployment Center*

5.   The App Service builds service as the Build Provider (Figure 11-16).

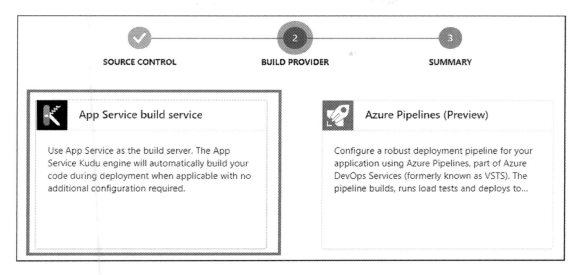

Figure 11-16.   *App Service build service*

6.   Click Finish

7.   Click on Deployment Credentials (Figure 11-17)

Figure 11-17.   *Get Deployment Credentials*

8.   Copy and Store the App Credentials securely (Figure 11-18)

   a.   Git Clone URL

   b.   Username

   c.   Password

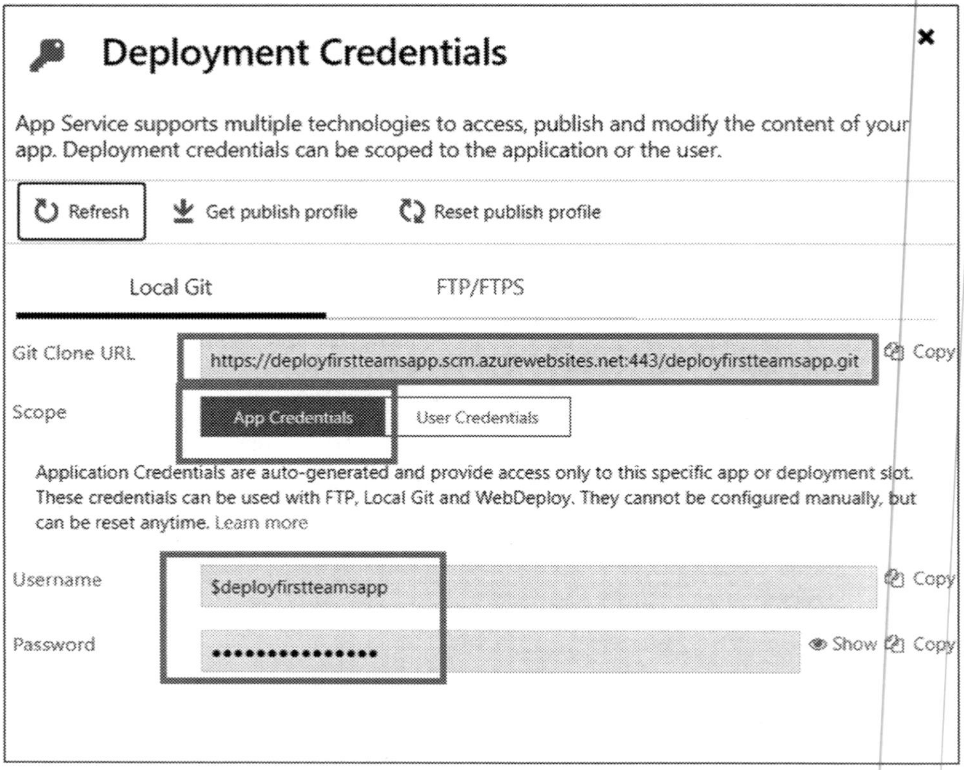

Figure 11-18. *Store Deployment Credentials*

9. Go to the Command Prompt

10. In your tab folder, initialize a Git repository using **git init**

11. Build the solution using **gulp build** to make sure you don't have any errors

12. Commit all your files using **git add -A && git commit -m "Initial commit"**

13. Run the following command to set up the remote repository:

```
git remote add azure  https://<username>@deployfirstteamsapp.scm.
azurewebsites.net:443/deployfirstteamsapp.git.
```

14. You need to replace it with the username of the App Credentials you retrieved in Deployment Credentials. You can also copy the URL from Options in the Azure Web App (Figure 11-19).

```
i.e., git remote add azure  https://$deployfirstteams
app@deployfirstteamsapp.scm.azurewebsites.net:443/
deployfirstteamsapp.git
```

15. To push your code use to Azure, use the following command:

```
git push azure master
```

16. You will be asked for your credentials the first time, so insert the Password for the App Credential.

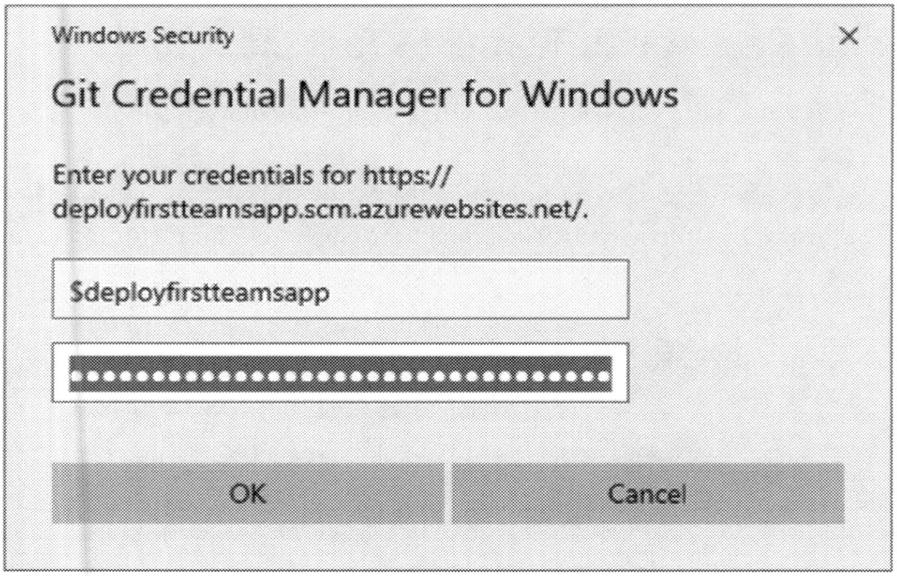

Figure 11-19. *Enter Deployment Password*

17. Wait until the deployment is completed and navigate to https://deployfirstteamsapp.azurewebsites.net/privacy.html to test that the web application is running (Figure 11-20).

```
C:\Jenkins\JPower4\Book\AppDeployment\deployfirstteamsapp>git remote add azure  https://$deployfirstteamsapp@deployfirstteamsapp.scm.a
zurewebsites.net:443/deployfirstteamsapp.git

C:\Jenkins\JPower4\Book\AppDeployment\deployfirstteamsapp>git push azure master
Enumerating objects: 42, done.
Counting objects: 100% (42/42), done.
Delta compression using up to 8 threads
Compressing objects: 100% (35/35), done.
Writing objects: 100% (42/42), 123.82 KiB | 4.95 MiB/s, done.
Total 42 (delta 3), reused 3 (delta 0)
remote: Updating branch 'master'.
remote: Updating submodules.
remote: Preparing deployment for commit id '77245c583e'.
remote: Running custom deployment command...
remote: Running deployment command...
remote: Handling node.js deployment.
remote: Start script "dist/server.js" from package.json is not found.
remote: Missing server.js/app.js files, web.config is not generated
remote: Looking for app.js/server.js under site root.
remote: The package.json file does not specify node.js engine version constraints.
```

Figure 11-20. *Deployment Started*

18. Done

19. Repeat step 11 for every commit you do and want to deploy.

Deploy the Package to Teams to Test the App

Now let's install the app in Microsoft Teams. In the browser, navigate to https://teams.microsoft.com and sign in.

Using the app bar navigation menu, select the More added apps button. Then select More apps followed by Upload a custom app and then Upload for me or my teams (Figure 11-21).

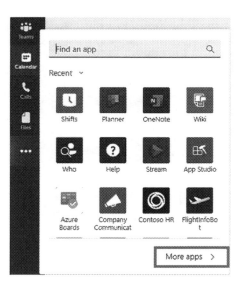

Figure 11-21. *Add apps to MS Teams*

In the file dialog that appears, select the Microsoft Teams package in your project. This app package is a ZIP file that can be found in the projects **./package** folder (Figure 11-22).

Figure 11-22. *Upload apps*

After installation, you will be able to see the app in the apps list (Figure 11-23).

Figure 11-23. *Personal apps installed*

Click the app, and Microsoft Teams will display a summary of the app (Figure 11-24).

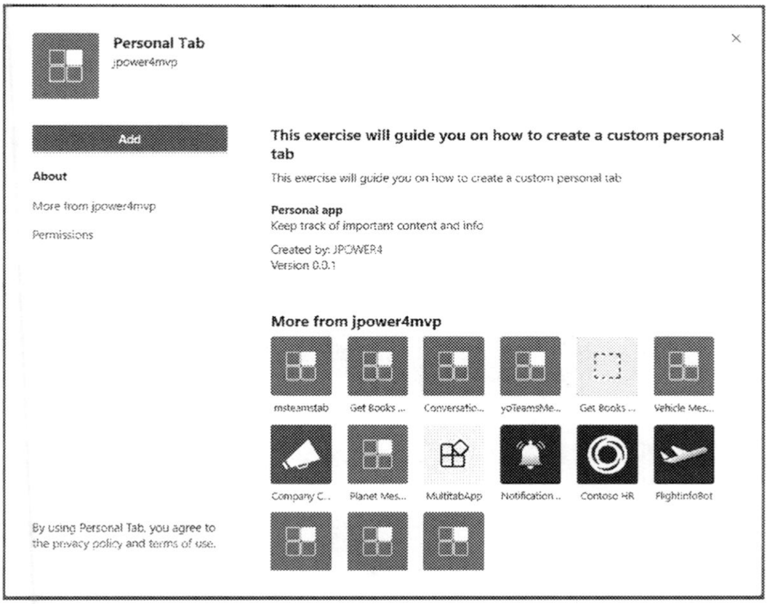

Figure 11-24. *Add the personal tab*

Testing the Deployed App

- Click the Add button to navigate to the personal tab to test.

- Also, you can pin the personal tab in the far-left navigation bar permanently.

- Or select the ... menu and choose your app from the list (Figure 11-25).

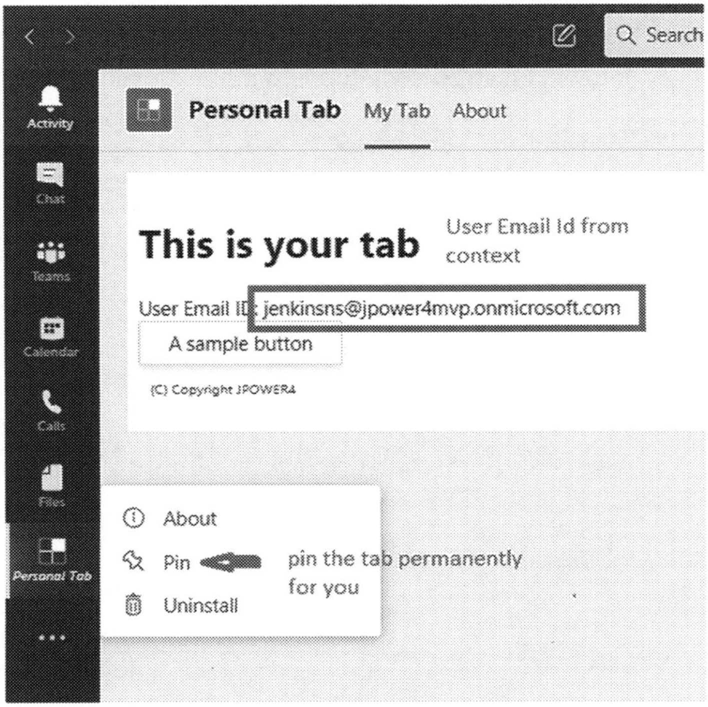

Figure 11-25. *Personal tab output*

In this exercise, you have deployed your code in the Azure Web App and installed the App in Microsoft Teams as a personal tab and tested it from a Microsoft Teams client.

Conclusion

In this chapter, you have learned various features of Deployment, Best Practices, and how to Deploy your code in an Azure Web App and install the App to Microsoft Teams using Yeoman generator (yo teams) and Git. You have also learned how to a Deploy Teams App in Azure using Git for Microsoft Teams.

This book has shown you how to build line of business apps for Microsoft Teams. While there are a lot of methods to develop Teams custom apps, yo teams is better when comparing it with other tools that can be developed and deployed easily without any dependency. This book has covered step-by-step builds of Messaging extensions, Bots, Tabs, Webhooks, and Connectors. It has also covered Surfacing SPFx with Teams and ready-to-use App Templates and deployment mythology.

Index

A

Adaptive cards
bot reacting, 93, 94
components, 88
creation, 88, 89
definition, 88
example, 89, 90
save/test bot, 92, 93
types, 88
updating, 90, 91
API *vs.* webhooks, 234
App Studio, 154, 155
App templates, 326
ability to customize, 326
benefits, 327
deployment, 328
FAQs, 329
License, 329
list, 327, 328
uses, 326
Authentication
Azure AD, 148
flow for tabs, 145–147
graph scope, 149
silent, 148
single sign-on, 149
tab context, 147
Azure active directory,
295–297, 299

B

Bot channels registration, 31
creation, 30, 31
search, 29
values, 30
webservice endpoint, 30

C, D, E, F

Channel/group chat, 160
install, 167, 168, 170, 171
mobile clients, 144
run locally, 165
test, 166
Visual studio code, 163, 165
Connectors, 237
manifest, 239
Team client, 238
Control library, 153, 154, 155, 165
Conversational bots
bot channel registration, 70–72
client secret, 74, 75
enable Teams channel, 73
group chats, 64, 65
ID/password, 74
installation
add apps, 83
personal bot, 85, 86
teams/channels, 84

© Jenkins NS 2021
J. NS, *Building Solutions with Microsoft Teams*, https://doi.org/10.1007/978-1-4842-6476-8